[handwritten] Champaign, Ill.
29 June 1981

Populist Vanguard

A HISTORY OF THE
SOUTHERN FARMERS' ALLIANCE

by Robert C. McMath, Jr.

The Norton Library
W·W·NORTON & COMPANY·INC·
NEW YORK

Books That Live
The Norton imprint on a book means that in the publisher's
estimation it is a book not for a single season but for the years.
W. W. Norton & Company, Inc.

Library of Congress Cataloging in Publication Data
McMath, Robert C   1944-
Populist vanguard.
(The Norton Library)
Original ed. published by University of North
Carolina Press, Chapel Hill.
Bibliography: p.
Includes index.
1.   National Farmers' Alliance and Industrial Union.
2.   Populism—United States—History.   I.   Title.
HD1485.N35M35   1977   338.1′06′275   77-14536
ISBN 0-393-00869-X

1 2 3 4 5 6 7 8 9 0

For Linda

Contents

Acknowledgments

I am deeply indebted to George B. Tindall for his advice and encouragement. He supervised an earlier version of this study and made helpful suggestions concerning the expanded work. His counsel and friendship have been, and remain, invaluable to me.

Others at Chapel Hill who helped guide this project included Donald G. Mathews, Gerhard Lenski, and Samuel S. Hill, Jr. (now of the University of Florida), all of whom helped me relate the Farmers' Alliance to the culture from which it sprang, and the late James Welch Patton, whose careful reading of the earlier manuscript saved me from a host of errors.

At an earlier stage, J. B. Smallwood, Jr., Robert A. Calvert, and Jack B. Scroggs, all of North Texas State University, stimulated my interest in the agrarian crusade. In the course of preparing this study, I have also benefited from the advice of many other scholars, including Lawrence C. Goodwyn, Sheldon Hackney, William F. Holmes, Melton A. McLaurin, Stuart Noblin, Stanley B. Parsons, Germaine M. Reed, Jean L. Rogers, William Warren Rogers, Joseph F. Steelman, Lala C. Steelman, Robert K. Whelan, and George-Anne Willard.

Matthew Hodgson, Malcolm M. MacDonald, and Gwen Duffey of The University of North Carolina Press offered incisive suggestions and expert editorial assistance. Carol Hulbary typed the final draft of the manuscript.

Archivists and librarians at the following institutions provided access to needed materials: Alabama State Department of Archives and History, Catholic University of America, Dallas Public Library, Duke University, East Carolina University, Emory University, Georgia State Department of Archives and History, Kansas State Historical Society, Library of Congress, North Carolina Archives and History Division, North Texas State University, Perkins School of Theology of Southern Methodist University, Tennessee State Library, Texas State Library, Texas Tech University, University of Alabama, University of Georgia, University of North Carolina at Chapel Hill,

University of South Dakota, University of Texas at Austin, University of Virginia, and the Virginia State Library. In addition Ruth C. Hale and her staff at the Information and Exchange Center of the Price Gilbert Library, Georgia Institute of Technology, were extremely helpful in securing materials through interlibrary loan.

The Georgia Tech Foundation and the Department of Social Sciences at the Georgia Institute of Technology have generously supported this project in its later stages. For arranging that support, I am particularly thankful to Patrick Kelly, head of the Social Sciences Department, and Henry S. Valk, Dean of the General College.

Finally, this book would never have been written without the help of my wife, Linda McFadyen McMath. She has shared the drudgery and the excitement of this undertaking from its beginning, and for both I shall always be grateful.

Introduction

On a June morning in 1891, a crowd of about one hundred people gathered at John R. Allen's farm on Donaldson's Creek eight miles north of Lampasas, Texas. The group included ten or fifteen surviving members of a local farmers' club formed there in the late 1870s. They were joined for a day of reunion by their friends and neighbors and by a few curious newspaper reporters. They thronged in and around a rough-hewn building that Allen and his neighbor, Lewis S. Chavose, had constructed twenty-five years before. Since that time, the structure had housed schools, churches, and all manner of community organizations. In 1877 Allen, Chavose, and neighboring farmers had gathered there to organize one of those voluntary associations to which rural and small-town Americans of the nineteenth century turned almost instinctively in times of economic and social upheaval. What made their club memorable after nearly fourteen years, and what attracted a reporter from the prestigious Galveston *Daily News*, was the fact that from their tiny band had evolved the National Farmers' Alliance and Industrial Union (NFA&IU), often called the "southern" Farmers' Alliance.

By 1891 the Alliance had reached and passed the height of its influence, having enrolled perhaps 1,500,000 members, three-fourths of them southerners. It had become a power in the economic and political life of the South and Midwest. At their reunion, the members of the first Alliance, mainly small farmers and their wives, were treated as celebrities. They posed for photographs of "The Last Meeting of the First Farmers' Alliance" and patiently recalled for reporters their memories of the beginning. At the end of the day, they helped take the old building apart, board by board. Its new owner planned to erect it temporarily in Lampasas and then take it to the Columbian Exposition in Chicago, where he hoped to display it as a shrine of the Alliance movement.

By the time the Columbian Exposition opened in 1893, the focal point of agrarian protest had shifted to the People's party, and the

Alliance was in shambles, but those who gathered at John Allen's farm in 1891 saw the Alliance as a burgeoning movement, ready to unite the farmers and laborers of the South and West for political action. The contrast between the inauspicious beginnings of the Alliance and its power in 1891 moved J. J. Hill, the reporter from Galveston, to write: "Thus I plied John R. Allen and his alliance brethren with questions with a view of accounting for the origin of the Farmers' Alliance. But the more facts elicited the greater became the enigma. Such a social and political product at the time and place, among such a people and under such circumstances, is inexplicable."[1]

The wisdom of J. J. Hill's admission is obvious to anyone who has tried to explain why a protest movement breaks out in a particular place among specific people. Recent efforts to explain the agrarian movement that culminated in the People's party have most often focused on its rhetoric or on the collective social and economic status of participants. Such efforts tend to minimize the development of the movement over time and also to minimize the role of individuals in it. It is important to see how agrarian protesters operated within an evolving organizational structure, the Farmers' Alliance. Generalizations about the social and economic backgrounds of Populists and their rhetorical style should be linked to the movement's chronological development within its institutional setting.

The "southern" Farmers' Alliance was one of three Alliances that flourished in the last two decades of the nineteenth century. A "northern" Alliance, officially entitled the National Farmers' Alliance, was organized in Chicago in 1880 as an outgrowth of a New York state farmers' organization. Under the leadership of Chicago farm journalist Milton George, this group attracted considerable attention across the Midwest in the early 1880s. A second organization, the Colored Farmers' National Alliance, originated in Texas in 1886 and recruited blacks into a counterpart of the all-white Alliance in the southern states. The NFA&IU, or southern Alliance, was by far the largest of the three Alliances and played a much more important role in the agrarian revolt of the 1890s than either Milton George's group or the black organization. From its Texas base, it spread across the South in the late 1880s, offering farmers salvation through economic cooperation. In 1889 it absorbed the strong state Alliances in Kansas and the Dakotas, and by 1891 it was organized in thirty-two states reaching from California to New York.

Of necessity this study deals selectively with the southern Alliance in those thirty-two states. I have dealt most extensively with the career of the Alliance in Kansas, Texas, Georgia, Alabama, and North

Carolina and with the development of the national organization. Extensive but less complete research in primary materials was conducted on the Alliance in the Dakotas, Tennessee, Mississippi, Florida, South Carolina, and Virginia. Information concerning the movement in other states was gathered from national Alliance sources (largely newspapers and proceedings) and from the voluminous scholarly literature on the agrarian movement.

The Alliance was one of many institutions that tried to make intelligible to the American farmer his social and economic situation and to enable him to cope with it. The answers it provided were convincing to a great many people. For a brief time in the late 1880s and early 1890s, the Alliance was one of the largest and most influential institutions in the southern and plains states; it, therefore, demands study in its own right. The significance of the Alliance, moreover, transcends its own career, for it provided the organizational base for political insurgency in the 1890s. In every southern state where the People's party became a viable political organization, a strong Farmers' Alliance gave it form and leadership. In addition, the southern Alliance formed the vanguard of successful insurgency in Kansas, Colorado, and the Dakotas.

To understand American Populism, one must understand the Farmers' Alliance, and to understand the Alliance, the place to begin is, as J. J. Hill knew, the Texas frontier.

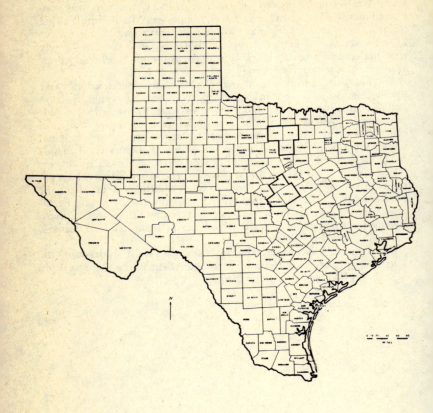

From Stanley A. Arbingast, *et al.*, *Atlas of Texas* (Rev. ed.; Austin: Bureau of Business Research, University of Texas, 1967). Outlined areas show Alliance strength before 1884 (Lampasas, Coryell, Hamilton, Parker, Wise, Jack).

Populist Vanguard

CHAPTER I

Frontier Beginnings

Settlers heading west from Fort Worth in the 1870s might almost have feared they had reached the edge of the earth. In a few miles, the familiar woodlands gave way to a strange, treeless prairie. Pressing on, they reached a vague but equally important line of demarcation, the farming frontier, beyond which open-range cattle ranching prevailed. In the course of their journey, they had also reached another invisible boundary, the cultural edge of the South.

In the 1870s these demographic, economic, and cultural frontiers stretched across Texas from Clay and Montague counties on the Red River down through Brown and San Saba.[1] Into this tier of counties poured an army of settlers from the South and Midwest, pushed by financial failure and pulled by a host of private dreams. Those too late, or too poor, to take up land along the tree-lined creek bottoms settled in the inhospitable cross timbers or edged onto the prairie. All found this new home to be a hostile place, violent and disorganized.

During and after the Civil War, the white man's efforts to "civilize" West Texas crumbled. Indian raids jeopardized outlying settlements until 1875. Deadly feuds continued throughout the 1870s and 1880s, despite the efforts of the Texas Rangers. Well-organized bands of desperados made stealing and murdering profitable enterprises, and the clash of two competing economic systems, cattle ranching and small-scale farming, compounded the difficulties.[2]

Settlers responded to the problems of the frontier as they had to social disorganization in their old homes, by forming voluntary associations. These ranged from vigilante groups to associations of stockmen, sheepraisers, or farmers, and to social institutions, including schools, churches, Masonic lodges—even literary societies—each struggling to bring civilization to the frontier.

The line separating these types of organizations was seldom distinct. For example, a club organized by farmers and stockmen near Lampasas in the late 1870s combined features of all three. It practiced vigilantism by protecting its members against rustlers, furthered their economic interests by helping them locate strays, and as a secret oath-bound fraternity helped meet social needs. The club was short-lived, but one of its members transplanted it to another frontier neighborhood in Parker County, one hundred miles to the north, and from it emerged the Farmers' Alliance.

Historians of the agrarian movement have not pinpointed the beginnings of the Alliance. Most suggest that it began in Lampasas in 1874 or 1875, although some argue that the Texas group sprang from similar organizations in Kansas or New York.[3] The uncertainty stems in part from the multiple sources of the Alliance movement and in part from the naturally obscure beginnings of such a group. The issue is further confused, however, by a controversy that raged in the 1880s and 1890s between competing "founders" of the order.

That dispute involved two points, the genesis of the Lampasas group and, more significantly, the degree of continuity between it and an Alliance that William T. Baggett formed in Parker County. The creation story that, with some modifications, became the standard Alliance line was first published by William L. Garvin in 1885. Garvin, who farmed and taught school near Poolville, Parker County, had joined the revived Alliance in 1880. He probably received his information concerning the Lampasas group from Baggett, who insisted that it began sometime between 1870 and 1875 and disbanded in 1879. Thereupon Baggett, who moved north to Parker County that year, founded a new organization, taking ideas from several sources, including the Grange and the defunct Alliance.[4]

Members of the Lampasas group remembered the beginnings differently. According to John R. Allen, A. P. Hungate, and other charter members, they formed the Alliance in September 1877 on Allen's farm. Lampasas Alliancemen argued that Baggett's group sprang directly from their own. Still smarting from a resolution adopted by the State Farmers' Alliance in 1888 which honored Baggett as "father of the Texas Alliance," they won from the state body in 1893 a decision that Allen "was the first person to conceive the idea of the Alliance organization."[5]

The ultimate wellspring of the Alliance, like that of most social movements, seems beyond discovery. Even A. P. Hungate, who interviewed Lampasas Alliancemen with the idea of writing an "official" history, had to admit, "It is not probable that the world will ever have a full and correct account of our origin and early development."[6]

Whatever its exact relation to the overall Alliance movement, an indigenous farmers' organization *did* develop in Lampasas County during the late 1870s. In that decade, Lampasas faced problems common to the frontier. The influx of small farmers quadrupled the county's population. The clash between ranchers and small farmers was apparently less bitter than elsewhere, but violence nevertheless abounded. Only weeks before John Allen called his neighbors together to form the first Alliance, Texas Rangers suppressed a long and bloody feud between two families in the county.[7]

To deal with social and economic upheaval, citizens of Lampasas formed all manner of associations. In the summer of 1877, the county boasted, in addition to a number of Protestant churches, two Granges, an immigration aid society, and lodges of the United Friends of Temperance, Masons, and the Odd Fellows. Most of these, however, were located in the county seat. The club that John Allen and his neighbors formed was among the first organizations of any kind in the sparsely settled northern section of the county. First calling their club the Knights of Reliance, they chose as president Lewis S. Chavose, a former Confederate captain and an established farmer and fruitgrower in the neighborhood.[8]

No sooner was the club organized than one of its officers, F. O. Yates, a large landowner, tried unsuccessfully to convert it into a local Grange. One of the members who opposed such a move was A. P. Hungate whose speech to the club revealed dissatisfaction with the Grange's self-help approach to agricultural problems. The Grange, he said,

might discover secrets of nature as would enable them to grow one hundred ears of corn where they now harvest fifty nubbins. But what benefit would that be if while engaged in that achievment, their negligence as citizens had allowed laws to find place upon our statute books that would render the fine ears worth less than nubbins. As Knights of reliance we stand upon a broader and stronger platform. We have undertaken the erection of a more comodious structure. We propose to employ the whole foundation of the Grange as a single corner stone of a grand social and political pallace, where liberty may dwell and where justice may be safely domiciled.[9]

The group remained an independent club but soon changed its name from Knights of Reliance to Farmers' Alliance. The club, which soon had forty or fifty members, sent out organizers to establish new lodges. William T. Baggett, then a schoolteacher in neighboring Coryell County, organized several lodges there. As affiliated clubs sprang up nearby, the original group on Donaldson's Creek took the name "Pleasant Valley No. 1." In February 1878 a county Alliance was organized at Pleasant Valley with Chavose as president, and in May lodges from Lampasas, Coryell, and Hamilton counties formed a "state" Alliance, again with Chavose as president.[10]

What sort of people joined this new organization? Information about them is scarce, and two of the founders later disagreed about their economic condition. Allen recalled that most "were in comfort-

able circumstances," but according to Hungate, "all were compara-
tively poor." Some of them left enough evidence to permit more
precise descriptions.[11] Almost all had arrived in Lampasas County
since 1870. The twelve members about whom something is known
came from eight different states, but except for two Hoosiers, all were
southerners. In 1880 nearly all owned their own farms. Most had
taken the state's offer of a 160-acre homestead, but several owned
substantially more land, with F. O. Yates's 1,400-acre holding being
the largest. The value of their land was roughly equal to that of other
farmers in the county.[12] Most of them combined stockraising with
general farming on a small scale. All of them raised cattle, and most
grew feed grain. By 1880 most were also raising a bale or two of
cotton. One, Captain Chavose, had a flourishing apple and peach or-
chard. In short, the early Alliancemen were not markedly different
from their neighbors. They represented a cross section of a farming
community on the Texas frontier.

The careers of two leaders suggest something of the group's diversity. John R. Allen was born in Tennessee in 1831.[13] When his
mother died eleven years later, he was sent to live with his grandfather, a Louisiana physician. When the grandfather reneged on a
pledge to train him in medicine, Allen moved to East Texas, where he
farmed until the outbreak of the Civil War. He served in the Confederate army and was mustered out as a second lieutenant, whereupon he
returned to his farm. After the death of his second wife in 1874, he
moved to Lampasas and began farming on Donaldson's Creek. By
1880 his small farm was valued at a respectable $1,200.[14]

Unlike Allen and most Lampasas Alliancemen, A. P. Hungate
was not a southerner. He was born on a farm in Indiana in 1842. Like
Allen, he received no formal education, but he was able to study medicine under a physician in Terre Haute. When the war came, he enlisted in the Indiana Volunteers, serving as a surgeon. Hungate did not
practice medicine after the war but instead opened a drug store. When
a fire destroyed his store in 1874, he packed up and moved to Texas,
where he settled near Donaldson's Creek. By 1880 his 160-acre farm
was valued at only $600. Unlike Allen, who remained a Democrat
until his death in 1899, Hungate became a Populist and, after the
People's party collapsed, a socialist.[15]

Like many subsequent Alliance leaders, both Allen and Hungate
were active farmers but also had skills and social standing that fitted
them for leadership. Allen was a successful farmer and acknowledged
community leader, while Hungate's professional and business experience and his gift for oratory made him a natural leader for any
community organization.

No single crisis moved these men to organize their club. John Allen's call was reportedly couched in the rhetoric of traditional agricultural societies. The neighbors were to meet "for the purpose of bettering the conditions of the agricultural classes." Hungate recalled that "there were about as many objects in view for organization as there were men participating." Some thought lawyers or merchants were at the root of their problems, while others wanted only to protect themselves against cattle thieves.[16] All agreed on the need for a system of finding strayed or stolen cattle, for barbed-wire fences had not been introduced in the county, and cattle grazed at will. Following the lead of the Grange, the club appointed two officers (called "Grand Smokeys") to record brands, report strays, and work for the apprehension of rustlers. Initiates to the club swore to report strays found on their property and to assist officers of the Alliance in maintaining "peace and harmony" in the county. As other Alliances sprang up, a system was developed whereby the local groups reported on strays to the county or state secretaries of the order.[17]

In a frontier county having few institutions to create a community out of the heterogeneous mass of settlers, the Alliance came to play an important socializing role. What a defender of the Alliance later said of rural Texas in general applied to Lampasas: "[W]ithout some common cause for the assembling of the families of each neighborhood together, [Texans] . . . being a land of strangers, would for a great many years to come, remain strangers to each other."[18]

The new group took the form of a secret society, replete with passwords, grips, oaths, and regalia. This pattern of organization reflected Grange influences but no doubt also stemmed from a generalized familiarity with fraternal organizations. Both the ritualism and the secrecy came to have practical significance in the economic and political dealings of the Alliance, but they first offered a feeling of community to isolated farm families. The local "lodge" provided a setting not unlike the Protestant churches to which most of its members belonged, within which shared values could be reaffirmed and new courses of action clothed with authority.

The most significant function of the Lampasas Alliance, and the one that led to its quick demise, was political. The birth of the Alliance coincided with the rise of the Greenback party, which in Texas began organizing at the local level early in 1877. By February 1878 the city of Lampasas had a flourishing Greenback club.[19] Throughout its career, the Alliance conducted a running debate on its proper relation to the exercise of political power. That debate began at Lampasas. John R. Allen expressed a wish rather than a fact when he stated in 1891 that the original group "did not let party politics come into the alliance." Some early members, probably including F. O. Yates, opposed any contact with politics, but A. P. Hungate envisioned the Alliance as a vehicle for "education" in antimonopoly principles which would act as a nonpartisan pressure group.[20]

One wing of the Lampasas order, led by L. S. Chavose, sought to make the Alliance a vehicle of political insurgency. At an early meeting, the Donaldson's Creek club adopted a constitution, supported by Chavose, that apparently committed the order to overt political action. No copy of the document has survived, but it was controversial enough to elicit from Hungate, author of a rival constitution, a warning that its publication would "be a death warrant to our organization."[21] The group did not publish the inflammatory document, and it was, in fact, modified, but Chavose's view prevailed, and the Alliance endorsed the Greenback party. Chavose, though an energetic organizer, made no effort to reconcile the conflicts that political involvement created within the order. The Alliance survived the trauma of the 1878 campaign and may have lasted through 1880, when the county experienced a bitterly contested election in which Greenbackers fielded a full county slate.[22] The Greenback ticket in 1880 included Chavose's lieutenant in the Alliance, John Reeves, and, strangely enough, F. O. Yates. If the Alliance had in fact survived until then, the decisive defeat of the local Greenback ticket would no doubt have killed it.[23]

What then was the significance of the abortive effort in Lampasas for the overall development of the Alliance? Parker and Wise counties, not Lampasas, provided the nucleus of leadership for expansion beyond the frontier. The cooperative enterprises that sparked the expansion also stemmed from the Alliance's second growth. Even the organizational structure of the order probably owed more to Baggett and his associates than to John Allen's neighborhood club. The Lampasas beginnings provided the Alliance with a myth of creation, appropriately vague, the exegesis of which helped fuel the ongoing debate about the proper course of action for the movement. Alliance leaders seeking a coalition of southern and midwestern farmers could point to the Lampasas experience as the beginning of intersectional cooperation. As the Texas Alliance became more class-oriented during the 1880s, leaders could describe it (incorrectly) as an organization born in the struggle between small farmers and wealthy cattle kings and the land-company agents. Most frequently, those who strove to maintain the order's "nonpartisan" posture could sermonize, as did W. Scott Morgan in 1889, that the Alliance "though originally organized for the protection of the farmers, had become, through the selfishness of some of its members, a means by which they expected to secure political prominence and lucrative positions."[24]

In the spring of 1879, William T. Baggett packed his schoolbooks and moved to Poolville, a new community in northern Parker County. Along with his books, Baggett took a copy of the Lampasas Alliance constitution. In short order, he organized a school, the first in Poolville, and a Farmers' Alliance.[25] Parker County was a likely spot for the Alliance to take hold. In the 1870s it experienced the usual frontier problems—mushrooming population, lack of social organization, and farmer-rancher disputes. At the end of the decade, the tensions were increasing. New settlers in Parker and neighboring Wise counties discovered that land companies and railroads had preempted much of the potential farming area. The introduction of barbed-wire fences and the enclosure of huge tracts heightened ill feelings between cattlemen and farmers to the point of armed conflict by the early 1880s.[26]

Immigrants to the Poolville area faced an additional strain. Settlers who filtered into the northern section of Parker County, mostly poor farmers pushed to the frontier by failure in the South or Midwest, encountered hostility from residents of the settled, relatively prosperous southern part of the county. County-seat bankers and merchants in Weatherford considered them poor credit risks, and editors branded them as shiftless and lawless. The settlers around Poolville and Springtown reciprocated in kind. They looked to Fort Worth rather than Weatherford for markets. They banded together politically against their neighbors to the south, sometimes challenging them for control of the county Democratic party and on other occasions turning to Greenbackism. Some even wanted to secede and form a new county.[27] Thus in Parker County, from which it would spread across the South, the Alliance was influenced not only by problems common to late nineteenth-century farmers and the uncertainties of the frontier but by local social and economic cleavages.

The new schoolmaster in Poolville, a twenty-six-year-old Georgian, had mastered the techniques of organizing people. Baggett had belonged to the Grange, as well as the Lampasas Alliance, and it was relatively easy for him to organize his neighbors into an Alliance in June 1879. Dreaming of bigger things to come, the group named themselves "Poolville No. 1." As Baggett later remembered it, the new Alliance faced the suspicions of farmers who had recently watched the Grange collapse and of townsmen who were edgy about agrarian insurgency: "We had to fight ignorance [and] superstition in a certain class in those little towns, and support the weak-kneed . . . and when the papers took the matter up they called us Molly Maguires, Anarchists, and Communists."[28]

The men whom Baggett persuaded to join the new organization were for the most part small farmers and stockmen similar to those who had belonged in Lampasas. At least one charter member, J. N. Montgomery, was a well-established, prosperous farmer, but the first president of the Poolville Alliance, Thomas Jefferson Womack, apparently failed to make a go of his farm, for by the end of 1879 he had moved west to Jack County and started over.[29]

The revived Alliance worked to recover strays, protect farmers from thieves and ranchers, and prevent eviction by "land sharks," land-company agents who sometimes used fraudulent land titles to remove settlers. Drawing upon Lampasas and Grange experiences, the Alliance developed an elaborate system for locating strayed livestock and for apprehending rustlers. The suballiances circulated lists of strays, and the order adopted a special brand to identify members' cattle. The early Alliance ritual included a series of signs for use in apprehending cattle thieves.[30] For a time, the new organization even retained the position of Grand Smokey to coordinate the pursuit of thieves.

In addition to recovering lost property, the new Alliance functioned as a vigilante group, meeting force with force to protect farmers' interests. In this regard, it resembled the land leagues and protective associations that had flourished on the middle border before the Civil War and along the frontier from Texas northward in the 1870s.[31] In the 1870s and 1880s, the Texas frontier had the highest concentration of vigilante groups of any region in the country. The extent of Alliance vigilantism is indeterminable, but accounts written years later lauded Alliance efforts to thwart land-company agents. By presenting a solid front and threatening to settle disputes "with Winchesters and revolvers," the Alliancemen routed the land sharks, or so the legend went.[32]

Alliancemen participated in the most violent confrontation between farmers and ranchers in the era. By 1880 ranchers were stringing barbed-wire fences to enclose ranges covering hundreds of thousands of acres. These fences, sometimes illegally placed and often lacking gates, prohibited access to water, farms, and even towns. In retaliation, farmers, operating in well-organized bands, began cutting fences and burning fence posts. The conflict reached such proportions that early in 1884 a special session of the legislature was called to deal with it.[33]

For many small farmers, the issue of fencing brought into focus the cause of all their ills. One group of fence cutters posted the following notice in a frontier county: "Down with the monopolies! They can't exist in Texas and especially in Coleman County. Away with your foreign capitalists! The range and soil of Texas belong to the heroes of the South. No monopolies, and don't tax us to school the nigger. Give us homes as God intended and not gates to churches and towns and schools. Above all, give us water for our stock."[34]

In 1883 the conflict became acute in Jack County, western outpost of the Alliance. When asked if the Alliance were "at the bottom of the 'fence-cutting trouble,' " the editor of the Alliance's journal emphatically denied that it was but had to admit that some members had been involved.[35]

In 1881 the young Alliance was confronted directly with a charge of vigilantism. In June the Weatherford *Times*, branding Alliancemen as "thieves, robbers, [and] murderers," claimed that they were to blame for a reign of terror in Parker, Wise, and Jack counties. Alliance leaders, fearing that the accusation would destroy their organization, demanded a public hearing. On 7 July fifty-seven Alliancemen met with a large crowd of Parker County citizens. Alliance leaders emphatically denied the charges, pointing out that the editor of the *Times* had made them only after losing Alliance patronage to his crosstown rival, the *Herald*. The editor of the *Times* failed to produce evidence to support his charges, and the citizenry, including Weatherford lawyer and future governor S. W. T. Lanham, agreed that his blanket denunciation of the Alliance was unwarranted, but the resolution that the assembled citizens adopted suggested that not all Alliancemen were blameless: "While we acknowledge that there may be a few unprincipled men who are members of the Farmers' Alliance . . . we most emphatically deny that the Alliance, as a body, recognizes mob law or anything that is not in strict accordance with the laws of our state."[36]

There is no substantial basis for challenging the Alliance's protestations of innocence, but in an atmosphere charged with violence where legitimate channels for the redress of grievances seemed to be closed, it would be remarkable if such an organization had remained clear of extralegal efforts to protect its perceived interests. In any event, the confrontation with the Weatherford *Times* actually helped the Alliance. As one leader put it, the conflict "has wonderfully advertised us and success has been the end of it."[37]

The stray-catching and vigilantism of the Alliance soon declined in importance, but during its frontier phase, the order also adopted a viable organizational structure that remained virtually unchanged throughout its career. Whatever its debt to the Lampasas Alliance, the new, more complex structure included most of the features common to voluntary associations in the United States.

By the early nineteenth century, a host of associations had standardized techniques for mobilizing rural and small-town Americans. The pattern included hiring secretaries and lecturers to recruit and organize members, developing a sympathetic press, and establishing local chapters. The new Alliance, like its Lampasas predecessor and the Grange, added to this pattern the secrecy and ritualism of fraternal organizations.[38] Virtually all of the Texas frontiersmen, northerners and southerners alike, were acquainted with this cultural pattern in one form or another—churches, Sunday school associations, fraternal lodges, agricultural and debating societies, and vigilante groups. The Alliance developed variations on the theme, but the general pattern was so familiar as to seem part of the way society naturally organized itself.

The key man in the missionary thrust of the Alliance was the lecturer-organizer, of whom schoolmaster Baggett was the prototype. On his own initiative, Baggett organized nine of the twelve lodges that had been established in Parker, Wise, and Jack counties by the summer of 1880. At that point, the new "Grand State Farmers' Alliance," an association formed in December 1879 among those twelve lodges, appointed specific members to carry on the work. These agents were to receive one dollar for each lodge they organized. (In 1881 the fee was raised to $3.25).[39] In 1881 the "state" Alliance appointed several deputy lecturers to organize in specific counties, usually the ones in which they lived or from which they had moved to the frontier. By the summer of 1883, twenty-six of these lecturers were at work in eleven counties, which covered the frontier and reached into central and eastern Texas.[40] By July they had organized 144 lodges (called subordinate Alliances).

But the recruiting system had its weaknesses. Paid according to the number of Alliances they could organize, the lecturers frequently remained in a community only long enough to explain the rudiments of the order's program, supervise the election of officers, reveal the "secret work," and collect the fee. By August 1883 only thirty of the suballiances they had organized were active enough to send delegates to the meeting of the state Alliance.[41]

Nevertheless, the lecturer-organizer was an essential figure in the Alliance's growth. He was to the Alliance what the circuit rider had been to early Methodism. He provided the necessary point of contact between troubled farmers and an organization that offered them relief. Most of the organizers came from the loosely defined class of rural professional men. To be sure, most of them were farmers, more or less, but many brought to their work skills and experience beyond that of most "horny handed sons of toil." For example, Dr. Owen G.

Peterson, who was living near Poolville when Baggett reestablished the Alliance, became a charter member of the lodge in his neighborhood and was soon commissioned as an organizer and assigned to develop a ritual for the order. In his native Illinois, Peterson had become a physician by "reading" medicine. At the age of twenty-two, he won election as county tax assessor and five years later had moved to Texas. In 1877 he began practicing medicine in rural Wise and Parker counties while operating a small farm. A man of varied interests, he conducted a neighborhood Sunday school and presided over a music society. At age thirty-five, Peterson had the energy, the expertise, and the social standing to be an effective organizer for the new Alliance.[42]

It was largely through the efforts of Peterson's neighbor, S. O. Daws, that the Alliance survived its decline in 1883. In 1881 Daws became an organizer in Parker and Wise counties. In 1882 he was elected state lecturer, then largely a ceremonial office, but at the time of his election, he called for the employment of a full-time "traveling lecturer." During the winter of 1883, the state president appointed Daws to such a post.[43] Daws, who was thirty-three when he began work for the Alliance, had little formal education but was a voracious reader and served as a lay preacher. In 1868, after service in the Confederate army, Daws moved from his native Mississippi to Texas. When the Alliance came to Wise County, he was already established as an "old settler" and therefore a man of importance. Daws operated a small farm, but from 1883 until 1896, he spent most of his time as a professional organizer for the Alliance.[44]

Daws, Peterson, and other Alliance organizers had skills and social standing that set them apart from the mass of small farmers, but too much should not be made of their elite status. Some had never been anything but farmers, although most had at least tried their hand at business or a profession. Furthermore, the distinction between farmers and rural teachers, preachers, and even doctors was often negligible. In many cases, the same pressures had forced them all to the frontier. The early organizers had skills and experience that suited them for their task, but they were tied by necessity and inclination to the culture of the dirt farmers.

Unlike its Lampasas forerunner, the revitalized Alliance reinforced the work of its organizers through a subsidized press. The early response of newspapers in Parker and Wise counties was either to ignore or condemn the new organization. When the Alliance began attracting followers, struggling editors, who suffered even more than farmers from overproduction, saw the value of supporting the order.

In February 1881 the Alliance came to an understanding with the editor of the Weatherford *Herald*, Lewis Wood, a peripatetic frontier journalist. Wood agreed to print Alliance notices and articles and presumably to support the order editorially. The Alliance, in turn, agreed to pay him a fixed sum and use its organizational network to enlist subscribers for the *Herald*. The arrangement apparently proved unsatisfactory, for in February 1882 the Alliance shifted its patronage to the Jacksboro *Rural Citizen*, and Wood moved his press further west to Mineral Wells.[45]

Joseph N. Rogers, who settled in Jack County in 1873, began publishing the *Rural Citizen* in 1880, as an outgrowth of a Sunday school magazine that he had published at his country home. When the Alliance began organizing in Jack County, Rogers editorially endorsed its activities. In February 1882 he accepted an offer similar to the one made to Wood, and the *Rural Citizen* became the order's official journal, an arrangement that lasted until 1886 when disagreement over the political stance of the Alliance forced a change.[46]

A subsidized press served two purposes for the young Alliance. First, it took the organization's message to more farmers than the lecturers could possibly contact. Second, the papers, through their network of "exchanges" exposed Alliancemen on the Texas frontier to similar movements elsewhere, while conversely, news of their venture found its way back across the South and into the Midwest. Through the *Rural Citizen*, Texas Alliancemen learned about the Chicago-based National Farmers' Alliance. During the spring of 1881, the paper quoted antimonopoly editorials from Milton George's *Western Rural*, organ of the National Farmers' Alliance, and advised its readers that they could obtain additional information on reform topics by writing to the Chicago paper. In its earliest description of Alliance activities in Jack County, the *Rural Citizen* mistakenly identified the Texas Alliance with the organization that "has assumed ponderous proportions in the Great West."[47]

Unlike many voluntary associations, including the "northern" Alliance, the Texas state Alliance maintained rather strict control over its local units.[48] As the Alliance expanded from its nucleus of a dozen or so lodges in the area around Poolville, the "state" organization took steps to insure conformity among the suballiances. In October 1880 the state Alliance, now headed by J. N. Montgomery, secured a state charter that listed the purposes of the organization as "encouraging agriculture, horticulture, and to suppress personal, local, sectional and national prejudices." On the basis of this document, the state Alliance issued charters to the suballiances.[49]

By early 1881 the Alliance had adopted a constitution that further strengthened the state body. It established methods of representation to county and state Alliances based on the number of dues-paying members, set membership requirements, and even outlined procedures for settling disputes through appeals to the state Alliance.[50] Under the constitution, membership was open to anyone over the age of sixteen, male or female, who believed in a supreme being and was a "farmer, farm laborer, a country school teacher, a country physician, or a minister of the gospel." The requirements were significantly altered the following year to limit membership to whites. Alliance leaders who helped make the change later said it had been done because the Alliance was a social organization "where we meet with our wives and daughters."[51] The initial lack of such Jim Crow restrictions probably owed more to the scarcity of blacks in West Texas than to enlightened racial attitudes.

By the 1881–82 period, the organizational structure of the Alliance, although not its program, was well defined. The expansion of the order into Jack County in 1881 demonstrated the organizing process that the Alliance would use in mobilizing farmers across the South. Two of the first lodges organized by William Baggett in 1879 were in Jack, but there was no systematic drive to attract support in the county until late in 1880. In September of that year, William J. Womack received permission to organize new suballiances. In 1879 Womack and his brother Jeff had moved to Jack County from Parker, where Jeff had been the first president of the Poolville Alliance. William, who was to spend the next six years pushing the Alliance west with the farmers' frontier, had a penchant for organizing. In addition to his efforts on behalf of the Alliance, he helped establish a neighborhood debating society and a Sabbath School Association in frontier Jack County.[52]

During the winter of 1880–81, William Womack formed a suballiance in his neighborhood. He then approached a group of "select gentlemen" in the nearby Post Oak community who formed an Alliance with Isom H. Steed as president. "Major" Steed was a successful cattleman and merchant and had recently opened a cotton gin at Post Oak. A local correspondent for the county's only newspaper soon noticed another of the lodges that Womack had organized, this one at Gunter's schoolhouse: "They have an organization here called the Farmers' Alliance of which your correspondent knows but little as yet; though they meet every other Friday night. [I] guess it is a good thing."[53] Favorable coverage by the *Rural Citizen* brought the Alliance to the attention of more potential members who were attracted to the order by conditions much like those in Parker and Wise counties. By July 1881 enough of them had joined to permit the formation of a county Alliance.[54]

In Jack County, the growth of the Alliance followed the classic pattern of voluntary associations. It utilized a paid organizer who enlisted the support of influential leaders and won the endorsement of a local newspaper. The organizer then formed his converts into local chapters, each linked to a central governing body.

But organization could not save the Alliance from a precipitous decline in 1883. In August only 30 of the more than 140 suballiances were active, and the state Alliance had virtually ceased to function. Leaders attributed the decline to conflict during the tumultuous election campaign of 1882 and the failure of early efforts to establish marketing and purchasing cooperatives.[55] The Alliance seemed about to go the way of other farmers' organizations, but worsening economic conditions on the frontier and the emergence of S. O. Daws as an energetic, capable leader reversed the decline. Within two years of its nadir, the Alliance had spread across much of the state.

CHAPTER 2

Expansion across Texas

In January 1884, as the Alliance seemed to be collapsing, state president William Garvin appointed his neighbor, S. O. Daws, as a "traveling lecturer" for the order. Daws received authority to revive dormant lodges, give public lectures on the work of the order, and recruit assistant lecturers. Unlike previous organizers, he was to receive a fixed salary of $50 per month.

When the state Alliance met in February, Daws had already reorganized fifteen dormant lodges. His appointment (and his salary) were renewed, with the stipulation that he would visit suballiances in the eight counties where they already existed and take the message beyond that West Texas enclave.[1] At that meeting of the state Alliance, Daws demonstrated the kind of rhetoric that was breathing new life into the order. He "gave a stirring lecture on the condition of American farmers and their duties as American citizens and their obligations to stand as a great conservative body against the encroachment of monopolies and in opposition to the growing corruption of wealth and power as exhibited in the present day and age."[2] By the end of February, Daws had revived the order in Parker and Wise counties and had moved on. A spokesman in Parker County reported the revival, noting that farmers and mechanics there "are determined to try and lift the yoke of monopoly and oppression from their necks."[3]

Clearly, Daws envisioned the Alliance as something more than a frontier protective association. The problems he described were those of commercial farmers, and the solutions he proposed began with a program of cooperative enterprise through which farmers could market their crops and purchase supplies. In the early 1880s, the economy of Parker, Wise, and Jack counties was shifting from stockraising and subsistence farming to commercial agriculture based on wheat and cotton. Resumption of railroad construction after the depression of the 1870s brought Weatherford, Decatur, and Jacksboro into the market areas of St. Louis, New York, and Liverpool.[4]

Lengthening lists of farms to be sold at sheriffs' sales bore witness to the fact that the problems that many settlers had fled Alabama or Indiana to avoid had caught up with them in Texas, and the growing popularity of antimonopoly and soft money schemes and of plans for circumventing middlemen suggested that more and more farmers were ready to seek some sort of relief. By the mid-1880s Alliance leaders and many farmers strongly believed the source of their problems to be the credit and marketing system of the cotton culture, in which the "furnishing merchant" loomed as the principal villain.[5]

These angry farmers were familiar with the cooperative efforts of the Grange. In 1882 the Alliance tried unsuccessfully to reach an agreement with the Patrons of Husbandry whereby Alliancemen could market their cotton through the Texas Cooperative Association, the business arm of the Grange.[6]

Following Grange precedent, county Alliances organized by Daws and his associates established "trade committees" that negotiated with local merchants, using the carrot of Alliance patronage and the stick of threatened boycotts to exact special rates for Alliance members.[7] Some county and suballiances also opened joint stock cooperative stores, often patterned after local Grange stores. In frontier Erath County, for example, the Alliance set up a joint stock cooperative encompassing marketing and purchasing functions. In 1885 Alliancemen there noted with pride that local merchants had been forced to recognize the Alliance as an economic power.[8]

The Alliance also ventured into cooperative cotton marketing with notable success. After failing to market their cotton through the Grange agency at Galveston, Alliancemen turned to controlling local markets. Despite increasing competition for the Texas cotton crop, farmers at interior points often found themselves at the mercy of local buyers who sometimes offered only goods in payment. During the expansion of the order during 1884–85, Alliance trade committees began "bulking" members' cotton for sale on a competitive basis.[9]

The Wise County Alliance initiated this practice. In September 1884 the Wise County brethren forced buyers to raise prices for Alliance cotton sold in bulk. In October, Alliancemen from Wise and surrounding counties brought almost three thousand bales of cotton to Decatur, the county seat, and sold them for 8.5 cents per pound, which was above the going rate.[10] The following year, the Wise County Alliance opened its own cotton yard in Decatur, on land provided rent-free by a local merchant. In an editorial that presaged the attitude of many southern townsmen toward the Alliance and revealed the symbiotic relationship between the Alliance and rural trade centers, the pro-

prietor of the *Wise County Messenger* urged local merchants not to op-
pose the cooperative cotton yard, predicting that "An Alliance cotton
yard will bring hundreds of bales of cotton to Decatur that will never
be seen here without such a yard." Decatur cotton buyers, viewing the
situation differently, refused to raise prices for Alliance cotton, and
farmers who sold their cotton through the Alliance yard that year received less than the prevailing rate.[11]

Recalcitrant buyers represented only part of the dilemma confronting the cooperative marketing system. Such a system was not
workable where farmers were committed to crop liens. Yet in 1885 one
Alliance spokesman claimed that the order's marketing activities had
raised the price of cotton by one-half to three-fourths of a cent per
pound. Cotton bulking could be dramatically successful, as in the case
of Collin County Alliancemen. They took their cotton to Dallas to sell
in a bloc, but when Dallas buyers refused to meet their terms, they
accepted a higher bid from an out-of-town buyer. Alliancemen also
began operating cotton gins and compresses, while in the wheat belt of
northern Texas, the order opened grain elevators and flour mills.[12]

The first and most successful of the flour mills opened in Denton
late in 1886. Like most of the cooperative ventures, the Denton mill
was financed by subscription of stock among Alliancemen. Throughout its career, it was chronically undercapitalized, but it enjoyed
capable business leadership and an expert miller, under whose super-
vision the mill produced prize-winning flour for many years, even
after the collapse of the Alliance.[13]

News of the Alliance's varied experiments in business, lumped
together under the rubric of "cooperation," soon filtered across the
state, carried by word of mouth, by the press, and by Alliance organizers. Failures were ignored or forgotten. Successes were described
in glowing detail to farmers made receptive by their own problems
with the furnishing merchant or the cotton buyer. In the cooperative
movement, the Alliance had at last found an appealing program that
would enable it to expand beyond the frontier.

The key to the cooperatives' success was solidarity. Large numbers of farmers had to unite in a cohesive organization with enough
muscle to command attention from wholesalers or buyers. The structure that the Alliance had adopted on the frontier made possible such
solidarity. The order had a capable, aggressive corps of lecturer-
organizers—many of them selected and trained by S. O. Daws—who
could articulate the anger and frustration of small farmers and mold
them into an effective force. The network of subordinate, county, and
state Alliances, along with the subsidized press, offered an ideal

setting for instruction in the techniques of cooperation. Its secrecy gave the Alliance an element of surprise in its business dealings. Finally, the fraternal intensity of the suballiance meetings and the evangelical fervor of Alliance rallies provided a social setting in which farmers could be persuaded to commit themselves to unproven economic programs.

This combination of a demonstrable need, a program of relief, and a viable organizational structure produced results with a speed that surprised the state's politicians and editors. When S. O. Daws took up his labors as traveling lecturer, the Alliance was largely confined to Parker, Wise, and Jack counties, but beginning in the spring of 1884, the order swept across the northern part of the state.[14] In Dallas County, organizer S. H. Tucker reported spending three weeks visiting farmers and laborers and "advocating the cause of the 'Farmers Alliance' of Texas." He found an "avenging spirit" among them and warned that they would not be "trampled on." Less than two months after his appearance in the county, forty-one Alliances had been organized and a trade committee was at work. Soon Dallas Alliancemen were linking forces politically with the powerful Dallas Assembly of the Knights of Labor.[15]

By August 1885 over 500 suballiances had been organized. By April 1886 the number organized, though not necessarily active, had increased to more than 1,650, with a reported membership of over 92,000. The rapid growth even took Alliance leaders by surprise. When over 600 delegates attended the annual meeting of the state Alliance in August 1885, state leaders had to devise a new system of representation to permit the orderly completion of business.[16]

One indication of the order's increasing popularity in 1885 and 1886 was the ease with which it rolled across the Grange strongholds in central Texas, routing the "revived" Patrons of Husbandry. The Alliance held a competitive advantage over the Grange on several counts. Its rhetoric was more militant and its cooperatives were unhampered by Grange failures. Furthermore, it cost less to belong to the Alliance. Men paid six cents in dues per month and women were admitted free.[17] The Alliance also simplified its ritual, giving it a more egalitarian cast than that of the Grange. Originally the Poolville Alliance, like the Lampasas group, had three "degrees," or levels of membership, but in 1882 the three were consolidated, making the Alliance, its supporters claimed, the first secret society with no "privileged class."[18]

As the Alliance pushed eastward onto the fertile blackland prairie and beyond, A. J. Rose, master of the State Grange, and other Grange leaders received frantic pleas for help. "No Grange at work in the county," wrote one local leader. "The Alliance completely over-shadows the Grange." Rose, who in 1882 had refused to cooperate with the Alliance in cotton marketing, thought the new organization would soon pass. "I am aware that the Alliance has spread over the country like a tornado," he consoled one local Grange official, "but it will soon subside." He did, however, admit to the secretary of the National Grange: "I am expecting to lose some members this year, but hope we will shine all the brighter. Politics, the Alliance, the Agri-cultural Wheel, K. of L. growth and c. [etc.] certainly hurt us."[19]

Rose harbored unrealistic dreams for the revival of the Grange and mistakenly believed the Alliance to be a front for political malcon-tents, but at the close of the century, he reflected rather accurately on the relation of the two organizations. He recalled that the Alliance sent out lecturers who told farmers that the Grange was "too slow" in solving their problems. The Alliance established cooperative stores, but, unlike the Grange, it made arrangements to provide credit for needy members. "By this scheme," recalled Rose, "they drew of[f] the membership of the Grange and also the support of the trade to the Grange stores."[20]

In 1886 the growing Alliance demonstrated its ability to mobilize large numbers of farmers for a specific purpose when a severe drought parched the western part of the state. Like their counterparts on the northern plains, many of the farmers who settled in West Texas during the 1870s were unaware that rainfall there was periodically inadequate for traditional farming. In 1886 the rains stopped. In the area west of Decatur, crops withered and cattle began dying of thirst. To make matters worse, cattlemen further west allowed their stock to drift east-ward in search of forage. Thirty thousand head of cattle pressed into Jack and Wise counties, where they broke into fields and destroyed the remaining crops.[21]

By summer, conditions were desperate. Congressman S. W. T. Lanham introduced a bill appropriating $50,000 to purchase seed grain for drought-stricken farmers. Congress passed the bill, but President Grover Cleveland vetoed it.[22] Private relief efforts met with varied success. The Merchant's Exchange of St. Louis sent a carload of provisions, and church groups and the Grange distributed supplies, but agents sent eastward by the beleagured counties to seek aid often had to deny claims from local boosters that no suffering existed. The Reverend J. A. Zinn, Alliance spokesman from Wilbarger County, cited such statements in Fort Worth papers as evidence of a conspiracy by cattlemen and land companies to starve the farmers out.[23]

The Farmers' Alliance coordinated one of the largest relief efforts. In the eastern counties, where bumper crops of wheat and cotton were being harvested, Alliancemen collected large quantities of grain and food stuffs for shipment west, coordinating their efforts through the state Alliance paper, the *Dallas Mercury*, and Alliance officials in the drought-stricken areas. In one such shipment, Dallas County Alliancemen sent eight thousand pounds of flour and meal to Coleman County. The relief efforts even reached farmers in Lampasas County, where an Alliance had been reorganized in 1884.[24]

While the drought-relief project was under way, the Alliance experienced a fundamental shift in its objectives. Since the Alliance's resurrection in Parker County, the order had maintained a nonpolitical posture. Some Alliancemen had challenged this policy, particularly in 1882, but when Daws began his work of reorganization in 1884 the order remained essentially nonpolitical. Yet two-and-one-half years later, the Alliance adopted a platform of political demands and launched a career in pressure group politics.

Several forces propelled the Alliance toward politics between 1884 and 1886. Independent political movements along the frontier continued to sweep local Alliances into their vortices. In addition the campaign for statewide prohibition attracted large numbers of Alliancemen, and, most significantly, the Alliance's emergence as an "antimonopoly" cooperative movement coincided with the largest, most violently class-oriented labor upheaval in the history of the state.

In the aftermath of the fencing wars of 1883, farmer-cattlemen conflicts spawned independent political movements throughout West Texas. In the spring of 1884, neighborhood "land leagues" coalesced into county-wide political organizations. In Jack County, prominent Alliancemen helped organize an insurgent group, the Commonwealth Immigration Society, while members of land leagues in adjacent Clay County formed a "People's party" and prepared to field candidates for county and legislative offices. Both groups opposed ownership of land by foreign syndicates and the fencing of large tracts. J. N. Rogers, a Democrat who professed a literal belief in the order's nonpolitical rule, felt constrained to quash rumors that the Alliance and the immigration society in Jack County were "about one and the same."[25]

Prohibition attracted some Alliancemen to political insurgency. Alliancemen were predominantly Baptists and Methodists, and leaders of these denominations were preaching a crusade against Demon Rum. In 1887 clergymen led (and most Democratic leaders opposed) a "nonpolitical" campaign to enact statewide prohibition. In the ensuing referendum, almost all of the thirty-two counties that voted dry were located in the area of the Alliance's greatest strength, along the Red River and in West Texas.[26] In 1886 and succeeding years, the miniscule Prohibitionist party sought support from the Alliance and Knights of Labor by adopting a platform that the ever-watchful *Dallas News* termed "revolutionary." In addition to demanding a prohibitory amendment to the state constitution, the platform condemned speculation in commodity futures, proclaimed (four months after a bloody railroad strike) that "labor is the creator of all wealth" and must be protected against the power of corporations, and denounced the Democratic party for giving away state land to "capitalists and cattle syndicates."[27]

From hindsight, it seems unlikely that the Prohibitionists could have assembled a viable political coalition, but amid the fluid political situation of 1886 such a conclusion was far from self-evident. In 1885 the state Farmers' Alliance and the two leading Alliance papers endorsed statewide prohibition. Rumors circulated during the early summer of 1886 that Alliancemen and Prohibitionists would combine to disrupt the state Democratic convention, but the coalition never materialized. The doctrinaire drys and the men seeking to lead the Alliance into political insurgency never really trusted each other. Their visions of what ailed America overlapped but remained fundamentally different.[28]

The Alliance's shift toward political action owed less to range wars and Demon Rum than to the growth of a powerful, class-oriented labor movement in Texas.[29] In the mid-1880s the Knights of Labor, espousing the concept of "one big union," won many converts, most of whom were employees of Jay Gould's railroad system, Galveston longshoremen, or farmers and farm laborers. The Knights sought redress of specific labor grievances and preached an antimonopoly gospel similar to that of the Alliance. In 1885 the order reached its apogee in the Southwest, after its strike against Gould's midwestern lines forced a reversal of a wage reduction. The organization mushroomed to include almost one-half of the nonfarm laborers in the state.[30]

In 1885 relations between the Knights and the Alliance became cordial. The two organizations had compatible objectives and their membership overlapped, particularly along the route of the Texas and Pacific Railroad and in the mining regions of West Texas. In August 1885 the state Alliance, meeting in Decatur, listened to speeches made by K. of L. officials and passed resolutions of solidarity. By the end of 1885, local cooperation between the two had taken such diverse forms as plans in Kaufman County to open a cooperative cottonseed-oil mill and in Palo Pinto County to field an independent slate for local offices.[31]

The issue of Alliance cooperation with the Knights and, concomitantly, of Alliance involvement in politics, erupted in a public debate among Alliance leaders. Early in 1886 some local Alliance leaders called for the order to support the Knights' boycotts against the Mallory steamship lines and against a Dallas dry-goods firm. In February, William R. Lamb, a protégé of Daws, asked (or ordered) state president Andrew Dunlap to proclaim Alliance support for the boycotts. When Dunlap refused, Lamb, acting on his own initiative, announced support in the name of the state Alliance. His actions drew fire from Dunlap and from editor J. N. Rogers. Local Alliances began lining up in support of each position.[32]

In a blistering rejoinder to Dunlap, published 11 March, Lamb condemned the state leaders for equivocating on the labor issue and restated his support for the boycott. Lamb was president of the militant Montague County Alliance, and the controversy with Dunlap pushed him into the leadership of the Alliance's growing left wing. He appealed to farmers as *laborers* whose interests lay with industrial workers. Manufacturers had united against them, he argued, and they must reciprocate.[33] Dunlap met Lamb's attack with a lengthy letter, published in newspapers hostile to the K. of L., in which he rehearsed the debate and condemned Lamb for exceeding his authority.[34]

As the argument over the boycotts began, a strike broke out on the Gould lines which threatened to engulf northern Texas in civil war.[35] Gould's manager, H. M. Hoxie, supported by a sympathetic press and judicial system, moved to crush the strike and the Knights of Labor. For weeks, striking trainmen disrupted rail traffic by disabling engines and intimidating nonstrikers. At least four men died in the ensuing violence.

Many Alliancemen, perhaps most, supported the strike. They gave food and money to the workers, held joint meetings with the Knights, and, in growing numbers, adopted resolutions similar to the one passed by the Red River County Alliance: "[W]e sympathize deeply in the misfortunes of the Knights of Labor in their struggle to feed and clothe their families, and ask them to meet us at the ballot box and help overthrow all monopolies."[36]

By early May, the strike had been crushed and with it the Knights of Labor, but the movement for independent political action continued, spurring new growth in the Alliance. With Alliances in county after county endorsing direct political action, many leaders feared that the order would become hopelessly divided and would be swept away like the Lampasas Alliance. Some tried unsuccessfully to revive William Baggett's nonpolitical rule. S. O. Daws offered a middle course, similar to that already taken by some West Texas Alliances and by earlier farmer organizations in the Midwest. Deploring efforts to turn the order into a "political machine," Daws suggested that Alliancemen come together in each neighborhood *as individuals* to form "antimonopoly leagues" for the purpose of nominating candidates. Thus the order would remain a nonpartisan "educational" agency, but Alliancemen could form political coalitions with like-minded individuals. Even before this crisis, Daws had argued that the Alliance's role in politics was to educate "workers and producers" concerning those governmental policies that, when enacted, would "secure to labor the full reward of its toils." "When farmers and laborers are thus educated," Daws had explained almost a year earlier, "true political action will naturally and unavoidably follow."[37]

One of the first Alliances to follow Daws's advice was the McLennan County Alliance, which voted in June to avoid partisan politics while agreeing "to organize anti-monopoly clubs and to vote for anti-monopolists for the legislature." The distinction between becoming a political machine and exerting political pressure escaped newsmen and Democratic politicians. Thus the Palo Pinto *Star* cited as proof of the Alliance's nonpolitical character a statement by W. F. Westellison that it was "contrary to the principles of the Farmers' Alliance to go into politics and if we ever prosper we must stand aloof of all political bearing *as an organization*." At the time he made the statement, Westellison was organizing an independent coalition of Alliancemen and Knights in Palo Pinto County.[38]

Not all Alliancemen heeded Daws's advice. Some opted for direct political action, while others eschewed politics altogether, but the "Daws formula," coupled with an announcement by the state Alliance in August that nonpartisan political education would be a major goal of the order, redefined the limits within which Alliancemen debated their collective role in politics. The question was no longer whether, but how the Alliance would exert political pressure.

In 1886 farmer-labor coalitions cropped up in at least twenty counties across northern Texas. In Comanche County, another of Daws's protégés, Thomas Gaines, organized one of the most successful of these groups, the "Human Party," which easily elected a full county slate. Although most of its leaders were Alliancemen, Gaines was careful to point out that they acted as individuals "and not by order of a secret society or any organization to which they belonged." Gaines avoided the rhetoric of the yeoman and appealed to the class interests of "labor," which for him included farmers. "The case as it stands," he wrote to the local editor, "is plainly understood to be an issue between capital and labor; and the present leaders of both the old parties are . . . in sympathy with and support the capitalists."[39]

Alliance cooperation with the K. of L. did not always result in political unity. In Dallas County, where the Alliance reportedly had five thousand members, Alliance and Knight leaders conferred in May and agreed upon joint political action, but not upon its form. In July ten thousand Alliancemen and Knights paraded through downtown Dallas to a rally at the fair grounds, where they heard the Reverend J. H. Jackson, state lecturer of the K. of L. and state chaplain of the Alliance, advise them to win political power by seizing the Democratic party. Apparently Jackson's Alliance constituency followed his advice but his brother Knights did not. In November, Jerome Kearby, independent congressional candidate, carried four of six Dallas wards but only one of thirty-three precincts outside the city.[40]

In August, while local Alliances were questioning how, or whether, the order should participate in politics, delegates to the state Alliance gathered in Cleburne to debate the same issue. The Cleburne delegates, like the Alliancemen whom they represented in the eighty-four counties, were sharply divided on the matter. However, the line of battle was not drawn between proponents of political and economic action.[41] The most radical political activists supported the cooperative program of the order; indeed, they had helped to establish it. Those who feared "that the Alliance was about to launch into politics" objected less to the adoption of legislative demands than to an independent coalition with the Knights of Labor. Many believed that such a coalition, which was gaining grass-roots support even while they deliberated at Cleburne, would receive the official sanction of the order.

The tenor of the state meeting bore out their fears. A committee dominated by the "political" faction called for the adoption of seventeen legislative resolutions, phrased as "demands," which were designed to correct "the onerous and shameful abuses that the industrial classes are now suffering at the hands of arrogant capitalists and powerful corporations." Although the immediate source of the demands was a series of resolutions adopted in July by the Alvord Alliance in Wise County, most of them ultimately derived from the ongoing antimonopoly and soft-money crusades.[42] The demands included granting the right of incorporation to cooperative stores and similar ventures (the previous legislature had repealed the law under which Grange cooperatives operated); the passage of laws to discourage large-scale engrossment of land, particularly by foreign syndicates; and the payment of taxes by corporations and land companies proportionate to those paid by farmers. Another resolution demanded payment of wages by corporations "according to contract" and abolition of convict labor outside prison walls. The federal government was called upon to begin unlimited coinage of gold and silver, to substitute legal tender treasury notes for national bank notes, and to establish an interstate commerce commission and a national bureau of labor statistics.[43]

Conservative delegates were particularly troubled by two of the resolutions. One called for a national conference of labor organizations "to discuss such measures as may be of interest to the laboring classes," and the other instructed the president of the state Alliance to appoint a committee "to press these demands upon the attention of the legislators of the state and nation." Centrists in the meeting, hoping to forestall both overt political action and a walkout by conservatives, succeeded in adding to the order's Declaration of Purposes a statement that the Alliance should "labor for the education of the agricultural classes, in the science of economical government, in a strictly nonpartisan spirit." In the emotion-charged atmosphere at Cleburne, the statement only added to the controversy.[44]

There were, nevertheless, a few harmonious moments at the meeting. All factions agreed upon a plan for coordinating the cooperative sale and shipment of cotton, and a conservative leader was put in charge of the project. Furthermore, Andrew Dunlap, who still opposed alignment with the Knights of Labor, was re-elected president. But in the showdown vote, the state Alliance adopted the platform of legislative demands by a margin of ninety-two to seventy-five.[45]

With the die thus cast, members of the minority faction secretly organized a rival Alliance, with the regularly elected state vice-president and treasurer at its head, along with an executive committee member and former secretary. They secured a charter from the state designating it the "Grand State Farmers' Alliance of Texas" (the charter under which the Alliance had operated since 1880 only mentioned operations in Parker County) and vowed to promote the Alliance as a "strictly non-political body." At the same time, leaders of the Cleburne majority published the demands as an official statement of the order's position.[46]

The Alliance had split in fact and in spirit. Although the movement was still vital at the grass roots, it faced collapse because of the factional dispute. Sensitive to such a possibility, leaders of both sides agreed to confer at Waco on 10 November.[47] After three days of conferences and informal discussions, they reached a compromise. The breakaway group agreed to hold their charter in abeyance temporarily and to recognize the regularly elected officials. In return, leaders of the majority faction, including several architects of Alliance political insurgency, agreed to submit to the suballiances for debate a resolution adopted by the breakaway "Conference Committee," which defined the Alliance as "strictly non-political" and suggested expulsion for any county or suballiance that allowed discussion of politics in its meetings. In short, the majority agreed to refight the battle of Cleburne.[48]

In an additional effort to restore harmony, three high-ranking officials resigned: President Andrew Dunlap, Vice-President D. J. Eddleman, and an executive committee member, J. H. Harrison (the latter two were also officers of the rival group). At the request of the resigning officers, Charles Wesley Macune, chairman of the executive committee, called a meeting of the state Alliance for January 1887 to fill the vacant offices, consider the recommendations of the Conference Committee concerning politics, devise plans for expanding the Alliance into other states, and deliberate "for such other purposes as the absolute necessities of the order may imperatively demand."[49]

The debate over "the Alliance in politics" continued in the Alliance press and in both the suballiances and the county Alliances. Opponents of the Cleburne demands denied that one set of Alliancemen had the right to impose their political views on the others. Supporters of the demands agreed with Chaplain J. H. Jackson that the demands did not commit the order to a particular political course. Pointing out that the breakaway order had not a single operating suballiance, Jackson predicted that the rank and file would uphold the demands.[50] Reports from the local Alliances bore him out. The Dallas County Alliance was one of many that endorsed the demands and condemned the Conference Committee resolutions. The secretary of one suballiance asked: "Are we going to shear the giant of his strength, by depriving him of the inherent right of every free man?"[51] As the called state Alliance meeting approached, supporters of the demands seemed to hold the upper hand.

When Charles Macune gaveled the state Alliance to order in Waco on 18 January, he faced an angry, divided convention, essentially the same group that had clashed at Cleburne. Then thirty-five years of age, Macune was a native of Wisconsin who had drifted to California and Kansas before settling in Milam County, Texas. He was practicing medicine there when the Alliance movement swept across the state. (He had "read" both medicine and law.) Macune may have edited an Alliance newspaper for a time in Milam County, which would make his meteoric rise in the order less baffling.[52]

Macune's presence at the helm was a happy accident for the Alliance. He had belonged to the Alliance less than a year and was not identified with either faction. He had steered a middle course on the political issue since Cleburne. In a letter to the *Dallas Mercury*, Macune upheld the right of the Alliance to discuss politics but had decried "petty partisanship." He advised the *Mercury*, now official organ of the order, to "deal in principles, not plans, subjects in the abstract and not in the detail of their execution."[53] Handsome, self-confident, and articulate, Macune was perfectly suited to the role of mediator. His mind ran more naturally to organization than to ideology. Macune thought big, but he was not a fiery or divisive orator. Indeed, his lengthy address to the delegates at Waco may have calmed the crowd by putting some of the brethren to sleep!

No sooner had Macune opened the session than he was besieged by procedural questions. What authority had he to call the special session? Would those who had resigned from their offices be allowed seats? He quieted the dissidents long enough to allow discussion on expanding the Alliance into other states, whereupon machinery was set in motion to consolidate the Alliance with the Louisiana Farmers' Union in a "national" Alliance.[54]

Macune, still presiding as temporary chairman, then delivered a lengthy address outlining what he believed to be the needs of the order, chief of which was an intensified effort to organize cooperatives to market and purchase goods. He told the delegates: "I hold that cooperation, properly understood and properly applied, will place a limit to the encroachments of organized monopoly, and will be the means by which the mortgage-burdened farmers can assert their freedom from the tyranny of organized capital." Macune's speech appeased the minority, which was outmanned but still powerful. They acquiesced in the election of two political insurgents, Evan Jones and Robert F. Butler, to the vacant positions of president and vice-president.[55] Factional leaders joined on a committee to perfect a state-wide system of cotton marketing, and the former critics of the Cleburne platform joined unanimously in its reaffirmation. Finally, the convention voted overwhelmingly to establish a sweeping program of cooperative marketing and purchasing under the leadership of a state business agent.[56]

A Waco reporter who had viewed the secret proceedings from a ladder perched outside a courthouse window wrote that the meeting had "as its prominent objective the pacification of the Cleburne defection. That minority faction suffered a Waterloo defeat, and appears to be reconciled. . . . Dissensions are all healed, and the order is stronger than ever." The Alliance press agreed. Praising Macune for his work of conciliation, the *Dallas Mercury* proclaimed: "To-day there was *no minority*, no majority, but a determined legion of honest, earnest men." A month later, evaluating reports from local organizers, the *Mercury* was convinced that the crisis had passed: "We have passed the Rubicon; we have tided over the shoals, and are now moving steadily forward."[57]

Both judgments were premature. In 1888 politics and cooperative failures would reopen the breech, but for the moment, both factions stood united under the joint banners of "cooperation" and "political education," and they were committed to spreading the Alliance across the cotton belt.

The twin goals of economic cooperation in Texas and expansion of the Alliance beyond the state were closely related. The greatest selling point for the organizers who fanned out across the South was the demonstrable success of cooperative enterprise in the Lone Star State. The keystone of the cooperative network was Macune's brainchild, a statewide cooperative exchange. In February 1887 Macune was elected state business agent of the Alliance, and in August he set forth a detailed plan of operation based on a capitalization of $500,000, to be financed by a $2 assessment on each member. Macune then began arranging to purchase supplies directly from manufacturers and sell cotton to mills and buyers in the Northeast and in Europe.[58]

The exchange, which opened in Dallas after that city made a generous offer of cash and land, was fundamentally different from the Grange agencies, which operated on the Rochdale plan. Instead of selling at prevailing market prices and then dividing the profits among stockholders, the Alliance exchange charged only slightly more than wholesale prices for supplies. To facilitate the marketing of Alliancemen's cotton, the exchange developed a system of cotton grading and an elaborate communications network with county Alliances. The Dallas office served as a clearinghouse through which Alliancemen sold directly to eastern and European buyers, thus avoiding local buyers' fees.[59]

It soon became apparent, however, that many members could not take advantage of these benefits because lack of capital forced them to mortgage their crops to country merchants. In a bold effort to break the cycle of indebtedness that tied farmers to the furnishing merchant, officials announced in November 1888 that the exchange would provide supplies for Alliancemen on credit in return for a pledge to market their cotton through the exchange. The exchange would accept notes signed jointly by needy members of the suballiances and by "responsible farmers," who would then take mortgages on the crops of their less prosperous brethren. Macune and his associates launched an intensive campaign, using lecturers and Alliance newspapers, to inform members of the plan. By March the exchange had approved notes amounting to over $200,000 and had begun issuing supplies based on the notes.[60]

Then the financial underpinnings of the exchange began to crumble. Although its plan of organization called for capital stock of $500,000, the paid-in capital of the exchange in March amounted to slightly over $20,000. At that point, Macune made frantic but unsuccessful efforts in Dallas, Fort Worth, Houston, Galveston, and New Orleans to secure short-term credit based on the joint notes. Meanwhile the exchange continued to authorize additonal notes, the value of which reached $420,000. By May anxious creditors were demanding payment, and the exchange was on the verge of collapse. Its impending fall threatened to destroy the Alliance. Charges and countercharges flew: Macune's critics claimed mismanagement and even fraud, while Macune and his supporters blamed the situation on "hidden, masked opposition to the exchange" from Dallas bankers and wholesalers.[61]

In an effort to raise additional capital from the membership, the executive committee of the state Alliance called upon the brethren to hold mass meetings on the second Saturday in June. On 9 June thousands of Alliancemen gathered in courthouses across the state and heard lecturers from the exchange explain how the bankers and the middlemen had combined to thwart their cooperative efforts. The lecturers raised an additional $30,000 at the meetings, enough to prevent the immediate collapse of the exchange but not enough to put it on a secure financial footing. In the closing months of 1888, the exchange became the center of controversy within the order, with the *Southern Mercury* lambasting Macune for his mismanagement of the agency. Macune resigned as manager in January 1889, and the exchange tried to retrench, but the weight of indebtedness and lack of patronage forced the liquidation of the exchange in December 1889.[62]

Both Macune and his critics were partially correct in explaining the exchange's failure. The proximate cause of its decline was the unavailability of short-term credit in the spring of 1888, but acceptance of the joint notes without sufficient capital reserve left the exchange in an untenable position. An independent audit revealed unwise but not dishonest managerial practices, for which Macune was not entirely to blame. Viewed from a broader perspective, the exchange failed because it had attacked head-on the credit system that dominated southern agriculture. The exchange was unable to muster sufficient capital for such a task, but the experience convinced many Alliancemen, including Charles Macune, that agriculture would remain depressed until the nation's financial system underwent major changes.[63]

If the exchange fiasco helped turn some Alliancemen toward political solutions, it turned others away from the movement. Many lost faith in the ability of the order to deal with economic problems. After the joint-note plan failed, some local Alliances were even plagued by disputes between makers of notes who were unable to redeem them and wealthier Alliance members who had cosigned them.[64] The collapse of the exchange precipitated a decline in Alliance membership from which the order in Texas never fully recovered, but before the exchange went under, the Alliance had been planted and was beginning to flourish across the cotton belt.

CHAPTER 3

Organizing the Cotton Belt

Almost from the beginning, Alliance leaders dreamed of building a movement that would cover the farming regions of America. Expansion beyond Texas began in earnest after the Waco meeting in January 1887, when the Alliance merged with the Louisiana Farmers' Union, but Alliances had sprung up in four other states and the Indian Territory before the establishment of the "national" Alliance. Late in 1886 organizers James Madison Perdue and J. W. DeSpain moved into southwestern Arkansas and northwestern Louisiana, respectively. Both were invited by local residents who expressed interest in the order. Perdue organized Alliances in Miller County, Arkansas, issuing charters from the Texas body, as did DeSpain in Desoto and Sabine parishes, Louisiana. Similarly, Texas organizers took the Alliance into the Indian Territory during 1886 and by April 1887 had formed a territorial Alliance. In Arkansas lack of coordination among early organizers resulted in the formation of two separate "state" Alliances, in addition to the well-established Agricultural Wheel.[1]

In 1886 Texas Alliancemen who were natives of Kentucky and Alabama launched the movement in their home states. The Texas Alliance dispatched F. T. Rogers to Kentucky for that purpose, and A. T. Jacobson returned to his home in northern Alabama where he established Alliances without authorization from Texas. By September, Jacobson had formed a "state" organization consisting of lodges in Madison County. He applied for a charter from the state Alliance of Texas, which was then in disarray. When no reply came from the Lone Star State, the Alabama Alliancemen obtained a charter from their own state legislature.[2]

These early recruiting efforts produced only meager results, but in two respects they foreshadowed subsequent organizing campaigns. First, through agricultural journals such as the Louisville *Farm and Home* and the Atlanta *Southern Cultivator*, news of the Alliance reached the Mississippi valley and the seaboard South. Secondly, the Alliancemen who returned to Alabama and Kentucky were but the advance party of an army of adopted Texans who followed them to homes in Mississippi, Alabama, Georgia, and North Carolina with the Alliance message.

The major thrust of Alliance expansion began at the called meeting of the Texas state Alliance in January 1887. At the Waco conference the previous November, both factions had agreed that extension of the movement beyond Texas should be considered at the January meeting. At about the same time, perhaps earlier than the first Waco meeting, John A. Tetts, secretary of the Louisiana Farmers' Union, wrote to Alliance President Andrew Dunlap proposing a merger. The Farmers' Union, similar in structure and program to the Alliance, claimed ten thousand members at the beginning of 1887, although a student of Louisiana agrarianism estimates its strength at around four thousand.[3]

When Tetts wrote to Dunlap, the state Alliance was in shambles and Dunlap was unable or unwilling to reply. In late November, Charles Macune, by then acting president, replied favorably to Tetts's suggestion. Following the edict of the Waco conference committee, he also corresponded with leaders of the northern Alliance. Macune appointed a representative to the meeting of the Farmers' Union on 11 January, and Tetts agreed to attend the state Alliance meeting in Waco with authority to effect a merger.[4]

When the delegates to the state Alliance arrived in Waco, they differed on many issues, but they agreed on expansion. Under Macune's leadership, they organized a separate conference consisting of two delegates from each congressional district in Texas—and J. A. Tetts. The conferees, who met at night after the sessions of the state Alliance, agreed upon a "merger" between the Alliance and Union, which amounted to an absorption of the latter by the former.

In effect the new group was the Texas Alliance reorganized for expansion. In January 1887 the Alliance probably had an active membership of over 100,000 and claimed to have 200,000 on its rolls. In some *counties*, the Alliance had more members than the Farmers' Union had altogether. The leadership of the "national" Alliance and the corps of lecturers who fanned out across the South were part of the group who had built the Texas Alliance. Tetts himself reported to his Louisiana brethren on the merger: "[T]he Alliance of Texas has acted most nobly and kindly toward us, as a body. We are so very small in comparison to them, that their whole action . . . has shown an entire absence of selfishness or arrogance."[5]

Upon Tetts's recommendation, the organization was named the

National Farmers' Alliance and Co-operative Union. Charles Macune was elected president, and under the provisions of the constitution that gave each state a national vice-president, Tetts became vice-president for Louisiana, along with J. M. Perdue and George B. Pickett of Texas. E. B. Warren and Robert F. Butler, both of Texas, were named secretary and treasurer, respectively.[6] Both the Texas Alliance and Louisiana Union adopted the plan of organization without dissent. The national organization borrowed $500 from the Texas Alliance, applied for a federal charter, and set out to organize the South.[7]

Some Alliancemen had also hoped to unite with the northern Alliance (officially the National Farmers' Alliance), but in 1887 the "southern" Alliance failed to establish satisfactory relations with the midwestern group and instead concentrated on recruitment in the cotton belt, the region to which its program of economic relief was best suited and from which most of its adherents had migrated.

In 1887 a great many southern farmers were ready to listen to any organization that promised economic relief. The problems of postbellum southern agriculture have been described in detail elsewhere.[8] Suffice it to say that southern farmers were increasingly tied to one-crop commercial agriculture, that lack of credit and other resources had led to the crop-lien system and was creating large-scale tenancy, and that in the systems of marketing and purchasing that evolved most small farmers—owners or tenants—had little economic leverage. Yet most southern farmers had not yet reached the depths of economic depression. Before cotton prices hit bottom in the 1890s, many farmers retained the capability, as well as the determination, to resist further erosion of their position.

Some students of farmer protest have correctly noted that poor judgment and ignorance contributed to the farmer's plight and that economic distress cannot in itself "explain" why one farmer protested while his neighbor did not.[9] Yet the fact remains that the mass of southern farmers lived in a state of economic, social, and political dependency. They did not understand the intricacies of the market economy, but they understood the furnishing merchant. One woman who watched the system work in southwestern Alabama wrote: "The furnishing man was the boss, pure and simple . . . his word was law. If there were any differences in a community or a family they were settled by 'The Man.' " Poverty and dependence on the furnishing merchant generated a climate of discontent. "All of us hated bankers and we hated merchants," recalled a native of rural South Carolina. "We hated them because they robbed us."[10]

The Alliance was not the first organization to address the problems of southern farmers. In the years since the Civil War, all manner of groups had proposed a wide range of remedies. Southern farmer organizations of the postbellum era fell roughly into two categories. On the one hand, the National Cotton Planters' Association, state agricultural societies, farmers' associations in Tennessee and the Carolinas, and even the Grange followed in the tradition of the genteel antebellum agricultural societies. They generally reflected the interests of large planters. On the other hand, the Agricultural Wheel in Arkansas and the lower Mississippi valley, the Farmers' Relief in Mississippi, and the Louisiana Farmers' Union were more nearly grassroots movements of small farmers. Rural southern assemblies of the Knights of Labor also fell in this category.

While the first group of organizations had roots in the agricultural societies of the 1850s, they were equally at home in Henry Grady's New South. During the 1870s and 1880s, they sought to increase farm productivity, regulate the marketing of cotton, control the type and quantity of farm labor, and stimulate governmental action on behalf of agriculture. They promoted scientific agriculture through meetings, fairs, and publications; sponsored efforts to limit cotton production and alter market arrangements; and pressured state governments to establish departments of agriculture and agricultural colleges.[11]

These organizations functioned comfortably within existing political, economic, and social structures. In addressing the problems of the southern farmer, they employed the rhetoric of self-help and uplift. With the exception of the farmers' associations in the Carolinas, they made little effort to mobilize the mass of small farmers for issue-oriented political action. Nevertheless, many of the groups, particularly the state agricultural societies in Georgia and Alabama and the Farmers' Assembly in Virginia (and the state departments of agriculture with which they enjoyed a semiofficial relationship), provided bases from which aspiring statesmen launched careers in traditional Democratic politics.

The high point of this conservative "agricultural-political complex" came with the Interstate Farmers' Conventions held between 1887 and 1889. The most important of these, held in Atlanta in August 1887, was called by leaders of the Georgia Agricultural Society and the Georgia Department of Agriculture to discuss problems of the cotton belt (meaning problems of large planters).[12] The delegates who gathered in Atlanta, all appointed by the governors of their states, represented the agricultural elite of the South. For example, leaders of the state agricultural society dominated the Georgia delegation, and many of the North Carolina representatives were active in the state Farmers' Association. The Tarheel delegation included several nurserymen, seed merchants, and managers of prosperous stock farms. The Texas delegation consisted largely of Alliancemen, including two principal architects of Alliance expansion, Charles Macune and E. B. Warren.[13]

The delegates listened to a series of addresses, including paeans to the rural virtues by Governor John B. Gordon and Henry W. Grady, and speeches on such subjects as recruitment of farm labor, use of fertilizers, and diversification of crops. After much debate, the group endorsed the abolition of crop-lien laws and the amendment of the national banking act to make land acceptable as security for loans. The delegates established a loosely structured Interstate Farmers' Association, which was to meet annually and discuss farm problems. They elected as president Leonidas LaFayette Polk, North Carolina farm editor and agricultural leader.[14]

Although the rhetoric and the interests of the agricultural elite prevailed during the Atlanta meeting, an undercurrent of discontent presaged the rise of a more aggressive grass-roots movement among southern farmers. Delegate Macune, riding the crest of Alliance popularity, called for a vigorous program of cooperative purchasing and marketing as an alternative to passing resolutions on "the farm problem." The chair gaveled another delegate out of order when he called for nationalization of railroad and telegraph companies. In a speech that set off intense debate, Alson J. Streeter of Illinois, a leader of the midwestern Alliance, who was to become the vice-presidential nominee of the Union Labor party the following year, urged this group of southern gentlemen to deal with their problems through political insurgency: "It may not suit you that there should be a third party in the land [applause] but let me tell you that it exists, and you cannot help it. . . . The question is, what are we going to do."[15]

The minority view at Atlanta reflected the emergence of a different kind of farmers' movement. Growing numbers of southern farmers could no longer be quieted by soft-handed politicians and editors who mouthed rustic platitudes or satisfied by the efforts of ephemeral groups such as the Interstate Farmers' Association. These angry men banded together in groups such as the Farmers' Relief, the Brothers of Freedom, and the Agricultural Wheel. By 1887 the Wheel was the second largest farm organization in the nation, following only the National Farmers' Alliance and Co-operative Union.[16] Both in their objectives and in their rhetoric these groups resembled the left wing of the Texas Alliance. More than the Alliance itself, they reflected the anger of the white mudsills of the South. Groups like the Wheel vigorously attacked the marketing and supply system of southern agriculture and supported political insurgency more readily than the Alliance. Unlike most of the genteel farm groups, they won mass support by organizing local chapters among small farmers. In mobilizing a sizable body of heretofore inert southerners, they posed an implicit threat to the prevailing power structure.

As the Alliance moved across the cotton belt, it absorbed both the genteel and mudsill traditions. Many leaders of the elite groups found their way into the Alliance, particularly in the Southeast. On the other hand, the mass movement that created the Wheel and the Relief merged with the Alliance, strengthening its left wing. The Alliance took its internal divisions along when it moved beyond Waco.

Following the organization of the national Alliance in January, President Macune called a meeting of all those desiring to organize Alliances in the southern states. In an effort to regulate the organizing process, Macune and a board of examiners screened applicants and gave them explicit instructions. After the first screening session, Macune reported: "The result of this teachers institute, for such it was in fact, has been to lead to more thorough unity of action in the work of organization, and the men who go out into other states will all teach the same thing in the same manner."[17] Many of the appointees needed no instructions from Macune. The initial group included S. O. Daws, J. M. Perdue, J. W. DeSpain, and other veterans of the Texas organizing campaign.

S. O. Daws led a team of six organizers to his native Mississippi. After six weeks' work there, they had chartered twenty-five suballiances and established working relations with a strong local group, the Agricultural Relief, which was absorbed by the Alliance in the fall of 1887. Little more than a year after Alliancemen entered the state, the master of the state Grange complained: "The Alliance has swept over the State like a cyclone. They have more than 70,000 members and are still organizing."[18]

The Alliance planned to send one organizer to each congressional district in the South. That goal was not reached, but those who did go soon recruited capable local assistants who carried on the work.[19]

By summer Alliance organizers were at work in all of the southern states except Virginia. Initially they were most successful in North Carolina, Mississippi, and Alabama. When the Texans moved into North Carolina in May 1887, farmers were already joining an association of farmers' clubs organized by Leonidas L. Polk, former state commissioner of agriculture, who was now editor of the *Progressive Farmer*. In 1886 Polk had laid plans for a statewide farmers' organization, modeled in part on the East Tennessee Farmers' Convention and on Benjamin R. Tillman's Farmers' Association in South Carolina.[20] The North Carolina association was similar in many respects to traditional agricultural groups, but, unlike most of them, it encompassed an extensive network of local clubs linked by county and state organizations and by the *Progressive Farmer*. Polk's group had demonstrated its political power when, in March 1887, it helped persuade the state legislature to create an agricultural college, which eventually became North Carolina State University.[21]

While the Farmers' Association was getting underway, the Knights of Labor were recruiting North Carolina farmers, black and white, through an appeal for independent political action. In the piedmont region, Knights mustered enough votes to elect State Master Workman John Nichols to Congress as an Independent in 1886, but in 1887 the K. of L. began losing the support of white farmers, many of whom were swayed by Democratic charges that blacks and Republicans dominated the organization.[22]

Alliance organizers entered North Carolina at an auspicious time. The Knights of Labor were losing strength, and Polk's association, which had awakened many Tarheel farmers to the need for "organization," had probably reached its peak with the establishment of the agricultural college. The association could have provided a political vehicle for Polk, whose charisma and enthusiasm had contributed to its growth, or for its president, Sydenham B. Alexander, but the clubs offered little practical relief to farmers beset by falling prices and unpredictable markets.

The first Texas organizer to reach North Carolina, the Reverend M. T. Sealy, began work in his native Robeson County, in the southeastern part of the state. With the help of a local farmer, Thaddeus Ivey, Sealy organized the first suballiance at Ashpole, and by June he had established twelve to fifteen lodges and a county Alliance.[23]

Working independently of Sealy, J. B. ("Buck") Barry, also a native of North Carolina, began organizing near Raleigh in Wake County, which, unlike Robeson, was a stronghold of the Farmers' Association and of the Knights of Labor. In his sixty-six years, Buck Barry had fought in the Mexican and Civil wars, joined the Texas Rangers, led vigilante groups against Indians and horse thieves, served in the Texas legislature, and operated a farm in Bosque County, Texas.[24] Barry had great success as an Alliance organizer in his native state. The manner in which Wake County farmers flocked into the order led him to marvel: "The farmers seem like unto ripe fruit—you can gather them by a gentle shake of the bush." By August, Barry and his assistants had established thirty suballiances in the county.[25]

The entry of the Alliance into North Carolina took Polk and his associates by surprise. They had known of the order before launching their own organization but had made no effort to contact its leaders. By July, however, Polk had learned of the Alliance's work and joined one of the suballiances that Barry had organized in Wake County. Polk's *Progressive Farmer* reported on the cooperative efforts of the Alliance in Texas and urged North Carolina farmers to join. In August, Polk met Macune and other Texas Alliancemen at the Interstate Farmers convention and discussed an offer previously made by the Texans to consolidate the Farmers' Association with the Alliance. In January 1888 the state Alliance of North Carolina formally absorbed the Farmers' Association, over the objections of some Association leaders who felt uncomfortable among the aggressive Alliancemen.[26]

The first meeting of the state Alliance, held on 4 October 1887, showed the extent to which leaders of the Farmers' Association were already caught up in the Alliance. At the call of organizer N. H. C. Elliott of Texas, delegates from six counties met and elected a slate of officers headed by S. B. Alexander, president; Thaddeus Ivey, vice-president; and L. L. Polk, secretary.[27] Alexander, a Mecklenburg County planter, had worked with Polk in the Grange as well as in the Farmers' Association. As secretary Polk became the chief operating officer of the state Alliance, and the *Progressive Farmer* became its official organ. The state Alliance drew up a constitution, patterned after that of the Texas Alliance, and adopted the "Macune Agency system," based on the Texas Alliance's cooperative exchange.[28]

From North Carolina the Alliance movement spilled over into neighboring states. In the fall of 1887, organizer M. T. Sealy shifted his efforts to South Carolina, beginning just across the state line from his North Carolina home. Supported by the national headquarters in Texas and by Tarheel Alliancemen, Sealy and two other North Carolina organizers began attracting farmers in Marion and Horry counties to the order, primarily by describing the blessings of Alliance cooperative buying. In July 1888, with three thousand South Carolinians already enrolled, Polk organized a state Alliance. Many Alliancemen were also members of Ben Tillman's Farmers' Association, but in South Carolina the Alliance was never able to absorb the association as had happened in North Carolina.[29]

Like the Carolina organizers, Alliancemen who arrived in Alabama in the spring of 1887 found other groups at work. In 1886 A. T.

Jacobson, the overanxious Texan, established an Alliance beachhead in Madison County. The Agricultural Wheel was active in Madison and other northern counties. By the time authorized Texas organizers reached Alabama, the Wheel had attracted a sizable following in the Tennessee Valley region.[30] By the summer of 1887, W. C. Griffith of Texas was attracting many farmers to the cause in northern and central Alabama, to the consternation of the Montgomery *Advertiser*. Reporting that Griffith had blamed the wealthy for hard times ("communism," cried the *Advertiser*), the state's leading newspaper marveled that Alabama farmers would listen to "an unknown Irishman from Texas." "The fact is," warned the editorialist, "that . . . because times are sometimes hard and obligations are pressing, they [the farmers] are disposed to run off after strange gods." An Alabama Allianceman replied that the charge of communism was an insult to the 2,500 members of the order in Limestone and Madison counties and to their respective presidents, both of whom were members of the legislature.[31]

The Alliance rapidly spread southward across Alabama, but not without opposition, particularly in the black belt. From Opelika, organizer J. M. Perdue reported that "The poor farmers . . . are so crushed under the crop mortgage system that they have lost almost all hope of bettering their condition." Perdue said that many were afraid to join the Alliance for fear that "the major or colonel will quit issuing rations to them." Despite such opposition, by August 1887 a state Alliance was in operation, absorbing the group founded by Jacobson. The Reverend Samuel M. Adams, a Baptist minister from Bibb County, was elected president.[32]

As the movement rolled across Alabama, it attracted some wealthy planters, community leaders, and officers of the state agricultural society. Most notably, the Alliance gained the support of Reuben F. Kolb, commissioner of agriculture and gubernatorial aspirant. Kolb recognized the political potential of a group that did in a few months what he had been unable to do in several years, despite his access to governmental resources, namely, to organize a sizable bloc of the state's farmers into a cohesive movement. In succeeding years, Kolb would try to harness that movement for his own purposes.[33]

In Georgia, where no other group had mobilized the mass of small farmers, the Alliance grew less rapidly than in North Carolina or Alabama, but the grass-roots efforts of the Texas organizers soon produced one of the strongest Alliances in the South. One of those organizers was J. B. Wilkes. Before the Civil War, Wilkes had moved from Georgia to Red River County, Texas, which in the 1880s became an Alliance stronghold.[34] Early in the summer of 1887, Wilkes returned to Heard County in west Georgia. Failing to win support there, he moved on to adjoining Troup County, where he established several subordinate Alliances. Before the end of the year, Wilkes and assistants chosen from among his recruits had introduced the Alliance in fifteen counties of west-central and southwestern Georgia.[35]

Wilkes's approach was simple. Upon entering a community, he called a meeting of local farmers, particularly inviting neighborhood leaders to attend.[36] He told how the Texas Alliance had reduced costs and increased income through cooperation, and then he organized those who were interested into a subordinate Alliance. Wilkes left behind him a trail of suballiances, all of which began demanding reduced rates from local merchants in return for exclusive Alliance patronage.[37] At first, this rudimentary form of cooperation was dramatically successful. When Alliancemen in Mitchell County forced warehousemen to reduce charges by 75 percent, a cautious townsman reported, "This work created some little excitement."[38]

Meanwhile, another returned immigrant to Texas was recruiting in southern Georgia and Florida. Oswald Wilson, even more than Charles Macune, was a man whom Henry Grady could have appreciated. He was a wheeler-dealer of the first magnitude. Wilson established a cooperative exchange in Florida and then dreamed of forming a national cooperative, with himself in charge. To that end, he formed an association of Alliance business agents, opened an office in New York, and backed a journal with the unlikely name of the *Wall Street Farmer*.[39] Before embarking on these ventures, Wilson found time to plant the Alliance in two south Georgia counties. In October 1887 a resident of Thomas County reported that the Alliance that Wilson had established there had recruited "between two and three hundred of the best farmers in the county."[40]

In December 1887 Alliancemen from seventeen counties met in Fort Valley to form a state Alliance. They elected a slate of officers headed by the Reverend Robert H. Jackson, made plans to spread the Alliance across Georgia, and approved in general the establishment of a state cooperative exchange.[41]

As local merchants began yielding to Alliance pressure, many farmers decided that economic salvation was at hand. One put it this way: "Farmers' Clubs are nothing more than social entertainments where farming is discussed. . . . Expositions are a benefit [only] to the cities in which they are held. . . . But in a well-organized alliance that means business . . . something practical [may be done]."[42]

Alliance trade committees succeeded only temporarily in bargaining with Georgia merchants. Some merchants refused to cooperate, particularly when credit was involved; others reneged on Alliance contracts; and still others, who did cooperate, sold their businesses or went bankrupt.[43] As a result, local Alliances began establishing merchandising and marketing agencies of their own. By 1888 many subordinate and county Alliances were operating cooperative stores. Some, following precedents set by the Grange and local agricultural clubs, adopted the Rochdale plan, whereby all transactions were conducted in cash and dividends were distributed to patrons at the end of the year. Most stores modified this plan by reducing prices rather than paying dividends, and some extended credit to members. Most stores sold goods—at higher prices—to non-Alliance farmers, including blacks.[44]

In addition to forming merchandising outlets, Georgia Alliances established their own cotton warehouses. In 1888 one such warehouse at Fort Valley overwhelmed its competitor by offering lower costs and a free dinner to all patrons. The competition was less than overjoyed, but one resident of Fort Valley remarked: "The people say hurrah for the Houston County Alliance, as it has brought . . . many hundreds of bales of cotton that would otherwise go to other markets."[45]

Many townsmen shared that attitude. To be sure, merchants denounced the cooperatives, and bankers often refused credit, but in countless Georgia towns, competition for rural patronage was a matter of civic life and death. Towns across the state, particularly in southern Georgia, competed for Alliance cooperatives as fervently as for other commercial and industrial enterprises. Even southern Georgia railroads seeking new traffic contributed land and capital to Alliance warehouses. For their part, Alliance leaders tried to ease tensions between townsmen and farmers by repeating New South shibboleths about agricultural self-sufficiency and by denying that the Alliance threatened honest tradesmen.[46]

By the fall of 1887, state Alliances were functioning in Texas, Louisiana, Missouri, Mississippi, Alabama, and North Carolina, and work was under way elsewhere in the South.[47] In every state, the organizers generally followed the same pattern. They took the message of economic cooperation directly to the farmers, appealing most successfully to small-farm owners and the more stable tenants. At the same time, the Texas recruiters tried to win support from existing agricultural organizations. The state Alliances reflected this dual emphasis. In most southern states, the Alliance soon outnumbered all previous farmer organizations, and a corps of new leaders emerged, but officers of conservative agricultural organizations figured prominently in the new group.

The organizing campaign of the Farmers' Alliance systematically ignored almost half of all southerners who were engaged in agriculture, for the Alliance excluded blacks from membership.[48] White Alliancemen shared the racial prejudices of their region, and for many the (black) "labor problem" was a major concern. Thus the Alliance's goals of cooperation among all farmers and the political solidarity of all producers collided with the South's racial institutions.

Generally speaking, Alliancemen distrusted any effort to organize black farm workers. Two groups that the Alliance absorbed, the Agricultural Wheel and the Florida Farmers' Union, accepted black members, but upon merging with the Alliance, they acquiesced in drawing the color line. Many Alliancemen strongly opposed the efforts of the Knights of Labor to recruit black farm workers. In its short-lived southern campaign, the K. of L. often pitted black farm workers against white farm owners and was charged with promoting a new "Black Reconstruction."[49]

White Alliancemen were less hostile toward a subsequent, more successful movement to organize blacks, the Colored Farmers' Alliance. The mobilization of blacks into an order paralleling the white Alliance began in central and eastern Texas in 1886, during the phenomenal expansion of the order. In fact several black Alliances sprang up independently of each other, taking their places among the multitude of black self-help organizations. In October blacks in Caldwell County organized a "Grand State Colored Farmers' Alliance" and passed a resolution requesting cooperation with the white Alliance. The white state lecturer attended their meeting along with E. B. Warren, then a local Alliance leader in Weatherford. They were invited to address "a large colored assembly of people" and, after satisfying themselves of the group's "utility and benefit," helped establish the new Alliance.[50]

A second black group with headquarters in Lee County, Texas, was sending organizers into other states by 1887. In December of that year, it reportedly began work in Louisiana, and its secretary was promising to send information to anyone desiring "to organize Alliances of this kind among the negro farmers in any part of the South." The principal organizer of the group, which by 1889 was known as the "Consolidated Alliance," was Andrew J. Carothers, a white Allianceman from Beeville. Carothers's group maintained a separate existence until 1890, when it merged with the best known of the black Alliances, the Colored Farmers' National Alliance.[51]

The forerunner of this third group was founded in Houston

County in December 1886.[52] All sixteen delegates to its first "state" meeting were black, including the man elected president, J. J. Shuffer, but they selected as "General Superintendent" (chief organizing officer) the Reverend Richard Manning Humphrey, a white Baptist minister. Humphrey was a native of South Carolina and had attended Furman University. He had farmed, taught school, and preached in Alabama and Tennessee before moving to Texas. After the Civil War (in which he rose to the rank of captain), Humphrey settled in Houston County, Texas, where he farmed and worked with local black churches.[53]

The Houston County group, with Humphrey as principal organizer, apparently mobilized large numbers of black farmers and farm workers in Texas and soon spread into other states. In a meeting at Lovelady in March 1888, its leaders organized the Colored Farmers' National Alliance, with the same officers as the black state Alliance. President Shuffer authorized Humphrey to establish cooperative exchanges in various states. During 1888 and 1889, organizers for the group, some black and some white, introduced the Alliance to blacks in the gulf and southeastern states. After merging in 1890 with Carothers's organization, Humphrey claimed that the Colored Alliance had a membership of 1,200,000.[54]

Humphrey and Carothers were not the only white leaders of the Colored Alliance. State superintendents in Alabama and Kentucky were also white, as was the superintendent of the North Carolina–Virginia group. However, those in Georgia, Louisiana, and Mississippi were black.[55] Some white Alliancemen acted as organizers, but apparently most were black. Most other officers of the order, including presidents, secretaries, and lecturers, were also black. Many were established community leaders. A white newspaper described Frank Davis, president of the Alabama Alliance, as a "solvent and successful negro farmer." The Reverend Walter A. Patillo, black secretary and lecturer of the North Carolina branch, was an ordained Baptist minister and had run for register of deeds in Granville County in 1884. The Reverend J. W. Carter, state lecturer of the Georgia Colored Alliance, was pastor of a Christian church in Thomasville and a Republican functionary.[56]

Viewed from the perspective of the white press, Humphrey was the movement's most visible spokesman, but it is not evident that he or other whites completely controlled the internal workings of the Colored Alliance. In 1888 a white Allianceman from Goldsboro, North Carolina, wrote to the *Progressive Farmer* that his neighbors were "somewhat excited over the announcement that negro Alliances were being formed in the State." In a reply that mirrored the ambivalent feelings of many white Alliancemen, the editor acknowledged that the Colored Farmers' Alliance was organizing North Carolina Negroes and then commented: "[W]e think the negroes had better let the Alliance alone . . . yet he that is not against us ought to be for us."[57]

Formal contact between the black and white Alliances was slight before 1890. In 1888 the National Farmers' Alliance and Co-operative Union encouraged state Alliances to allow blacks the use of their cooperative exchanges. Alliances in Alabama, Louisiana, and Tennessee were among those that adopted such a policy.[58] Mollified by assurances that the Colored Alliance did not threaten the political and social status quo, white Alliancemen tolerated and in some cases supported the organization of rural blacks for economic cooperation.

White cooperation with black Alliancemen took place within the limits of white supremacy. Probably few white Alliancemen would argue with the *Southern Mercury*'s observations on the "race problem in the South": "The MERCURY is in favor of securing to the negro every right which belongs to him under the constitution and laws of the country, and this would imply political equality. But that provision of the constitution which made him a citizen did not make him a whiteman. This is a whiteman's country, and it must remain so just so long as Caucasian superiority is permitted to assert itself."[59]

Cooperation with the Colored Alliance played only a minor role in the southern Alliance's whirlwind expansion. During 1887 and 1888, the Alliance's promise of economic relief, presented through a relatively efficient communications and organizing network, brought southern farmers flocking into the order. In December 1888, when the National Farmers' Alliance and Co-operative Union held its second annual meeting at Meridian, Mississippi, representatives were present from every southern state, with the exception of Virginia, and also from Kansas and the Indian Territory. The order claimed to have over 400,000 members in more than 10,000 suballiances.[60]

At Meridian, the Alliance made a preliminary agreement to merge with the Agricultural Wheel. When the state Alliances and Wheels ratified the merger the following year, the membership almost doubled, with most of the increase coming in Arkansas, Tennessee, and Missouri.[61] The program that the order endorsed at Meridian gave further indication of its growth in the South. The Alliance encouraged cooperative efforts at the state and national levels and set in motion plans to regulate the marketing of the South's cotton crop.[62]

The dream of organizing the cotton belt was within reach, but the rapid expansion was so far based more on promises than on performance. By the end of 1888, the Alliance had the numerical and organizational strength to try to redeem its pledge of salvation through cooperation.

CHAPTER 4

Cooperation in Business and Politics

The remedy that Alliance organizers proposed to farmers across the cotton belt was the establishment of cooperatives. Many to whom they spoke knew something about the subject, for the Grange and local farmers' clubs had already experimented with cooperation. Local Alliance trade committees appeared in the wake of the Texas organizers, and soon there sprang up a multitude of cooperative stores, warehouses, gins, and elevators. In South Carolina, where the order was relatively weak, the legislature granted charters to twenty-one such cooperatives.[1] Few of these local agencies survived for very long. Many were poorly managed, most were undercapitalized, and all faced the perils common to small businesses in the late nineteenth-century South. Yet the short-range success of local cooperatives, coupled with the promise of even greater benefit to be derived from statewide cooperation, caused the Alliance to flourish in almost every southern state by 1888.

Alliance organizers recommended the opening of state cooperative agencies modeled on the Texas exchange, but before any of the state Alliances could act, Macune's exchange collapsed. After the failure of the Texas model, the various state Alliances launched diverse programs of their own, beginning with the one in Mississippi.

As quickly as S. O. Daws and his associates organized suballiances in Mississippi, the brethren began forming embryonic cooperatives, restricted at first to the purchasing of supplies in bulk from wholesalers and to making trade agreements with local merchants. One county Alliance in eastern Mississippi even tried to get local physicians to reduce their charges to its members.[2]

Soon after the state Alliance had been organized, the state business agent, W. R. Lacy, began operating a rather modest commission agency, buying cotton bagging, plows, staples, and other goods for local Alliances. A more ambitious state cooperative agency opened its doors at Winona in October 1888. The agency, which operated on a cash basis, never prospered. Early in 1890 the floundering agency was moved to Memphis and merged with the state Alliance cooperatives of Arkansas and Tennessee.[3]

A more successful cooperative exchange was operated by the Georgia Alliance. The Georgia exchange enjoyed capable, experienced leadership. Its first president was Felix Corput, son of a Belgian physician, who had moved with his parents to Georgia in 1850. Corput worked as a store clerk in his youth and later became an officer in the Confederate quartermaster corps. He had been mayor of Macon between 1881 and 1884 and in 1886 had taken up farming, developing one of the best vineyards in the state. Corput was prominent in the Georgia Alliance from its beginning and was instrumental in organizing and financing the exchange.[4]

Bearing in mind the collapse of the Texas exchange, Corput and his colleagues adopted a more cautious plan than Macune had followed. Their exchange would provide only selected items, principally fertilizer and farm implements. It would accept only cash or commercial paper but would encourage local alliances to provide credit for needy members. The election of exchange trustees by the participating suballiances would, it was hoped, insure grass-roots support. Architects of the Georgia exchange, perhaps again drawing on the Texas experience, believed that its primary mission was not to do extensive business, but, by offering lower prices, to compel local merchants to make similar reductions.[5]

Plans for the exchange were approved in June 1888, but lack of funds prevented their implementation until late in 1889. Most Alliancemen had little cash to spare for the project, and controversies involving the exchange slowed contributions. Many backers of local cooperatives perceived the exchange as a rival. In addition, exchange officers became embroiled in intrigues within the state Alliance. President Robert H. Jackson of the state Alliance opposed Corput's leadership, while Vice-President Leonidas Livingston supported him.[6]

Finally, in November 1889, the exchange opened in Atlanta. Two months later, it established headquarters in a building at Hunter and Forsyth streets which was provided by the *Atlanta Constitution*.[7] The exchange initially offered fertilizer and a few other items to Alliancemen at reduced rates, later adding groceries, hardware, drygoods, and seeds on a limited basis. Fertilizer sales represented a large percentage of the total.

Charles Macune, the Alliance leader most knowledgeable about cooperation, upheld the Georgia exchange as a model.[8] It *was* the most successful of any in the South. Its leaders struck a balance between over-expansion, which would have caused a speedy collapse as in Texas, and fiscal timidity, which would have rendered the exchange useless to impoverished farmers. The Georgia exchange was adequately capitalized through subscriptions of stock and income from wholesale commissions. It survived the defalcation of its business agent in 1891 and even the political rending of the Alliance during 1891–92, but collapsed in 1893, by which time the Alliance itself was virtually defunct.[9]

In contrast to the exchanges in Georgia, Mississippi, and Alabama, several state Alliances adopted an agency system in which the state business manager acted strictly as a commission agent, providing goods for cash or on consignment from manufacturers and wholesalers. Alliances in Florida, Tennessee, Arkansas, and North Carolina adopted variations of this plan.[10]

In the summer of 1888, Leonidas L. Polk, secretary of the North Carolina Alliance, urged Tarheel Alliancemen to establish a fund of $75,000 to be used as a surety in transactions of a state business agency. Polk and others claimed that such a capital fund would give manufacturers and wholesalers confidence in the agency, and, since interest from the fund would defray operating expenses, the agency could provide goods at cost, albeit for cash. Alliance officials began soliciting contributions through the county and suballiances, but by December only $4,700 had been paid into the fund. Many members expressed dissatisfaction with the plan and demanded the establishment of a cooperative system that would benefit them more directly by extending credit. In January 1889 the state president warned that, unless an attractive plan were adopted soon, the Alliance movement would collapse.[11]

Only part of the agency's problems stemmed from its conservative fiscal policies. After several months of floundering, W. A. Darden, state business agent, confessed that he was "in the dark" about how to proceed, and he even suggested that contributions should be refunded and the project abandoned. Angered by Darden's inertia, the agency's trustee demanded that he be replaced, charging that "he does not seem to have had any business experience beyond buying on time at a country store."[12] Renewed pleas from Alliance leaders brought forth additional contributions (still far short of the $75,000 that had been asked for), and the agency began operations later in 1889—with a new business manager.[13]

The agency purchased a variety of goods for members, including food stuffs, farm implements, seeds and fertilizer. Local Alliances could place orders with the agency in Raleigh, and lecturers visited suballiances armed with samples and order books. In its first year of operation, the agency conducted a business of almost $350,000, about three-fifths of which represented fertilizer sales.[14]

Alliancemen with ready cash could purchase supplies at substantial savings, but the agency offered goods on credit only when the manufacturer or wholesaler would accept notes for his merchandise. Furthermore, the trustee of the Business Agency Fund adhered strictly to the rules and allowed no part of the fund to be used for buying goods in advance of order.[15] State president S. B. Alexander noted in August 1889 that dissatisfaction with the exchange was working to the benefit of local cooperative stores, many of which extended credit. As support for the exchange decreased, the number of cooperatives owned by local Alliances increased, and so did the animosity between them and the state agency. Many, perhaps most, of the local stores dealt directly with wholesalers rather than patronizing the agency, and they were continually competing with the agency for the limited capital that Alliance members had to invest. Local stores and Alliance tobacco warehouses probably attracted more support for the Alliance in North Carolina than the state agency.[16]

Elsewhere in the South, statewide cooperative efforts met with only limited success, serving principally as commission agencies for funneling goods to local and county Alliance cooperatives. Those that remained solvent for more than a year or two did so by following conservative financial policies that greatly restricted their usefulness to all but the minority of farmers who could pay cash for their supplies.

The South Carolina exchange, located first in Greenville and later Columbia, stayed in business until 1899, long after the Alliance itself had withered away, but it operated strictly on a cash basis.[17] The Louisiana Farmers' Union operated a Commercial Agency in New Orleans between 1888 and 1893 which was modeled on the state Grange's Rochdale-type agency. Like the South Carolina exchange, it did not materially improve the economic condition of most farmers in the state.[18] The Tennessee Alliance supported agents in Memphis and Nashville under a system similar to the North Carolina Agency. Yet the most effective cooperatives in Tennessee were local operations.[19]

In some states, the order's internal conflicts blocked cooperative enterprise. Arkansas agrarians, divided until 1890 into three competing organizations, were unable to do more than give feeble support to the Tennessee Agency in Memphis, even though one of the Arkansas "state" Alliances had previously drawn up grandiose plans for a state exchange that was to be capitalized at $500,000.[20] The exchange that Oswald Wilson opened at Jacksonville, Florida, failed to unite southern Florida citrus growers and cotton farmers from the northern counties. Even Wilson's opening of a branch exchange in New York City to provide a new outlet for Florida fruit did not attract citrus men to the order. Many Florida cotton growers themselves chafed under the exchange's "cash only" policy. Furthermore, the Florida exchange suffered from the personal feud between Wilson and state Alliance President B. F. Rogers, which was exacerbated by Wilson's efforts to build his own private empire, independent of the state Alliance.[21] In the South as a whole, the promise of the statewide Alliance cooperatives far surpassed their performance.

The promise of cooperative purchasing and marketing attracted blacks to the Alliance movement, as it did whites. Colored Alliance leaders planned a network of exchanges similar to the white state exchanges. In his brief history of the black organization, R. M. Humphrey wrote that he had established exchanges in Houston, New Orleans, Mobile, Charleston, and Norfolk.[22] They proved to be even more ephemeral than their white counterparts. The most successful seems to have been the exchange at Norfolk managed by J. J. Rogers, a white North Carolinian who was state superintendent for North Carolina and Virginia. Its plan of operation called for members to contribute to a fund with which Rogers would finance the purchasing of supplies and the marketing of cotton. Rogers not only planned to provide these services for the black Alliancemen of North Carolina and Virginia, many of whom lived within the Norfolk market area, but he also solicited cotton sales from white Alliancemen, claiming that Norfolk was the natural port for North Carolina cotton. The exchange survived at least until 1892 but then became the focal point of a controversy within the Virginia Colored Alliance. Rogers's critics claimed that he had profited personally from the exchange. They denounced him for merging it with the white exchange system in Virginia and for charging higher prices than other cooperatives. When Rogers refused to undergo an investigation, R. M. Humphrey removed him from office.[23]

More than their white counterparts, black Alliancemen lacked the financial resources to operate cooperatives. If they were to benefit substantially from economic cooperation, they would have to receive aid from whites. Despite the barriers of racial prejudice and perceived class interests, white and black Alliances did work together in a limited way. White Alliancemen did not lose their faith in white supremacy, nor did those who were so inclined stop thinking of themselves as employers, but the experiment in cooperative enterprise convinced some that it was in their interest to include black farmers in their plans.

Some Alliance leaders argued openly that the economic interests of black and white farmers were the same. One white leader of the black Farmers' Union in Louisiana stated this argument in its most self-interested terms: "We cannot afford to create division in the ranks of labor, and it is certain that if the colored people are not organized as they wish to be, in harmony with the Farmers' Alliance and Farmers' Union, they will be used by our opponents to defeat us."[24]

In 1888 the white national Alliance encouraged state Alliances to allow blacks the use of their cooperative facilities, and Alliances in Alabama, Mississippi, Louisiana, and Tennessee were among those that adopted such a policy. Quite possibly more black Alliancemen patronized white-owned cooperatives than those established by their own order. In one Mississippi delta county, black patronage of a white Alliance store and a Colored Alliance boycott of non-Alliance merchants helped precipitate a massacre in which, apparently, Colored Alliance leaders were systematically murdered. No remaining evidence indicates that the white Alliancemen who opened their store to the blacks protested the killings.[25]

A resolution debated by the Texas state Alliance defined the limits of interaction between the two Alliances. It suggested "that no effort be spared by our order to secure a more thorough co-operation in all commercial or manufacturing enterprise allowing each organization to retain in the fullest sense its social features unimpaired."[26] Until 1890 relations between the black and white organizations remained that limited.

What impact did the cooperatives have upon the Alliance in the South? To begin with, they attracted farmers to the order in droves. The mere announcement of plans to open exchanges and warehouses persuaded many to join, and the occasional dramatic success that followed further stimulated interest. If southern farmers experienced a revolution of rising expectations in the late 1880s and early 1890s, that revolution stemmed in part from the Alliance's massive experiment in cooperation. Over one million farmers listened to agents of the exchange explain how cooperation could raise them out of poverty or heard the secretaries of their suballiances read from the Alliance newspaper that the agency could get supplies for them cheaply and find higher prices for their cotton, wheat, or tobacco.

The cooperatives, particularly the state exchanges and agencies, gave the Alliance much of its internal cohesion. Leaders of the state exchanges had to combat both rural inertia and the dissipation of capital and energy in local schemes. State leaders sent out a wave of lecturers to promote the exchanges, subsidized newspapers to advertise them, and even tried to bring local cooperatives under their control. The cohesion forged in the cooperative movement would form the basis for such political solidarity as the Alliance subsequently achieved.

There were temporary successes, but the cooperative system could not overcome the established mercantile and credit practices of the South. It soon became apparent that cooperation would not bring salvation.[27] As early as 1889, there were signs of disillusionment among the brethren. Some Alliancemen dropped out of the movement; others protested that the managers of the cooperatives had cheated them; many, however, came to believe that something must be seriously wrong with the nation's financial system if farmers in combination could not gain the advantages enjoyed by other economic interest groups.

While state exchanges were opening across the South, the Alliance undertook another form of economic cooperation, this time on a regional scale, which brought the order its most clear-cut success. In 1888 a cartel monopolized the supply of jute bagging, the most widely used covering for cotton. During the cotton-growing season, the retail price of bagging rose steadily, doubling by late summer. Political and agricultural leaders responded to the crisis, but the most forceful action came from the Alliance.

By August and early September, Alliancemen were discussing the bagging issue in Texas, Tennessee, Florida, Georgia, Mississippi, and North Carolina, with Alliance leaders calling for a boycott of jute bagging.[28] However, it was then too late in the season to secure a substitute. The only successful effort against the trust that year seems to have come from Macune, who secured ten carloads of jute bagging at a price substantially below retail prices in Texas. He offered the bagging for sale at the Dallas exchange and in leading cotton-producing counties in the state, whereupon Texas merchants lowered their prices.[29]

In 1889 the same cartel controlled the importation and manufacture of jute. This time southern farmers fought back. In March, Mississippi Alliancemen laid plans to open a bagging factory. In April the Georgia Alliance voted to substitute cotton bagging for jute. The Georgia brethren had been quarreling about other matters, but reportedly they were united, 100,000 strong, on the bagging issue.[30]

The Georgia Alliance also urged the national organization to call a boycott of jute bagging. President Macune was at first cool to the idea, but late in May he met in Birmingham with state business agents and other Alliance leaders to discuss the problem. The group passed resolutions that called for the substitution of cotton bagging for jute. At the request of the Birmingham conferees, Macune appointed an Alliance cotton committee to direct the effort.[31]

Resolutions came easier than boycotts. Major cotton markets in Liverpool and elsewhere hesitated to accept the substitute bagging because it was less durable, and when they did accept it, they refused to pay a higher price per bale, even though the cotton wrapping constituted a smaller percentage of the total weight than jute. Furthermore, the limited supply of cotton bagging was itself expensive. Nevertheless, national Alliance leaders issued instructions for local Alliances to vote on the bagging issue and (assuming that they supported the boycott) to proceed with cotton bagging, even if merchants reduced the price of jute. National leaders found several companies willing to supply cotton bagging, the largest being the Lane Mills of New Orleans and West Point, Georgia. By November a factory owned by the Alabama exchange was producing the substitute, and Mississippi Alliancemen were proceeding with their plans to establish a similar factory.[32]

The planned Mississippi bagging factory never opened, but the campaign to establish it involved a mixture of agrarian cooperation and New South boosterism. In April, Alliance leaders leased a building at the state penitentiary at Jackson and also acquired the services of between twenty-five and fifty convicts to operate the bagging factory. The Jackson Board of Trade (which, incidentally, opposed the use of convict labor in the undertaking) subscribed $5,000 to the factory in return for partial control. Other outside interests, including the *Atlanta Constitution*, also contributed. By April 1890, $25,000 had been contributed to the factory, but that was less than half the amount required to open it. By then the antijute campaign was waning, and the Alliance quietly dropped the project. In Mississippi, as in other states, funds badly needed by the cooperative exchanges were used to finance the bagging fight.[33]

By harvest time in 1889, Alliance leaders had been unable to provide enough cotton bagging to cover the entire southern crop. Macune and others thought they could secure enough bagging if farmers could hold part of their cotton off the market for a few months. Thus the bagging campaign coalesced with a long-standing goal of southern agriculturalists, raising the price of cotton by preventing a glut on the market at harvest.

At its Meridian meeting in December 1888, the Alliance had adopted a plan for gathering crop statistics and for regulating cotton marketing. Alliance leaders now merged that program with the drive to substitute cotton for jute. The national cotton committee instructed members to hold their cotton in September if possible and to sell no more than 10 percent of it in October. An influential southern editor said of this bold scheme, "If the resolutions adopted by the Farmers' Alliance of the Southern States shall prove effectual, we may look for a commercial revolution."[34]

But the plan to withhold cotton foundered on the rock of credit. The same farmers who could not afford to pay cash for supplies could not hold their cotton, which in many cases was already owned by landlords or secured by liens. Despite efforts to provide short-term credit to needy Alliancemen, the plan to hold the cotton crop failed.[35]

Where cotton bagging was readily available at harvest time the antijute campaign was more successful. Bowing to Alliance pressure, leading American cotton exchanges agreed to accept the substitute bagging and to allow a tare differential from jute, even though the dominant Liverpool exchange refused to do so. Across the South, thousands of suballiances voted to use cotton bagging, and some took literally the instructions from national headquarters to "expel any members who belong to the ranks of the enemy." Alliancemen dramatized their support in various ways. In Cameron, Texas, the brethren held a mock funeral for the last roll of jute bagging in town. In North Carolina and Georgia, Alliancemen and their brides were married in clothes made of cotton bagging. One such ceremony in North Carolina was performed by the chaplain of the state Alliance and took place during the state fair "in the presence of thousands of enthusiastic witnesses," including the governor.[36]

The crusade against jute was particularly successful in Georgia and South Carolina. Over half of the crop in Georgia was covered with cotton in 1889.[37] During the summer of 1889, jute prices dropped to premonopoly levels. Low jute prices in 1890 caused most farmers to forsake the substitute bagging, despite Alliance efforts to effect a permanent change. In 1894 and 1895, after the collapse of the Alliance, jute prices rose once again, but in 1889 Alliancemen defeated a real live trust.[38]

At first glance, the jute bagging issue seems like a tempest in a teapot, but to cotton farmers operating on the narrowest of margins it was crucial. For the Alliance itself, the campaign had great significance. The order now had a single, clear-cut issue on which it could draw the line between "producers" and "monopolists." To anyone who watched the price of jute spiral during 1888 for no apparent reason, the antimonopoly rhetoric of the Alliance made a great deal of sense. The world was divided into two camps, those who supported and those who opposed the trust. As Tom Watson of Georgia put it: "Well might outsiders say to the 'jute combine' as every Monday morning they raise the price on the Southern Farmer, 'Hit him again, he's got no friends!' What shall we do? Grin and Endure it? I say no. . . . This, as well as all other combinations of this kind, is clearly illegal, and ought to be promptly and effectually crushed by Congress."[39]

Although it clearly defined the enemy, the issue on which the fledgling Alliance took a stand neither divided its membership nor led to reprisals from the holders of power in southern society. In Georgia genteel Democrats like W. J. Northen joined Tom Watson in condemning the distant trust. The words that Watson put in the mouths of monopolists could have been said by southerners of the jute trust itself, "Hit him again, he's got no friends!" Merchants, factors, editors, and other townsmen had no reason to support the trust, and by joining the fight against it, they deflected some of the agrarian hostility aimed at them. Henry Grady's own paper editorialized: "The CONSTITUTION enters this fight with the farmers and it will stand with them to the end."[40]

Finally, the contest with the jute-bagging trust demonstrated to the south the power of the Farmers' Alliance. Within weeks after their leaders had decided upon a course of action, Alliancemen in thousands of isolated farming communities knew the details of the plan and were pledging to turn their backs on the traditional method of wrapping cotton in favor of an untried and questionable procedure. And they won. Their success attracted a new wave of recruits to the order. Wrote one South Carolina Alliance leader: "It seems to me that the Alliance is about to swallow up Everything. *Our* bagging *Spark* seems to have set fire to the whole farming country."[41]

In the jute fight and in their other cooperative undertakings, Alliancemen maintained a symbiotic but distrustful relationship with the South's towns and cities. The cooperatives were formed to circumvent existing channels of commerce, but they required the kind of financial backing that could usually be found only in the towns. Conversely, leaders of crossroads communities and burgeoning commercial centers distrusted the cooperative movement, but their towns depended heavily on rural patronage. Consequently, cooperation like that between the Mississippi Alliance and the Jackson Board of Trade was fairly common. Civic leaders from competing towns vied with each other to provide land, buildings, and capital to the exchanges. Railroads in Alabama and Georgia even lowered rates for exchange traffic and assisted in the establishment of Alliance warehouses.[42]

Most Alliance leaders used their newfound proximity to financial power to do good. A few also did well. Exchange agents in Georgia and Tennessee embezzled funds from the cooperatives that they managed. Oswald Wilson, promoter of the Florida exchange and self-styled architect of a nationwide cooperative network, made an agreement in 1891 with the National Cordage Company, backer of the defunct jute trust, to front an organization that would buy out Alliance cooperatives and form a national network of stores. Critics of the plan charged, with apparent justification, that it would have destroyed the cooperative movement. Between 1889 and 1893, Charles Macune enjoyed a style of living in Washington which neither his Alliance salary nor profits from his newspaper, the *National Economist*, could have supported. A wealthy Texas Allianceman, R. J. Sledge, aided Macune financially, but Macune also received a loan of $2,000 from Patrick Calhoun, an official of the Richmond Terminal Company. Macune's opponents charged that the loan represented only a small part of his indebtedness to railroad interests. One of those who harbored such suspicions was Macune's successor as president of the national Alliance, Leonidas L. Polk.[43]

Even if charges of malfeasance against Wilson, Macune, and others were all true, the cooperative movement did not fail because of their wrongdoing but because of the enormity of the agricultural problems that it confronted. Alliance purchasing cooperatives in the South and in the plains states addressed themselves to the problems of farmers who were caught up in the process of commercialization. Their approach, although too limited to solve those problems, was essentially reasonable. The state cooperative exchanges and the Alliance's bagging campaign sought to reduce the cost of items that were of strategic importance in commercial farming. In the worn-out cotton lands of the Southeast, that meant chemical fertilizer and jute bagging. In the plains states, as will be discussed later, it meant coal, binder twine, and farm machinery. Similarly, local cooperative stores and the state agencies tried to provide savings on food stuffs and other supplies that southern farm families were increasingly incapable of producing for themselves. The pianos, the sewing machines, and all the other eye-catching consumer goods that the agencies offered to farmers and their wives were frosting on the cake. Alliancemen patronized the cooperatives because they believed that these new merchandising outlets could make the difference between commercial survival and annihilation.[44]

While the Alliance was building its cooperative empire, a similar but more class-conscious group, the Agricultural Wheel, was establishing a strong base in the Mississippi Valley. The merger of the Alliance and Wheel in 1889 produced a quantum jump in the strength of the Alliance and helped move it toward political activism. Unlike the Alliance's absorption of the Louisiana Farmers' Union, this merger united organizations of approximately equal strength. The Wheel was strongest in Arkansas, its birthplace. Before the merger it outnumbered the Alliance there and in Tennessee, Missouri, and Kentucky. It also had a large following in Alabama, with smaller units in Texas, Mississippi, Wisconsin, and the Indian Territory.[45]

Representatives of the Wheel and Alliance agreed to hold their national meetings simultaneously at Meridian, Mississippi, in October 1888 to discuss a merger, but a yellow fever epidemic forced President Macune to postpone the meeting of the national Alliance. The president of the Wheel, Isaac McCracken, had second thoughts about the merger and moved the meeting of the Wheel to St. Louis.[46] McCracken was not alone in his distrust of the Alliance. "We do not desire to swallow up the Alliance, neither do we wish to slide down into the capacious maw of that body," wrote a leading Wheel editor in Kentucky. "The Wheel has too much at stake to be willing to give up everything." Despite such misgivings, the joint meeting was rescheduled for December, in part through the efforts of Alliance and Wheel leaders in Tennessee, where the two orders had already established working relations.[47]

At Meridian committees of the two organizations agreed upon terms of consolidation, subject to ratification by three-fourths of the state bodies. The proposed constitution, essentially that of the Alliance, provided for a rather loose confederation of state organizations. The new group would be called the Farmers' and Laborers' Union of America. Its leadership reflected the balance between the two groups: Evan Jones of the Alliance and Isaac McCracken of the Wheel were elected president and vice-president, respectively, with other posts being divided between the two orders.[48]

In most states, the merger was effected without difficulty.[49] In Texas, however, it encountered strong opposition. Early in 1889 the Texas state Alliance was largely controlled by men who had been part of the conservative minority at Cleburne. They distrusted both the national Alliance leaders and the Texas Wheelers, many of whom were committed to political insurgency. Because of mutual distrust, the Texas Wheel and Alliance did not merge until May 1890. In Arkansas, where the relative strength of the two orders was reversed, the merger also faced opposition. There the presence of two competing Alliances further complicated the situation, and final settlement was not reached until 1891.[50]

By September 1889 the required number of states had ratified the

merger, and Macune, McCracken, and Jones announced the consolidation. With this declaration, the Alliance (the name Farmers' and
Laborers' Union was short-lived) was well established in every southern state, claiming a membership of over three quarters of a million.[51]

By 1888 politically active southerners were aware of the Alliance's potential for influencing elections and public policy. While
Alliance leaders were for the most part careful not to involve the order
directly in the electoral process, they advocated the education of farmers in "the science of economical government," which, as in Texas,
was everywhere susceptible to a multitude of interpretations.[52]

In several states, the Alliance quickly became an element in the
equation of traditional Democratic factionalism. In Mississippi, Chick-
asaw County publisher Frank Burkitt and other leaders of the Democratic party's "agrarian" wing joined the Alliance and by 1888 were
using it as a political base. The following year, opposition from
Mississippi Alliancemen forced the front-running candidate for governor to withdraw from the race. In 1888 North Carolina leaders
boosted the gubernatorial candidacy of S. B. Alexander, president of
the state Alliance. When Alexander failed to win the nomination,
Alliancemen supported him for U. S. Senator over the incumbent,
Matt Ransom.[53]

Political "friends of agriculture" were soon making the rounds of
Alliance picnics and rallies, and in 1888 and 1889, Alliance blocs
emerged in state legislatures. In Mississippi, Georgia, and Tennessee
lawmakers elected with Alliance support seemed to be moving toward
unified action, but in fact they lacked agreement on issues.[54]

By early 1889 some southern Alliance leaders were trying to
define substantive political issues on which to judge candidates. Most
state Alliances adopted lists of legislative resolutions similar to the
Cleburne demands but made little effort to force compliance. In 1889
Alliance leaders in North Carolina and Virginia tried unsuccessfully to
make state regulation of railroads a stand-or-fall issue, and in Alabama
the jute-bagging issue became a dividing line between the Alliance and
Democrats aligned with the *Montgomery Advertiser*.[55]

A few Alliancemen in the southeastern and Gulf states advocated
political insurgency in 1888 and 1889. In Mississippi and Alabama,
a handful supported the miniscule Union party in 1888, while in Tennessee, some Alliancemen and Wheelers, influenced by the Arkansas
Wheel, called for the establishment of a farmers' party. In North
Carolina an early and consistent advocate of independent political
action called upon Alliancemen to "ignore Democratic, Republican
[or] Independent . . . partisanship and . . . coalesce in one solid
phalanx."[56]

In Texas the campaign of 1888 found the Alliance weakened by the exchange debacle. Most who remained in the order turned to political action. In many counties, they used their numbers and discipline to control the Democratic party. Elsewhere the trend toward insurgency continued. Moving beyond the scattered efforts of 1886, Alliance insurgents formed a statewide organization, linking themselves at the national level with the new Union Labor party. The state organization, established at a "nonpartisan" convention in July, was dominated by the Alliance's left wing. The convention nominated Evan Jones, then president of the state Alliance, for governor, but Jones declined to run. With his refusal, the insurgents lost their best opportunity to win the governorship. The Democratic candidate in 1888 was Lawrence Sullivan Ross, a lackluster politician, whereas in 1890 Democrats nominated the popular state attorney general, James Stephen Hogg, who endorsed most of the Alliance platform.[57]

The involvement of Texas Alliancemen in political insurgency again generated friction within the order. At the close of the campaign, the state executive committee noted that many Alliance lecturers had contributed to the controversy by endorsing the insurgents. In an effort to regroup Alliance forces, the *Southern Mercury* called upon members to "turn your political excitement into Alliance enthusiasm."[58]

In the South as a whole, the Alliance was not yet committed to issue-oriented politics. No single symbol had focused political concern. Furthermore, President Macune, by inclination a centrist, had avoided championing a particular issue. But farmer discontent remained high, and success in the jute-bagging fight strengthened confidence in the Alliance's ability to effect change. By the end of 1889, the Alliance was interpreting its mandate for "political education" more aggressively.

What sort of message, or rhetoric, was in fact being transmitted to the rank and file? The message became more sharply focused after 1889, but throughout the career of the Alliance, its rhetoric dealt more with proximate solutions to specific problems than with resolving cosmic issues. If comparative weight of words is the standard of measurement, Alliance spokesmen were much more concerned with marketing and purchasing cooperatives and with federal monetary policy than with restoring a Jeffersonian Arcadia or with building a proto-socialist society. To use the categories of Murray Edelman, they dealt more with "referential symbols" (e.g., statistics and "objective" economic systems) than with "condensation symbols," those which "evoke the emotions associated with the situation."[59] The line between referential and condensation symbols was, however, often imprecise.

The subtreasury plan was a technical marketing and monetary system, but it acquired an emotional significance, and support for it became a test of loyalty to the movement.

Alliance spokesmen also drew on a wide range of rhetorical traditions to defend and win support for their cause. They called for the unity of all "producers" against monopolists, appealed to history (ancient and American), echoed familiar soft-money ideas, and warned of conspiracies against liberty.[60]

Alliance newspapers and lecturers also appropriated the venerable tradition of the yeoman farmer. On ceremonial occasions, spokesmen for the order extolled the virtues of rustic life and warned that the Republic "can not survive the degradation of the American farmer." Yet the Alliance relied on that tradition to a lesser extent than had previous farm organizations. Many Alliancemen would have agreed with one of the North Carolina brethren who suggested that each Alliance should "appoint a 'rotten egg' committee to inflict that punishment on every political speaker who compliments the farmers and tickles their vanity by telling them that 'they are the back bone of the country, the salt of the earth, &c'."[61]

The universal idiom of the rural South was neither Jeffersonian nor conspiratorial. The language of evangelical Protestantism, the rhetoric of Methodist camp meetings and Baptist revivals, informed popular southern culture. Alliancemen adopted the language of Zion to explain the depression of southern agriculture and to clothe their movement with the legitimacy of culturally sanctioned symbols. At a time when most leading churchmen of the South were using the received religious tradition to support the economic and political status quo, Alliancemen employed the same tradition to advocate change.

Speaking before a Senate committee in 1890, Leonidas L. Polk voiced a popular explanation for agricultural depression: "We protest, with all reverence, that it is not God's fault. We protest that it is not the farmers' fault. We believe and so charge that it is the fault of the financial system of the Government."[62] The evangelical fervor of Alliance meetings and the oft-repeated biblical justifications for reform assured many brethren that their cause was just. Wrote one Alabama Allianceman: "On that rock [belief in God] is the Alliance founded, and its efforts will be to carry out the will of God upon earth." In Texas an Alliance lecturer and former Methodist minister read to his audience a biblical denunciation of usury and declared: "This is the Alliance gospel. It is the gospel for the masses. You may call me a calamity howler if you will, but if I am one so was Nehemiah. So was Jesus."[63]

At the heart of the revivalistic message was the notion that when one hears the truth preached to him he is obligated to make a personal response. Alliance preachers, like other reformers, turned the traditional appeal for repentance into a call for men and women to join in the struggle for justice, as perceived by the Alliance. The rhetoric of repentance and commitment, with its insistence upon separation from sin, helped the Alliance to distinguish friend from foe and became increasingly common in Alliance speechmaking as the order moved toward political insurgency. In the heat of the first Populist campaign in 1892, a third-party Allianceman from Virginia told the brethren that Jesus had called his disciples to separate themselves from the evils of the world. Applying the commandment to Alliancemen and the Democratic party, he exhorted: "Our order demands of us our best service. It says: 'Whoso loves his party more than me is not worthy of me.' "[64]

For Alliancemen who were, as one Texas churchman and reformer put it, "Bible people," religious rhetoric had a powerful appeal. Its use provided assurance at the most profound level of their understanding that the Alliance cause was just. At a time when for many of them the prevailing myths of southern and American culture were proving inadequate to explain the conditions of life, the message of the Farmers' Alliance, steeped in the familiar language of Zion, helped to render intelligible both their situation and the movement on whose success they staked their fortunes.[65]

The fact that Alliancemen appropriated the familiar rhetoric of evangelical Protestantism rather than developing a new set of symbols does not mean that they were simply trying to preserve a fading rural Arcadia. Since the outbreak of the Second Great Awakening, the symbols of pietistic revivalism had proven remarkably elastic, capable of supporting both the cause of order and the cause of freedom. By linking the prophetic tradition of social justice with pietistic immediatism, Alliancemen imparted meaning to this set of symbols which was novel for the South. As used by the Alliance preachers, the familiar religious rhetoric provided both a new locus of meaning in a situation that was being rendered unintelligible through the unresponsiveness of prevailing institutions and a tool for promoting economic and political change.[66]

The Alliance gospel was not, by and large, preached to individuals but to groups. It was within the community of the true believers that the Alliance faith was shared.

CHAPTER 5

Brothers and Sisters:

THE ALLIANCE AS COMMUNITY

In 1888 a Texas Alliance lecturer reported on a rally that he had recently attended: "We held an old-fashioned experience meeting," recalled T. M. Smith. "We all owned up like men, told our respective shortcomings, and made good resolutions for the future. In that meeting I saw brethren embrace each other in loving embrace, and to this day, the effects of that meeting are plainly visible in Navarro County." At about the same time, the secretary of a North Carolina suballiance reported to state headquarters: "You cannot imagine what a kindred feeling has sprung up among us, how much more courteous to each other we are. . . . Bless the name of the Alliance . . . it is next to religion with us, as its Constitution partakes so much of the faith, hope, and charity commended in the Bible."[1]

Observers of the Alliance were struck by its moralistic tone and revivalistic fervor. In every formal statement of the order's objectives, ethical and social concerns were paramount. The Alliance was to improve conditions "mentally, morally, [and] socially," as well as financially. In florid language borrowed from the Grange, the brethren were admonished to "visit the homes where lacerated hearts are bleeding; to assuage the suffering of a brother or sister; bury the dead; care for the widows and educate the orphans; [and] to exercise charity toward offenders."[2]

Was this kind of talk just so much window dressing, and did the outpourings of emotion at Alliance meetings merely reflect yearnings for a lost Arcadia? The evidence suggests that neither was the case. Throughout its career, the Alliance, particularly at the local level, was a cohesive social institution as well as an agency for political and economic action. Its leaders, including those of the insurgent left wing, considered the "social" aspects of the movement to be essential.[3] The Alliance functioned as a community within which participants reaffirmed shared norms and values and made plans to implement them through specific economic and political programs.

This affirmation of community in the Alliance began with the idea that members shared common beliefs and interests. Thus, to understand the Alliance's social function it is essential to know how that community was defined (i.e., what requirements were set for membership) and who actually joined and led the movement. The order's constitution limited membership to rural whites, including ministers, teachers, and doctors, but made no distinction between large planters, tenants, and farm laborers. Merchants, bankers, lawyers, and other undesirable sorts were barred, as were townsmen. Alliance leaders tried, with varying zeal and effectiveness, to untangle the web of economic and social relationships linking rural southerners in order to maintain the purity of the Alliance as a "producers'" organization. Acting on orders from state presidents, some suballiances expelled or refused membership to townsmen and to farmers who had mercantile or banking interests,[4] but more often when local squires petitioned for membership, the suballiances chose to forget that they operated a store, held stock in a national bank, or practiced law on the side. For example, Senator John B. Gordon of Georgia, railroad lawyer, business executive, and gentleman farmer, encountered no difficulty in joining a suballiance near his DeKalb County home.[5]

In addition to imposing racial and occupational restrictions, the Alliance, like other secret societies, made adherence to cultural norms and values a test of admission. Prospective members had to "believe in the existence of a Supreme Being" and be of "good moral character." These requirements, like the occupational ones, were sometimes winked at, but not always. In North Carolina the state president ruled ineligible men who made and sold whiskey or who "wilfully and persistently" violated state laws. One Tennessean was denied admission for allegedly mistreating his wife.[6]

Many suballiances tried to regulate the conduct of their members. The bylaws of one North Carolina lodge stated that "This Alliance shall require and cultivate morality among its members, and any member violating the moral laws in common use may be dealt with as in the wisdom of the order may seem best." Often lodges did not allow members to participate in meetings if, when they whispered the password to the doorkeeper, he detected the smell of whiskey on their breath. A Mississippi suballiance expelled two members for eloping because the man left behind a wife and four children and numerous unpaid debts.[7]

Constitutional requirements for membership, while reflecting Alliance aspirations, do not reveal what sort of people actually joined. Alliance records have not survived in sufficient quantity or quality to permit rigorous analysis of the "typical" member, but the movement was apparently most attractive to a middle range of rural southerners, including not only full-time farmers but also rural teachers, preachers, and doctors, many of whom operated farms.[8] Relatively few wealthy planters seem to have participated, and, particularly in the Southeast, the Alliance did not actively recruit the most impoverished tenants, although the Alliance did include a lower stratum of rural southerners than the Grange and most local agricultural societies. The poorest rural white southerners lacked even the nominal amount of cash required to join the order and to participate in its cooperative undertakings.

Scattered evidence suggests that more Alliancemen owned farms than not, at least in the Southeast. A survey of South Carolina Alliancemen taken in 1888 showed that 55 percent were farm owners and 31 percent were tenants, the remainder being teachers, doctors, ministers, and merchants (presumably managers of Alliance stores). Records of local Alliances and statements of Alliance leaders suggest a similar pattern elsewhere. One contemporary observer of the Alliance in Texas stated that most of its members were tenants, but even in the Lone Star State many Alliancemen were landowners.[9]

Landownership, however, does not tell the whole story. In several states, including Virginia, North Carolina, and Texas, the Alliance was strongest in the most economically depressed sections, where landowners and tenants alike suffered economic distress. In North Carolina the Alliance was strongest in those areas that were most dependent upon commercial agriculture, either cotton or tobacco. Those areas were among the most severely depressed in the state.[10] Some Alliancemen were experiencing an alienation from the prevailing southern culture which would lead them to revolt against established political and social institutions. Many of the farm owners who joined faced economic ruin and were willing and able to fight, and some of the poorest members had only marginal loyalty to cultural norms in the first place.[11]

To approach the question of membership another way, in much of the South the areas of greatest Alliance strength were those that most closely resembled the frontier—either recently settled or economically and socially disorganized. In Alabama the Alliance was strongest in the impoverished and remote Tennessee Valley and in the newly settled wire-grass counties of the southeast. In Mississippi the order took root in the isolated hill country. Similarly, in Missouri the order was strongest in the newly settled southeastern lowlands. In Georgia the stronghold of the Alliance was a crescent-shaped region stretching across the upper piedmont, down along the Alabama border, and then east into the wire grass, an area skirting the tidewater and older plantation regions and including sections that were then experiencing extremely rapid growth.[12]

In many of these areas, ties with prevailing southern institutions were relatively weak. Here the Alliance organizers were in their own element. Their system of operation, like that of the Methodist circuit rider, was particularly suited to mobilizing people amid the social disorganization of the frontier. Agrarian protest in the South, as in the West, was in part a frontier phenomenon, not because the frontier was the seedbed of democracy, but because unsettled conditions in the frontier-like regions encouraged new forms of social organization. Indeed, on the southern frontier of the 1880s the Alliance, like the church, was a principal agent of social organization.[13]

One thing is certain about Alliance "men." As many as one-fourth of them were women, mostly the wives and daughters of men who joined the order.[14] Alliance leaders issued glowing reports of women's contributions to the movement and recounted the benefits that membership offered women. A Texas Alliancewoman proclaimed that "the Alliance has come to redeem women from her enslaved condition. . . . She is admitted into the organization as the equal of her brother, and the ostracism which has impeded her intellectual progress in the past is not met with." Addressing a crowd of Mississippi Alliancemen on the Alliance's success in promoting temperance, a national Alliance leader remarked: "Here [in the Alliance] is woman's greatest field; here she can wield the greatest influence. These splendid records are but the influence of women upon our membership."[15]

Despite such pronouncements, the Alliance was run by and for men, and suggestions that women should become more than dutiful wives and domestic workers evoked sharp criticism. One Mississippi brother huffed: "We have a sister in our Alliance that talks too much. What shall be done about it? . . . It was never intended that ladies should take that course in the Alliances." An anonymous sister in Tennessee complained about "those old drones, who think women only fit to cook, wash, scrub and wait on men, [and] values them only a little higher than the animals he works." In many suballiances, women took little part in discussions and received attention only when they prepared a community dinner or performed similar chores.[16]

Yet, like the southern churches, which also opposed a redefinition of women's role, the Alliance did afford women some opportunity for self-expression. As Alliance spokesmen pointed out, the biweekly sub-alliance meetings provided relief from the isolation and monotony of farm life. The Alliance, unlike the Grange, had no offices that were reserved for women, but local Alliances occasionally elected women to office, usually as secretary or lecturer. However, no woman held office in the national Alliance until Mrs. R. A. Southworth of Colorado was elected as one of four regional lecturers by the moribund order in 1894. (Mrs. Southworth was the wife of a prominent Colorado agricultural leader.) Only in Texas did women serve as officers of a southern state Alliance. There Mrs. Mary M. Clardy of Sulphur Springs became assistant state lecturer in 1892 and Fannie Leak of Austin, a staunch Populist, was elected secretary in 1895.[17]

For reasons rooted in their culturally sanctioned roles, those women whose voices were heard in the Alliance were more apt than men to express their feelings about religion and the home. They helped make the Alliance a spiritual crusade in which economic reform, the conservation of traditional values, and the preservation of the family farm were molded into a single righteous endeavor. As one enthusiastic sister announced, "I am going to work for prohibition, the Alliance and for Jesus as long as I live." The lecturer of a Louisiana lodge admonished her sisters to attend meetings faithfully, to educate their children in reform principles, and above all to pray for the Alliance: "God has promised to hear the cry of the oppressed. Petitions from every family alter should arise to Him who is ever ready to hear. If He be with us none can withstand us."[18]

Taking her cue from the women's missionary societies, Mary Clardy urged Texas Alliancewomen to hold a day of prayer to coincide with a national Alliance gathering in 1892. She encouraged the sisters to spend the day of 16 February "at some friendly parlor [or] at some well warmed church" reading Scripture and praying. Then, suggested Mrs. Clardy, they should take a collection for the purchase of reform tracts and newspapers.[19]

The Alliance and the People's party in the South had no spokeswoman as fiery as the Kansas pythoness, Mary Elizabeth Lease, but some southern women capably represented the radical wing of the order. Mary Clardy was one, and another was Mrs. Bettie Gay of Columbus, Texas. After her husband's death in 1880, Mrs. Gay managed a large farm and also found time to speak and write for women's suffrage, prohibition, the Alliance, and the People's party. A locally prominent Baptist, she represented her congregation at the state Baptist convention in 1886. Mrs. Gay was in the forefront of the fight to save the Texas exchange; she was an early supporter of Macune's subtreasury plan; and in 1892 she became an advocate of the People's party.[20]

Mrs. Gay's essay on "The Influence of Women in the Alliance," written in 1891, reveals the way in which the Alliance perpetuated the traditional role of women, but at the same time, it suggests that a strong-willed woman could work through the Alliance to change that role. She wrote that the position of women in the order "is the same as it is in the family—the companion and helpmeet of man" and that their presence in Alliance meetings tended to "place a premium upon politeness and gentility." She also pointed out that women have an abiding interest in economic reform, for they "are the chief sufferers whenever poverty or misfortune overtakes the family," and that, through the teachings of the Alliance and contact with "educated reformers," they have been able to overcome the debilitating belief that misfortune strikes because God so ordains.[21]

Women like Bettie Gay influenced the tone of the Alliance crusade, but the people who dominated the movement in the South were all men. The leadership of the Alliance, like that of other protest movements, came primarily from a higher socioeconomic stratum than the rank and file.[22] Such movements naturally capitalize on the expertise and prestige of recognized leaders. Alliance organizers across the South consciously recruited community leaders to take charge of state and local Alliances, and particularly in the Southeast, the leadership included many members of the interlocking economic, political, and social elites.[23]

Some Alliance leaders owned large plantations and had related business interests, including stores, gins, and warehouses. Some were officers of the prestigious state agricultural societies; others were influential lay churchmen. Based on information gathered on ninety-five southern Alliance leaders, almost one in five were college graduates, having attended the state universities of Louisiana, Arkansas, and North Carolina, such southern colleges as Vanderbilt, Mercer, and Randolph-Macon, and even Princeton, Oxford, and Aberdeen. About half of the Civil War veterans among them (a substantial number) had been officers in the Confederate army.

In addition to these men of property and standing, the Alliance drew much of its leadership—especially its lecturers, business agents, and editors—from the ranks of rural teachers, ministers, physicians, and journalists. They possessed communicative and administrative skills badly needed by the Alliance and usually commanded considerable respect in their communities, although they typically were no more than marginal members of the "ruling class."[24]

There are few collective biographies through which to compare Alliance leaders and other southern leadership groups (in fact, there are no truly comparable groups), but based on the available evidence concerning the region's political leadership, officers of the alliance ranked somewhat lower in economic and social standing.[25] That pattern prevailed in one instance in which precise comparison is possible, the Georgia House of Representatives of 1890, which included sixty officers of county and local Alliances. When compared with their non-Alliance colleagues in the House, they ranked substantially lower in wealth, education, professional standing, and legislative experience.[26] However, of the sixty Alliance legislators, twenty-nine had previously held local office, sixteen had attended or graduated from college, and sixteen had professional or business experience. As a group, the Alliance leaders in the House were older, and substantially more of them were Confederate veterans than were non-Alliancemen.

As the Alliance moved toward political insurgency after 1890, its leadership began to divide along the fault line of class. With few exceptions, most notably in Virginia, Alliance leaders whose primary identification was with the South's ruling class stayed with the Democratic party, while those most likely to support the People's party were teachers, preachers, and physicians, whose personal backgrounds and positions within the Alliance kept them in closer touch with the grass roots. In Georgia, for example, the Alliance's top leaders recoiled from making such a break, and leadership of the third-party movement devolved upon lower level Alliance leaders and farmer-oriented politicians like Tom Watson.

The bifurcated nature of Alliance leadership can be seen in the careers of H. S. P. ("Stump") Ashby of Texas and Elias Carr of North Carolina. Harrison Sterling Price Ashby, a founder of Texas Populism, was born in Missouri in 1848. His family claimed to be descended from Virginia cavaliers, but they had no wealth to show for it. During the final months of the Civil War, young Ashby served in General Joe Shelby's Confederate command, after which he set out for Texas to seek his fortune. There he worked as a cattle driver, Texas Ranger, and school teacher. He even flirted with an acting career before discovering a call to the ministry. After completing a theological reading course, Ashby was ordained to the Methodist ministry, and for fifteen years he served a succession of rural pastorates in western and north-central Texas. One of his first preaching assignments was in Stephenville, where Thomas L. Nugent, future Populist candidate for governor, was a member of his congregation.[27]

With close ties to the rural folk, Ashby was easily caught up in the Alliance movement and in the Knights of Labor. His organizing ability and forceful oratory won him the position of state lecturer in the Alliance. Ashby supported the early efforts of the Alliance's left wing to promote political insurgency, and when a statewide People's party emerged in 1891, he was among its leaders, serving first as chairman of the party's state executive committee and later as Populist candidate for lieutenant governor. Ashby's political activities, his criticism of the church for supporting the economic status quo, and an un-Methodist fondness for drink led to his being "located" (removed from the itinerant ministry) in 1888.[28]

Although he held important administrative positions in the Alliance, Ashby's greatest contribution to the cause was as a public speaker. On the hustings, he exercised the skills of his various callings to dramatize the plight of the farmers in a culture where powerful institutions, including the church, were insensitive to their needs. At one rally, he told Alliancemen that if Christ had been like most modern preachers he would have advised the rich young ruler differently. Instead of commanding him to sell all he had and give to the poor, "he would have advanced down the aisle, seized him with both hands and said Colonel, come up and consider yourself saved."[29]

In 1900 Ashby joined a host of Texans who, pushed by the boll weevil and pulled by the lure of new land, moved north to the Indian Territory. In his new home, Ashby renewed his involvement in radical agrarian politics, this time as an ally of Democrats William H. ("Alfalfa Bill") Murray and Charles N. Haskell. Before his death in 1923, Ashby served three terms in the Oklahoma legislature, where he established a reputation as "one of the most fiery debators" in that body.[30]

In contrast to "Stump" Ashby, Elias Carr of Edgecombe County, North Carolina, typified the gentleman farmer. Descended from Revolutionary army officers and an antebellum congressman, Carr was educated at the Universities of Virginia and North Carolina. After college he returned to the family estate, where for thirty years he enjoyed the life of a country gentleman. He experimented with scientific agriculture and received the homage due the local squire, including a seat on the Board of County Commissioners.[31]

In 1886 Carr's interest in agricultural reform took him to St. Paul, Minnesota, as a delegate to the National Farmers' Congress. He subsequently dismissed that organization as being "of doubtful utility" because of its "short sessions, constant changing of members, and an itching to discuss intricate political problems."[32] Carr was more impressed with the Farmers' Alliance. When an Alliance organizer reached Edgecombe County in 1887, Carr was elected president of the first suballiance. With his statewide reputation as an agricultural spokesman (he was president of the North Carolina Farmers' Association that Leonidas L. Polk had helped form), Carr became at the outset a powerful figure in the state Alliance, and during 1889–90 he served as its president.[33]

Carr steered a middle course on politics in the Alliance. Rejecting the advice of other gentleman farmers to keep the Alliance completely out of politics, he helped make the order a powerful pressure group in North Carolina. He even endorsed the subtreasury plan, which many regular Democrats vigorously opposed. However, Carr's ties with Democratic leaders made a break with the party unthinkable for him, even when those leaders failed to support the Alliance platform. In 1890 he strongly supported incumbent Senator Zebulon Vance for reelection, despite Vance's rejection of the subtreasury plan.[34]

When, in the cataclysmic spring of 1892, the Alliance moved toward political insurgency, Carr held back. "I am an Allianceman now and forever," he confided to Polk, who had already crossed the Populist Rubicon, "but not a Third Party man by any means."[35] Carr's loyalty—and the Democrats' need for a "farmer" candidate—won him the party's nomination for governor in 1892. After easily defeating lackluster Republican and Populist nominees, he served creditably as governor and then retired to his estate in Edgecombe County, where he spent his remaining years.[36]

In the end, the gap between men like "Stump" Ashby and Elias Carr proved unbridgeable. The Alliance could not establish a classless consociation of all farmers and rural people. Yet the organization did constitute a fairly cohesive community, bound together by shared values and behavior patterns, similar economic perspectives, and white solidarity.

This community of the true believers assembled in several well-defined social settings, the most important of which was the biweekly meeting of the suballiances. In countless rural neighborhoods, Alliancemen and their families heeded the exhortation of their national lecturer: "Can not we lay everything aside for one day in every two weeks and take our families, meet our friends and neighbors and make Alliance day our pleasure day? . . . Give this day to kindness, and good-fellowship, to the advancement of each other socially, mentally, morally and discuss plans for your financial benefit. Come close to each other, mind and body; be united."[37] The men and women who gathered on Saturday afternoons in churches, schools, and homes sang hymns and Alliance songs, observed the rituals of the order, conducted business, listened to lectures on subjects ranging from "Grasses and Clover" to "monopolies . . . and their relation to National affairs," and generally enjoyed each other's company.[38]

The rituals that the local Alliances practiced included "exemplifying the secret work"—repeating the oath of allegiance while making the prescribed hand signs—and initiating new members. The Alliance initiation ceremony drew on the familiar rituals of the Grange and fraternal organizations but was less elaborate than either. It was less involved than that of the Grange because the Alliance lacked its gradation of membership, or "degrees." Unlike the rituals of most fraternal groups, it did not require ornate regalia.[39] In the Alliance ceremony, the initiate was conducted around the meeting room, where he received instructions from officers of the lodge in the duties of membership. He then repeated the obligation, in which he swore to support the constitution of the Alliance, act in harmony with other members, and keep the secrets of the order. Finally the president explained to him the signs and passwords.[40]

In some of the fraternal organizations to which many Alliancemen belonged, the formal initiation was accompanied by a mock ceremony called "riding the goat," in which the new member was subjected to a series of farcical tricks. Some local Alliances apparently adopted such a practice. When Senator John B. Gordon joined an Alliance near his home in DeKalb County, Georgia, the Athens *Banner* published a vivid, but fictional, description of his initiation, in which the senator was made to change into farmers' clothing to remove the taint of politics and was then whacked with a "subtreasury plank" by the "supreme spanker." Alliance papers treated the story of Gordon's initiation as a joke, but similar antics were not unknown in some suballiances.[41]

Some students of the agrarian movement have suggested that, as the Alliance became politicized, its social function declined in importance. Evidence from national, state, and local Alliances suggests just the opposite.[42] Initially, the activities of many suballiances revolved almost entirely around business cooperation. Only when interest in the cooperatives began to wane did they try to make their meetings more socially attractive. In the years following 1890, local Alliance leaders placed increased emphasis on recreational activities, first to counteract the decline of the cooperatives and to support the work of political education and later in an attempt to revive the order after the divisive campaign of 1892.[43]

In January 1892 the *National Economist*, official organ of the national Alliance, began publishing a series of "Economist Educational Exercises" to be used in open meetings of suballiances. Each lesson contained information about the nation's economic ills and the Alliances's proposed remedies and was accompanied by instructions for conducting the meetings (like a "class in history or civil government"). The *Economist* advised each lodge to "have plenty of music" and to find other ways of making the public sessions appealing. "A first class teacher, man or woman, will make the best instructor," suggested the editor. "If you haven't a teacher try to get one into your Alliance."[44]

Just after the elections in 1892, the editor of the *Progressive Farmer* told North Carolina Alliancemen: "Now is the time to revive the interest in the Alliance. . . . [A]bove all induce your friends and neighbors to join in with you[,] thereby aiding in the social enjoyment of your meetings."[45] Such pleas appeared in the Alliance press after every biennial election, but in 1892 the message had a special urgency. In an effort to keep the all-important suballiances functioning, leaders turned to the old standbys of the agricultural clubs and debating societies. Elizabeth A. Dwyer, a staff writer for the *National Economist*, drew on her experience in "several literary and economic clubs" to suggest interesting topics for debate, including workingman's insurance, liquor laws, and a flexible currency. National lecturer Ben Terrell urged the brethren to "Make your suballiance a home improvement club; make it so jolly, so pleasant for all, that no one could afford not to be a member."[46]

The traditional activities of local farmers' clubs, which had never completely disappeared from the Alliances, became more important in local meetings during the order's declining years. An Alabama lodge held a cattleraising contest among its members, and Texas suballiances were encouraged to discuss such topics as accounting procedures on the farm and the profitability of various breeds of livestock.[47]

The suballiance was the focal point of the order as a social institution, but ingatherings of the Alliance community were not limited to the local meetings. In the summer and fall, many suballiances and county alliances held joint picnics to which the public was invited. In October 1890 over 1,500 people attended one such picnic held in Vance County, North Carolina. A brass band composed of local black Alliancemen opened the festivities with a rousing concert, after which the manager of the County Alliance warehouse discussed the merits of cooperative tobacco marketing. After consuming a staggering dinner, those who were still able listened while a procession of aspiring statesmen praised the Alliance and its platform.[48]

In Texas the Alliance, and later the People's party, adopted another organizing technique from evangelical Protestantism, the camp meeting. Alliance camp meetings never caught on elsewhere, but in the Lone Star State, they served an important social and political function.[49] At a time when most Protestant groups in Texas were forsaking the old-fashioned camp meeting for more refined indoor revivals, the Alliance picked up the practice to attract support from the rural population. During July and August, farmers gathered by the thousands in camp sites across the state to sing and pray and receive the Alliance gospel. To one such meeting came a host of over two thousand Alliance supporters—men, women, and children—who pitched their tents and lived together for five days of spiritual, social, and political refreshment. A similar gathering ended in an "experience meeting," with members testifying to "what the Alliance had done for them." An Alliance official reported: "Many backsliders became warmed up and resolved to again join our ranks, and [the meeting] ended in a general Alliance revival."[50]

The daily routine of the encampments typically followed that of church-sponsored camp meetings. At one meeting, the day's activities began at ten o'clock with a prayer by the chaplain, followed by group singing until eleven-thirty. After lunch, the group reassembled with the singing of a hymn and listened to speeches on cooperatives and politics until five.[51]

After the final session of the day, campers enjoyed a variety of recreations. Despite opposition from the more puritanical brethren, the evening's entertainment usually included dancing. Alliancemen forbade the sale of liquor on their camp grounds, but enterprising merchants managed to traffic in the vile substance within reach of the thirstier campers. A reporter at one Alliance camp meeting observed that "one prominent speaker, on account of too much 'iced tea' was unable to fill the engagement last night."[52]

Despite such lapses, not unheard of at church camp meetings, the farmers' encampments had a pronounced revivalistic flavor. A reporter's impression of one of the largest Alliance-Populist gatherings could be repeated for many others: "To one coming suddenly and unexpectedly upon this encampment just before the opening morning speaking, the singing of the lively songs to popular sacred tunes would have much more the general appearance of a good old-fashioned Methodist camp meeting in full blast than that of a political gathering."[53]

The farmers' camp meetings functioned for the Alliance as similar gatherings had for the churches. In such a meeting, Alliancemen could renew their spiritual commitment to the order. Amid the fervor

CHAPTER 6

The "Southern" Alliance Goes West

The Texas frontier was a meeting point of the American South and West. The early Farmers' Alliance, with its mingling of rebels and yankees, wheat farmers and cotton planters, was itself a microcosm of that juncture. The backtracking from the frontier which led Alliance organizers into the Southeast might also have spread the movement into the midwestern and plains states, but for a number of reasons, the initial expansion of the Alliance was eastward into the cotton belt.[1] Thus the Texas-based order became known as the "southern" Farmers' Alliance, an appellation that caused, and continues to cause, confusion about its role in the national farmers' movement of the 1890s.

Beginning in 1888 and 1889, the "southern" Alliance began recruiting in the West, and by the end of 1890, approximately one-fourth of its members lived outside the old Confederate states, most of them in Kansas and the Dakotas. An examination of the Alliance's expansion beyond the South and of the relationship between the "southern" and "northern" Alliances sheds light on both the agrarian revolt as a whole and on the subsequent evolution of the Alliance in the South.

In 1880 an organization that came to be known as the northern or northwestern Farmers' Alliance was established in Chicago. This group had no connection with the Texas Alliance, and while the two shared an interest in antimonopoly politics, the Chicago-based body never developed the aggressive cooperative system that characterized the southern Alliance. The nucleus of the northern Alliance—officially the National Farmers' Alliance—was formed by Milton George, an agricultural journalist and sometime Cook County farmer. George's purpose was to bring farmers together in a loose alliance that would lobby for railroad regulation and antimonopoly legislation.[2] George was influenced by a similar organization that had flourished briefly during the late 1870s in western New York state as a political coalition of Grangers and other farmers. An officer of the New York group was elected first president of the "national" Alliance in 1880.[3]

Although never president of the organization, George was its mainstay. He financed the Alliance out of his own pocket and advertised it through his popular farm journal, the *Western Rural and American Stockman*. Indeed, some critics claimed that George promoted the Alliance to boost his paper's circulation.[4] Spurred by George's advertising campaign and the ease of organizing (local agricultural clubs or interested farmers simply requested a charter, which they received free of charge), the Alliance grew rapidly during 1881. When the order held its second annual meeting in October of that year, delegates were present from Illinois, Indiana, Iowa, Kansas, Nebraska, Michigan, Minnesota, and New York. They represented around 24,500 members, the majority of whom lived in Nebraska and Kansas.[5]

Some local lodges attempted to establish rudimentary purchasing cooperatives, but at the state and national levels, the northern Alliance's objectives were largely political. Despite its lofty goals, the Alliance was short-lived in most communities. Rising wheat prices reduced the movement's urgency. The Alliance's lack of focus, effective leadership, and strong organizational structure contributed to its virtual collapse in 1882. At the end of that year, the national secretary claimed 100,000 members for the order, but in fact it was moribund. After a sparsely attended session in 1883, no further meetings of the national Alliance were held until 1886. Even the *Western Rural* seemed to lose interest in the movement.[6]

Nevertheless, remnants of the Alliance survived in Minnesota, Nebraska, and the Dakota Territory. During 1884–85, when western wheat prices again declined, the order experienced a revival, beginning in those same states. In Nebraska and Minnesota, aggressive state leaders linked the Alliance with statewide antimonopoly campaigns. In Dakota the Alliance attracted support through an ambitious program of economic cooperation.[7] Climbing back on the Alliance bandwagon, Milton George resumed his practice of chartering local lodges upon request and began distributing thousands of "honorary" memberships.[8]

Thousands of farmers in the plains states and upper Midwest responded to these renewed efforts, and when the national Alliance met in November 1886, George claimed that its membership exceeded 500,000. In fact, his estimate was highly inflated, perhaps by five- or tenfold. In addition to actual active members, the figure apparently included everyone who joined the order in its first burst of activity, plus all those to whom George had extended honorary memberships, and even the 150,000 Texas Alliancemen.[9]

The northern Alliance had affiliates throughout the Midwest, but its only strong state organizations were in Nebraska, Minnesota, Iowa, and the Dakota Territory. In 1887, in response to pressure from leaders in those states, the order adopted a new constitution that tightened its organizational structure and made the Alliance less dependent upon George. Some of those same leaders, including Jay Burrows of Nebraska and August Post of Iowa, assumed control of the national Alliance. Despite these organizational changes, the northern Alliance could not significantly expand its base of support in the West.[10]

Milton George's broadcast appeal for members even attracted some attention in the South. As early as 1882, George was issuing Alliance charters to local farmers' clubs in Arkansas. His chartering of a black club in Prairie County, Arkansas, gave rise to the claim that George was responsible for the formation of the Colored Farmers' Alliance. Such a claim seems unjustified, although George's relationship to the Colored Farmers' Alliance remains unclear. There is no apparent connection between the Prairie County club and the various black organizations in Texas from which evolved the Colored Farmers' National Alliance. Yet in 1889 R. M. Humphrey, national superintendent of the Colored Alliance, reported that George's *Western Rural* would handle job printing for his group free of charge.[11]

By 1885 George and other leaders of the northern Alliance knew about the Texas Alliance, which by then claimed 50,000 members. George was either unaware that the Texas group was totally independent of his own or he sought to obscure that fact. Until the end of 1886, Texas Alliance leaders were also uncertain about the nature and scope of the northern group. In December 1886 Acting President Macune appealed through the *Western Rural* to "men in all other states of the Union who are taking a prominent part in the organization of agriculturalists" to consider "the expediency of co-operation between those associations that are seeking to accomplish the same objectives."[12]

Despite the exchange of similarly cordial correspondence in 1887 and of fraternal delegates to their respective meetings that year, the two Alliances took no immediate steps toward consolidation. Nevertheless, some leaders of the Texas (now southern) Alliance held to the belief that their movement should expand northward, either by merging with existing organizations or by establishing rival Alliances in the western states. Ultimately, the southern Alliance employed both techniques in a drive that brought into the fold strong affiliates in Kansas and the Dakotas, as well as smaller units elsewhere north of the Mason-Dixon line. These southern expansionist efforts accentuated an economic cleavage within the northern Alliance which roughly followed the line of demarcation between the newer wheat belt and the areas of corn and hog production. In many respects, wheat farmers and small stockraisers of the western plains states had more in common economically with southwestern Alliancemen than with members of the northern Alliance in the more settled midwestern states.[13]

The first western target of Alliance expansion was Kansas. In the Sunflower State, the northern Alliance had flourished briefly during 1881–82 but then withered away. It reappeared briefly in 1888 but never became a major power in its own right. By 1889 the "revived" northern Alliance had only about 2,500 members.[14] That body was clearly incapable of mobilizing Kansas farmers, but declining commodity prices in the mid-1880s, coupled with a crippling drought and the subsequent collapse of the land boom during 1887–88, made Kansas a fertile field for a new agrarian organization that could promise some hope of relief.[15]

In May 1888 W. P. Brush of Clay County, Kansas, received an organizer's commission from the southern Alliance and began work in southeastern Kansas. The previous summer a Texas Allianceman had started organizing in the same area, but poor health had forced him to leave without establishing a beachhead for the Alliance. By July, Brush had formed several suballiances in Cowley County, commissioned some of the new Alliancemen to spread the work into adjoining counties, and established contact with William Peffer, the influential editor of the *Kansas Farmer*. Peffer had for years advocated the formation of such a group, and his support of the Alliance, expressed through his paper, hastened its expansion across Kansas.[16]

From its base in southeastern Kansas, the Alliance spread rapidly over the eastern two-thirds of the state. By the spring of 1889, the state secretary reported that new Alliances were being organized at the rate of more than twenty a week. When the state Alliance held its second annual meeting in August 1889, it claimed over 25,000 members in thirty counties. By the following spring, Alliance organizers had pushed to the western edge of the state and were reporting marked success in the southwestern counties. At the end of 1890, estimates of membership exceeded 100,000.[17]

In the course of its expansion across Kansas, the southern Alliance completely overshadowed the older northern group. Late in 1889 the state branch of the northern Alliance was absorbed by the southern order, which was roughly ten times as large. The polite term "consolidation" was used, but the officers of the "merged" Alliance were those of the southern affiliate, the new order patronized the cooperative agencies already established by the southern group, and it

promptly aligned itself with the National Farmers' Alliance and Industrial Union.[18]

The Alliance program was presented to Kansas farmers, as to
their southern counterparts, through well-developed communications
channels, which included subsidized newspapers and traveling lecturers, a corps of skillful and highly motivated men. (In addition to
their zeal for the cause, they were paid according to the number of
lodges they organized.) They promoted the Alliance not only with appeals to economic and political programs but by evoking the biblical
imagery that informed much of rural American culture. Like their
spiritual predecessors, the Methodist circuit riders, they organized
their converts into cohesive social units, the suballiances, where the
newfound Alliance faith could be shared and strengthened.

The Alliance had an even more important quasi-religious function in Kansas than it did in the South. In the late 1880s, the leading
Protestant denominations in Kansas were focusing their attention on
town churches. The inability of impoverished rural people to support
ministers or church organizations, coupled with interdenominational
competition for the allegiance of the more affluent townsmen, resulted
in the abandoning of many country churches. Consequently, for
many rural Kansans the Alliance literally became the church, the one
available institution within which they could interpret their experiences in terms of a meaningful value system. As William Peffer said of
the suballiances, "These meetings to a large extent, and in many
instances wholly, take the place of churches in the religious enjoyment
of the people."[19]

The new Alliance gospel was in part a political one. The movement emerged in the burned-over district of Kansas heterodoxy, political as well as religious, and its early leaders included veterans of
third-party crusades who encouraged political action.[20] In 1889 Alliancemen in Cowley and Jefferson counties adopted political platforms
and endorsed independent slates for county offices. By March 1890
many Alliancemen across the state had come to believe that the order
could no longer function as a pressure group within the GOP. Under
the leadership of President Benjamin H. Clover, the Alliance began
moving toward political independency at the state level.[21]

To perceive the Alliance as exclusively political is, however, to
misunderstand the nature of the mass movement upon which Kansas
Populism was based. Earlier in the 1880s, organizations based exclusively on support for antimonopoly and soft-money demands had
failed to attract Kansas farmers.[22] As in the South, the Alliance
became a significant force in Kansas by advocating a rigorous program
of economic cooperation.

When organizer Brush began his work, prominent Texas Alliancemen were telling Kansans that cooperation through the Alliance would reduce the cost of their supplies and increase their prices for livestock and commodities.[23] By the end of 1888, the Cowley County Alliance was saving money for its members by buying coal and food in bulk, and soon thereafter, cooperative stores sprang up around the county, each receiving goods from an Alliance exchange in Winfield, the county seat. By the spring of 1889, the Alliance exchange in Winfield was doing so much business that local merchants held an indignation meeting at which one irate shopkeeper pledged $2,000 of his own money to help destroy the Alliance competitor.[24]

Local cooperatives appeared across the state with the expansion of the Alliance. Much "cooperation" consisted of no more than buying in bulk from Kansas City or Chicago jobbers or pledging Alliance support to a single local merchant. At first, according to W. P. Brush, most local Alliances stuck to cooperative purchasing of a few staple items and the sale of grain and livestock.[25] But soon more ambitious cooperative ventures were launched, including cooperative stores, grain elevators, and even a fire and hail insurance company. Some Alliance stores adhered to the Grange's Rochdale plan, which required cash payment for goods, but others tried to alleviate the farmers' most pressing problem by extending or arranging credit.[26]

Cooperation soon expanded beyond the local and county Alliances. Kansas Alliancemen dreamed of building a statewide cooperative network, perhaps similar to the one that flourished briefly in Texas, like the agency that the Alliance and Agricultural Wheel had established in Tennessee, or like the Alliance exchange that was then aiding farmers in the Dakota Territory. Promoters of all three conferred with Kansas Alliancemen in 1888 and 1889.[27]

At its formation in December 1888, the state Alliance employed a business agent, who initially worked to secure markets for wheat and to coordinate cooperative purchasing.[28] However, leading Alliancemen, including Stephen McLallin, editor of the Meridan *Advocate*, were soon promoting a more ambitious scheme. In August 1889 the state Alliance approved plans for a cooperative exchange that was to operate warehouses, elevators, and stockyards, as well as coordinate the purchasing of supplies for members of the Alliance. The agency was to be financed through the sale of stock to suballiances and individual members and to be controlled by a network of local and county trustees separate from the hierarchy of the Alliance itself. Local cooperatives would be expected to channel their purchases through the state exchange.[29]

At first, Kansas Alliancemen hesitated to support the exchange with hard cash. Many were afraid to gamble their meager resources on a venture that might never open, or so it seemed to the editor of the Meridan *Advocate*, who complained that members were "far too penurious" in their support. In addition, conflicts arose between backers of the state system and existing local cooperatives, both of which were soliciting cash and patronage from Alliancemen.[30]

When the necessary capital was not forthcoming, officers of the exchange altered its rules to make the purchase of stock both easier and more advantageous to the members. In March 1890 the State Alliance Exchange of Kansas opened for business in Topeka, though not on the grand scale envisioned in its charter. It functioned primarily as an agent or broker for the purchase and sale of goods. Under the management of C. A. Tyler, state business agent, the exchange was prepared to handle the sale of livestock and grain and to provide certain staple supplies, primarily binder twine.[31] The exchange sold livestock at the Kansas City stockyards through the American Livestock Commission Company, a cooperative commission agency that the Alliance had established in conjunction with the Kansas state Grange and the state Alliances of Missouri and Nebraska.[32]

For a time, the state exchange succeeded in saving Alliance members substantial amounts on the purchase of farm machinery, twine, and other supplies. In 1891 W. H. Biddle, president of the state Alliance, asserted that in the preceding year the exchange had saved Kansas farmers $300,000 on one item alone (presumably twine). In its first eight months of operation, the exchange sold almost $470,000 worth of livestock for Alliancemen through its Kansas City outlet.[33] The state exchange, as the capstone of a cooperative network, provided Kansas farmers with a straightforward inducement to join the Alliance. By joining, they could save money on supplies and make better profits on the products of their labors.

Unlike Kansas, where the southern Alliance built its own organization from the ground up, the Alliance in the Dakota Territory flourished as an affiliate of the northern body before seceding to the NFA&IU. Yet from its inception, the Dakota Alliance more closely resembled the southern organization than the northern. In 1881 Milton George chartered the first local Alliance in the territory, but it was not until 1884–85 that the movement began to flourish there, stimulated by falling wheat prices and discrimination by railroads and grain elevators. The collapse of the Dakota land boom in 1886 further spurred its growth.[34]

The Alliance was particularly successful in the central counties of southern Dakota and the Red River valley in the north. Both regions were, by Dakota standards, settled areas. Like the central sections of Kansas and Nebraska where Populism flourished, these areas were populated by farmers who were well enough established to weather the first blasts of depression but were, nevertheless, vulnerable to fluctuations of the market and to exorbitant freight and elevator rates.[35]

The Alliance first attracted Dakota farmers by promising to deal with their economic problems through cooperative enterprise. As in Kansas, cooperation was at first rudimentary, with suballiances arranging bulk purchases of coal and binder's twine. In 1885 efforts to coordinate local purchasing and marketing ventures led directly to the establishment of a territorial Alliance. Cooperative enterprise remained a central feature of the Dakota Alliance and a principal concern of its leaders. Henry L. Loucks, president of the territorial Alliance, was personally involved in several cooperative schemes, including a plan to open a terminal grain elevator in Minneapolis. The territorial business agent, Alonzo Wardall, was probably as influential in the Alliance as President Loucks.[36]

In January 1888 the Alliance opened a joint stock cooperative agency, headquartered in Aberdeen, which it called the Dakota Farmers' Alliance Company. Despite its undercapitalization, the Alliance Company handled over $350,000-worth of merchandise in its first year of operation, with binder twine accounting for more than half of its sales. The company distributed large amounts of coal, barbed wire, and farm machinery, and smaller quantities of numerous other items. At a time when the price of binder twine was skyrocketing (like bagging, it was a jute product), the Alliance company sold it for one-third less than the prevailing price. By the summer of 1889, twine prices in non-Alliance stores had dropped sharply, for which the Alliance took credit.[37]

Unlike many other cooperatives, the Alliance Company was able to extend or arrange credit for some of its patrons. In addition to accepting farmers' personal notes, the company arranged loans on a limited basis through Sioux Falls capitalists, but the demand for credit exceeded the local supply, and in 1889 Alliance leaders tried, unsuccessfully, to obtain loan capital from British sources.[38]

The most well-received cooperative undertaking of the Dakota Alliance was its insurance program. Unhappy with high rates and unreliable adjustments, Alliancemen in 1887 established the Alliance Hail Association. Capably led by Alonzo Wardall, the insurance department subsequently branched out into fire and life insurance. Wardall employed local agents who not only sold policies but also organized new suballiances throughout the territory. In 1888 alone, his agents reportedly established 103 lodges. Similarly, lecturers employed by the Dakota Farmers' Alliance Company formed suballiances in many counties. Cooperative agents elsewhere, most notably in Texas, also organized suballiances and provided county-level leadership for the movement, but this tendency was most pronounced in the Dakota Territory.[39]

In addition to launching insurance and purchasing cooperatives, Dakota Alliancemen tried to establish their own marketing outlets, first by opening local elevators and warehouses, and then, when pressure from railroads and large elevator companies rendered them useless, by attempting to build their own terminal facilities at Minneapolis. Under the leadership of Henry Loucks, Alliancemen in Dakota and Minnesota laid plans in 1887 for an Alliance-controlled elevator company that would ship hard winter wheat directly to English millers. A lack of capital and the concerted opposition of established elevator companies killed the project, but out of its demise, and from Alliancemen's growing anger at what they perceived to be discrimination by the elevator companies, came louder demands for governmental regulation of the region's transportation and marketing systems.[40]

Specifically, Dakota Alliancemen looked to the territorial legislature for help. In 1885 Alliance pressure helped establish a Territorial Railroad Commission. When the commission proved to be ineffectual the Alliance began a systematic drive to elect legislators who would support more stringent measures. In 1886 and 1888, working primarily through the major parties, Alliancemen seemed to have elected enough sympathetic legislators to insure passage of strong regulatory bills, but the legislatures of 1887 and 1889 failed to take forceful action, partially because the "Alliance" legislators were divided and inexperienced, and partially because their skillful opponents were able to sidetrack key bills.[41]

Despite its failure to force enactment of effective regulatory legislation, the Dakota Territorial Alliance was one of the strongest Alliance organizations in the Midwest, but it was an anomaly within the northern Alliance. The cohesive territorial organization stood in contrast to the loosely knit state bodies elsewhere in the region. The Dakota Alliance alone developed a strong cooperative system. By mid-1889 its leaders recognized that their group had more in common with the southern Alliance, which was then taking Kansas by storm, than with the northern Alliance. In June delegates to Alliance conventions in North and South Dakota considered joining the southern Alliance when it met in St. Louis, and in October the South Dakota Alliance voted to do just that. Early in 1890 the North Dakota Alliance also switched, giving the southern Alliance jurisdiction over three of the strongest state organizations in the Midwest. (The Dakota Territorial Alliance had divided before statehood was acquired.)[42]

In 1889 and 1890, organizers for the "southern" Alliance fanned out across the western United States from Illinois and Michigan to Washington, Oregon, and California. Those recruiting drives failed to produce Alliances as strong as the ones in Kansas and the Dakotas, but in several western states, particularly Colorado and California, viable state organizations emerged which addressed the economic and political grievances of small farmers and later provided a nucleus for political insurgency.[43]

For the southern Alliance, the addition of new state affiliates in the Dakotas, Kansas, and elsewhere in the West meant not only an increase in membership but also an increase in the pressure for vigorous political action. Some western Alliancemen were veterans of the third-party crusades of the 1870s and 1880s. Others, having failed in the late 1880s to achieve their political objectives through the existing major parties, were now ready for insurgency. Some, including Henry Loucks, had been so radicalized by their struggle with railroads and grain elevator companies that they were insisting on government ownership of railroads and other "public necessities."[44]

At the end of 1889, the career of the "southern" Alliance and, indeed, of the entire farmers' movement had reached a critical juncture. The Alliance (still officially known as the Farmers' and Laborers' Union of America) had mobilized almost a million rural people in the South. Alliance leaders hoped to double the movement's strength at their convention in St. Louis through mergers with the northern Alliance, the Knights of Labor, and the Farmers' Mutual Benefit Association, an organization similar to the Alliance, which was strongest in Illinois and neighboring states.[45]

Politically, the southern Alliance was still without well-defined objectives, but there was a growing awareness among southern Alliancemen that the cooperatives would not usher in an agrarian utopia and that positive governmental action was needed to solve the problems of American agriculture. Partially because of their experience in the cooperative movement, including the war on the jute-bagging trust, Alliancemen were beginning to perceive the solutions to those problems in terms of corporate regulation and changes in federal monetary policy. If the cooperatives could not redress the inequities of marketing and supply systems and alleviate the credit squeeze, then government would have to do the job. When delegates to the national

Alliance arrived in St. Louis early in December, they sought not only the enlargement of their organization but a political redefinition of its goals.

The series of meetings that followed proved important both for what happened and what did not. The long-awaited merger of the two Alliances, which seemed assured by advance negotiations, failed to materialize.[46] Representatives of the northern organization insisted upon retaining the name "Alliance" and objected to the southerners' exclusion of blacks and to their secrecy and ritualism, but these differences were resolvable. The southern group obligingly changed its name to the National Farmers' Alliance and Industrial Union of America (which it retained until its demise) and agreed to make racial restrictions optional with the state Alliances. The northern Alliance had already altered its constitution to make secret meetings possible, though not mandatory.[47]

There were, however, more substantial conflicts. The southern Alliance had pursued some political-economic policies that were inimical to the interests of farmers in the old Northwest. In particular, leaders of the two Alliances had clashed over federal regulation of cotton-seed oil-based substitutes for butter and pork lard.[48] An unspoken but more fundamental stumbling block to merger was the relative strengths of the two orders. Attendance at their respective conventions dramatized the numerical superiority of the southern Alliance. The NFA&IU also had a cohesive structure and a network of cooperative exchanges that the northern Alliance could not begin to match. Some leaders of the latter group had favored union, among them its president, Jay Burrows of Nebraska, but, like the leaders of the Agricultural Wheel, they had no desire to "slide down into the capacious maw" of the southern Alliance. Unlike the Wheelers, they lacked the strength to avoid such a fate if merger were effected. Spokesmen for the northern Alliance agreed to confederation but not consolidation of the two orders, but southern Alliancemen balked at anything short of outright merger. Thereupon, the discussions were broken off. Charles Macune, who was deeply involved in the negotiations, believed that August Post, secretary of the northern Alliance, played a major role in blocking the union. Macune thought that Post, who was also a Republican party leader in Iowa, had been politically embarrassed by Alliancemen's desertion of the GOP in his home state and, therefore, wanted nothing to do with an organization composed largely of southern Democrats.[49]

What *did* happen at St. Louis proved to be more significant than the failure of the two groups to merge. Following the breakdown of negotiations, representatives of the Alliances in Kansas and South Dakota were admitted to the NFA&IU. In a dramatic closing session, they, along with a scattering of other midwesterners, took their seats as delegates. With their admission and a decision to push the organization into the midwestern and Pacific states through grass-roots recruiting, the "southern" Alliance broke out of its regional shell. The order's new president, Leonidas L. Polk, a lieutenant in the army of the late Confederacy, was to become a tireless spokesman for sectional reunion under the Alliance banner.[50]

At St. Louis the NFA&IU, in conjunction with the Knights of Labor, which was almost moribund but highly politicized, adopted a seven-point platform that concentrated on the reformers' trinity of finance, land, and transportation and that included a demand for public ownership of "the means of communication and transportation." In a related step, the Alliance established a national legislative committee that was to coordinate farmers' lobbying efforts in Washington and to cooperate with its counterpart in the Knights of Labor.[51] The groundwork for such cooperation had been laid through correspondence between Alliance leaders who were also Knights of Labor and Terence V. Powderly, general master workman of the K. of L. Less than a month before the St. Louis meeting, Alliance leaders had addressed the General Assembly of the Knights of Labor and appealed for unity of action. Powderly, who had previously sought cooperation with the northern Alliance, readily agreed.[52]

The most far-reaching action taken by the Alliance at St. Louis came just before the close of the meeting when a special committee on monetary reform called for the federal government to adopt the free coinage of silver and to establish a system of subtreasuries, which would provide storage for nonperishable crops and extend low-interest loans to be secured by the stored crops.[53] Many of the delegates had already left when the report was presented, but those who remained adopted it with little discussion. The subtreasury plan, which had been developed by Charles Macune, became in most southern states *the* issue that propelled the Alliance into politics, first in an effort to commit the southern Democracy to its enactment and, failing that, in an effort to establish a new party.

Alliance spokesmen continued to affirm the "nonpartisan" nature of their organization, but critics inside and outside the order recognized the political significance of the St. Louis meeting. The order's new members in Kansas and South Dakota and its allies in the Knights of Labor were firmly committed to political action, many of them to the establishment of a new party.

The growing support for political action and the lessening of Texas control over the national Alliance were demonstrated in the fight for the presidency of the NFA&IU. Evan Jones of Texas, president of the Farmers' and Laborers' Union, declined to seek reelection as head of the reorganized body. A three-way race developed among Macune, who had maintained de facto control over the order during Jones's tenure; Isaac McCracken, former president of the Wheel and a leader of political insurgency in Arkansas; and Leonidas L. Polk of North Carolina, who had emerged as the most influential Alliance leader in the Southeast. After four ballots, Macune withdrew, and on the fifth, Polk defeated McCracken by a majority of only eight votes.[54]

Polk had been campaigning for the presidency since summer. Following a trip through the deep South, he confided to a North Carolina friend: "I find that all the States east of the Mississippi are a unit for me as President of the Farmers and Laborers Union. . . . If tendered to me under conditions that will allow freedom of effort and energy I shall accept it, believing that I shall be able to do much in advancing the important work of organizing the new States."[55]

Despite his defeat in the presidential race, Macune became chairman of the powerful executive and legislative committees. From this new base and through his paper, the *National Economist*, which was the official organ of the Alliance, Macune turned his attention to the enactment of the subtreasury plan. The changing nature of the Alliance movement was dramatized by Macune's shifting stance. The architect of the Alliance's cooperative experiment, who had told prospective members that the order was "a strictly white man's non-political secret business association," now sought to commit the Alliance to political action.[56] Macune remained a centrist, but the center had moved.

CHAPTER 7

The Alliance in Politics:

SOUTHERN INTEREST GROUP AND MIDWESTERN INSURGENCY

As soon as the Alliance began attracting farmers in large numbers, it became, perforce, a political institution. Yet only slowly did the movement focus its political concern on specific issues. To be sure, southern state Alliances affirmed the order's political platforms, which were variations on the Cleburne themes, but at first they made no serious effort to impose their demands on potential officeholders. In 1890 the Alliance found an issue, the subtreasury, which generated substantial support among its southern members and provided a possible means of extricating the order from the traditional friends and neighbors politics of Dixie. Meanwhile, western members of the NFA&IU, embittered by previous failures with the kind of pressure group tactics that their southern counterparts were now employing, helped launch a new political crusade, the People's party. In the short run, both southern and western approaches seemed to be successful. The ultimate failure of the former would convince many southerners, previously unmoved by pleas from the West, that political insurgency offered the only hope of reform.

During its first ten months of publication, Charles Macune's *National Economist* discreetly avoided all economic panaceas. But the issue of 28 December 1889 greeted readers with a headline proclaiming: "EUREKA! Key to the Solution of the Industrial Problem of the Age." There followed a description of the subtreasury plan that Macune had introduced in St. Louis.[1] The plan called for the establishment of federal subtreasuries along with warehouses and elevators in which farmers could store certain nonperishable commodities. Upon depositing his crop, a farmer would receive negotiable treasury notes equal to 80 percent of the crop's value. He would pay 1 percent interest per month on the notes, plus minimal storage fees, but could withdraw his crop for sale at any time.[2]

The subtreasury plan addressed those problems of southern agriculture with which the cooperative exchanges had been grappling. Under its provisions, the government would provide short-term credit at low interest, thus giving the farmer more independence in marketing his crop. Not only would the system end the deflationary glut of commodities on the market at harvest time, it would, its advocates claimed, create an expanded, flexible currency that would reverse the decline of farm prices. The plan was complicated. Its critics called it impractical and unconstitutional. It did challenge southern Democrats' belief in limited government, but to many southern Alliancemen who had been educated by the cooperative experiment, the jute-bagging fight, and the campaign to withhold cotton from market, the plan seemed to justify Macune's banner headline.[3]

The authorship of the subtreasury scheme has been disputed by historians, as it was by Alliancemen. Four days before the St. Louis meeting opened, Harry Skinner, a North Carolina lawyer, outlined a similar proposal in *Frank Leslie's Illustrated Newspaper*, but as one student has pointed out, the Alliance would hardly have adopted such a sweeping plan on the basis of an article in a current magazine.[4] Leonidas L. Polk of North Carolina was a member of the monetary committee at St. Louis, but there is no evidence in Polk's extant correspondence that Skinner had discussed the subject with him. One historian who has studied the plan's antecedents describes, as did the Alliance press in 1890 and 1891, similar systems that operated briefly in France and Russia in the nineteenth century. However, Alliance spokesmen who referred to the European systems—and to supposed biblical and classical antecedents—seemed more intent on justifying their proposal than explaining its origins.[5]

Macune and those who had watched the career of Alliance cooperatives had ample basis for devising the plan out of their own experience. They were convinced of the need for a major change in the marketing and mercantile systems of the cotton belt and equally convinced that only the federal government had the resources to bring about such a change. Regardless of who devised the subtreasury scheme, it was Macune, more than any other man, who made it the principal issue on which the Alliance based its political career.[6]

Strategy for promoting the subtreasury plan and the St. Louis demands emanated from the Alliance's legislative committee in Washington, a committee that Macune chaired. Alliance leaders pursued two lines of attack. First they arranged the introduction of subtreasury bills in Congress and circulated petitions among local Alliances calling for their adoption. When it became apparent that the fifty-first Congress would not pass the bills, they urged local and state Alliances to elect congressmen and legislators who were pledged to support the St. Louis demands and the subtreasury.

To understand how national Alliance leaders orchestrated the subtreasury campaign, it is important to know how power was distributed in the Alliance. Delegates to the St. Louis convention vested more authority in the national leadership than it had previously held. Ultimate control remained with the state representatives in annual meeting, but considerable power was given to the new executive and legislative committees, both of which were to be chaired by Charles Macune.[7]

Despite his loss of the presidency to Polk, Macune retained effective control of the national organization.[8] In addition to heading its most powerful committees, he edited its official newspaper, the Washington *National Economist*. After the collapse of the Texas exchange in 1888, Macune, then president of the national Alliance, had received permission to establish a paper in Washington which would serve as the order's official voice. In March 1889, with $10,000 borrowed from Texas Allianceman R. J. Sledge, Macune began publication of the *National Economist*.[9] Macune also established the Alliance Publishing Company as a job printing affiliate of the *Economist*. Operating from the four-story headquarters building of the Alliance on North Capital Street in Washington, the *Economist* and the publishing company poured out a flood of material, including histories of the order, Alliance almanacs, and tracts on the subtreasury plan and other issues.[10] Neither the *National Economist* nor the Alliance Publishing Company were financial successes (the *Economist* lost $16,000 in its first twenty months of publication), but they provided Macune with an invaluable platform from which to address the membership.[11]

In January 1890 Leonidas L. Polk arrived at the Washington headquarters to begin work as president of the NFA&IU. Like Macune, Polk had grown accustomed to command. In North Carolina, he had dominated in turn the Agricultural Commission, the Baptist state convention, the Farmers' Association, and the Alliance. When he stepped down as secretary of the North Carolina Alliance, one relieved Tar Heel remarked: "We now have a sec[retar]y and not a boss."[12]

But in Washington, Polk lacked the resources to supplant Macune in fact as well as in title. The treasury of the national Alliance was empty because of the confusion over payment of dues that had prevailed since merger with the Agricultural Wheel. Polk could not even draw his full salary, much less assemble a staff equal to the corps of writers and lobbyists who managed Macune's multifaceted operations. In contrast to Macune's "gang," as one detractor called them, Polk employed only a personal secretary and occasional clerical help. Furthermore, Macune had already seized the initiative in the Alliance's legislative campaign. He, rather than Polk, made contact with Knights of Labor lobbyists and began mapping a plan of action. From the outset, relations were cool between Macune's entourage and Polk's supporters. After Macune made a controversial (and uninformed) statement on the Conger lard bill, Polk's secretary wrote: "Macune is not a safe leader. We are in hot water a good deal on account of his hot headed blunders. . . . Macune was the head so long that he feels that it is hard to give [up] the position of leader."[13] Because Macune was so thoroughly entrenched, Polk spent his first months in office following the Texan's lead on the subtreasury.

The first phase of the subtreasury campaign began in February 1890, when Representative John A. Pickler of South Dakota and Senator Zebulon B. Vance of North Carolina introduced subtreasury bills. Vance, who was facing reelection, privately opposed the subtreasury plan, but he nevertheless submitted the bill at the urging of Alliance leaders. Macune and Polk circulated copies of the bills and sample petitions to the suballiances, along with instructions for signing the petitions at local meetings and returning them to national headquarters for distribution to congressmen. In addition, lecturers made the rounds of the local Alliances to explain the subtreasury. At one meeting of a strong suballiance in North Carolina, the brethren turned out in record number to hear their respected county president praise the subtreasury. At the close of his address, he circulated a petition calling upon Congress to enact the plan, and, according to one member, "It seemed that every one wished to sign it first." Five months after the introduction of the bill, over 1,500 suballiances in North Carolina alone had endorsed it. Macune claimed that petitions bearing nearly one million signatures eventually reached Congress.[14]

In addition to directing the petition campaign, Macune testified before the Senate Agricultural Committee on behalf of the subtreasury bill and arranged committee appearances for other Alliance leaders, including President Polk and Superintendent R. M. Humphrey of the Colored Alliance.[15]

Although temporarily overshadowed by Macune, Polk clearly enjoyed his newfound place in the Washington limelight. As titular head of a large and as yet unfathomed farmers' movement, he received courteous attention from farm state congressmen. "They say we are so silent and quiet and dignified that they dont understand it," he confided to a friend. "They fear that it is a consciousness of a strength of powers behind us, that they have not comprehended. Generalship and diplomacy are indispensable in tackling Congress and we are doing our best."[16]

As agreed upon at St. Louis, Alliance leaders coordinated their legislative efforts with the Knights of Labor, represented in Washington by Ralph Beaumont, a veteran political insurgent, labor organizer, and lobbyist. After Beaumont's first meeting with Macune and Alonzo Wardall, the other member of the Alliance legislative committee, he and Terence Powderly, the general master workman, were optimistic about their liaison with the Alliance. "Stand by the Alliance men," instructed Powderly. "[A]ll that we do will not bear the fruit of successful legislation but it will agitate and educate."[17]

This solid legislative front was soon cracked. The Knights' leaders had no enthusiasm for the subtreasury, although they supported it publicly. Beaumont was distressed by the "National Economist fellows'" excitement over the scheme, which he believed to be an inadequate basis for political cooperation between farmers and laborers. Nevertheless, Beaumont reported to Powderly, "I am not disabusing their minds but saying 'Aye My Lord' to every thing." Conversely, Alliance leaders had little interest in the land-reform measures that Powderly believed were essential for the reconstruction of the American economy.[18]

For Powderly, a Pennsylvania Republican, friendship with southern Alliancemen did not come easily. Powderly grew suspicious that pleas from the Alliance's left wing for labor to launch a third party were a trick to destroy the Knights of Labor. In April 1890 he warned an associate: "The Farmers' Alliance there would like to have us start the ball rolling and wreck us so that there would be but one industrial organization existing [the Alliance]. I have fathomed some of them."[19]

Despite the tension between Knights and Alliancemen, their joint venture had considerable influence on leaders of the NFA&IU. It taught some of them, including Charles Macune, a great deal about congressional lobbying, and under the umbrella of Alliance-Knight cooperation, some Alliancemen, including Alonzo Wardall, could work to establish a farmer-labor party, while others, including Polk, began to perceive the need for such a movement.

By April 1890 the subtreasury bill was neatly buried in committee, despite what Polk thought to be an outpouring of public support for it. Polk vented his frustration in an angry letter to Senator Zebulon B. Vance of North Carolina. Demonstrating a stubborn commitment to the subtreasury—and enormous egotism—Polk requested that

Vance arrange for him to address a joint session of Congress on the subtreasury bill. Polk went on: "I would like to stand before [North Carolina Senator Matt] Ransom and others who are sneering at us and you and say some things that I would not say in Committee. We are not lobbyists—this is all we shall do about it. We shall say our say and leave it with Congress."[20]

After Polk's anger cooled, he remained convinced that only a political awakening of the "great Alliance Mass" could counter the influence of "The *Money* power of this Country and England" upon *both* political parties.[21] Two years before southern Alliancemen would begin forsaking the party of white supremacy for the strange god of Populism, Polk, his perception of American politics influenced for the first time by men like Ralph Beaumont, was beginning to think the unthinkable—that the Alliance's political objectives might not be obtainable within the existing party system.

Congress's failure to act on the subtreasury bill left most of its southern supporters angry but not yet willing to leave the Democratic party. Instead, they attempted to win control of the southern Democracy from the grass roots up as a step toward enacting their platform. Third-party advocates were quick to point out the logical flaws of such an approach. A Republican President sat in the White House, and a Republican Congress had killed the subtreasury bill without a floor vote. Even those Democrats most hostile toward the Alliance were beyond the reach of southern voters, but for most Alliancemen no alternative seemed plausible. As Terence Powderly put it, "They have not had their brains knocked out yet."[22] Until southern Alliancemen battered their heads against an unyielding wall of Bourbon resistence, there was no real possibility of their leaving the Democratic party.

In the summer of 1890, southern Alliancemen optimistically launched a drive to elect congressmen and legislators who would support the St. Louis platform and the subtreasury. Many prominent Alliancemen endorsed the subtreasury plan, but efforts to commit the order to its support, and by implication to place loyalty to the subtreasury above loyalty to the Democratic party, encountered strong opposition. The Mississippi Alliance endorsed the subtreasury over the objection of a substantial minority. In Texas the left wing of the order won an endorsement by a three-to-one margin and used the issue to regain control from the "Cleburne minority." Alliancemen in North Carolina, Georgia, and Florida passed similar measures, but the Alliances in Virginia and Missouri voted not to support the plan.[23]

In almost every southern state, the subtreasury was opposed by Alliance leaders who were involved in traditional Democratic politics.

The drive to separate friend from foe along the fault line of the sub-treasury was weakened by the order's dependence upon old-line leaders and by its integration into the mainstream of southern society. For many leading Alliancemen and their political allies, the first order of business was the preservation of existing power relationships. When the Alliance began to challenge the standing order, these men drew the line.

The case of Georgia is instructive on this point. In April the state Alliance executive committee demanded that all candidates take a stand on specific state and federal legislation, including the subtreasury plan. Democratic leaders perceived these demands as a threat to the party, particularly the subtreasury plank, which one loyalist called "that iniquitous subtreasury bill."[24] Alliance leaders in the state were not of one mind on the issue. W. J. Northen, conservative "Alliance" candidate for governor, alternately opposed and vaguely approved the subtreasury.

The real test of support for the measure in Georgia was its reception at the grass roots. Late in the spring, the county Alliances took up the debate. Many endorsed the subtreasury enthusiastically and pledged to support only candidates who would work for its enactment, but other Alliances rejected the subtreasury, some because of Northen's coolness on the issue and the opposition of Governor John B. Gordon, whose senatorial candidacy most Democratic regulars (including Alliancemen) were pledged to support. Some county Alliances avoided political pronouncements altogether, while others took a stand only to be fatally divided as a result. Although the state Alliance endorsed the subtreasury in August, the huge Georgia Alliance was unable to present a united front on what its national leaders believed to be the movement's most important issue.[25]

As primary returns began coming in during the summer and fall of 1890, the Alliance seemed to have wrought a major change in southern politics. In state after state, Alliancemen were able by weight of numbers and by virtue of their superior grass-roots organization to control Democratic primaries and conventions and to exact pledges of support from candidates. Alliancemen or candidates elected with their support apparently dominated the legislatures of Mississippi, Alabama, Tennessee, Georgia, Florida, South Carolina, and North Carolina. In addition several southern governors and congressmen owed their elections to the Alliance. In Georgia and the Carolinas, nineteen of twenty-seven congressmen reportedly supported the Alliance. Their number included the presidents of the Alliances in all three states.[26]

The apparent control of the Alliance over the southern Democracy was illusory. Most leading politicians either opposed the subtreasury or sidestepped the issue. In private many balked at being tied to the Alliance demands. "The sub-treasury bill is the dangerous question," growled Senator John Reagan to James S. Hogg, who had just been elected governor of Texas without supporting it. "They [the Alliance] ought to throw Macune and his set overboard. If he is not being paid to try to break up the Democratic party he is doing that work as effectively as if he was." In Alabama one Democratic leader wrote to another that "a Congressman must leave his official oath behind to live up to the demands of that organization."[27]

The difficulty of forcing candidates to support the subtreasury plan is illustrated by Alliance efforts to win an endorsement from Henry St. George Tucker, congressman from the tenth district of Virginia and a candidate for reelection in 1890. In September, Alliances in Tucker's district asked him to support the St. Louis demands and the subtreasury "uninfluenced by any party caucus." When Tucker did not reply, the brethren sought help from Charles Macune, who called at Tucker's Washington office. Failing to reach him, Macune wrote the congressman twice to ask for his "prompt attention" to the matter. Tucker ignored both letters. He was quietly making enquiries among his Alliance friends, one of whom told him that supporters of the subtreasury were in the minority in his district. Thus assured, Tucker replied to his inquisitors that he could not endorse the subtreasury because the state Alliance of Virginia had voted against it.[28]

A more decisive showdown over the subtreasury came in North Carolina, and it set the Alliance against Zebulon B. Vance, a seemingly invulnerable fixture in state politics, who was seeking a third term as United States Senator. In February 1890 Vance introduced the subtreasury bill in the Senate at the request of Macune and Polk, which brought him a flood of appreciative letters from Alliancemen.[29] Vance, however, had serious reservations about the bill, and in May he announced that he could not support it. Vance had misjudged the depth of Alliance support for the subtreasury. Opposition to his reelection materialized with a speed and intensity that took him and his advisors by surprise.

Since early spring, county Alliances had been preparing to seize the local Democratic primaries and name Alliance candidates to the legislature. Alliancemen expected to see substantial legislative action on their behalf, including the election of a United States Senator who supported the subtreasury. Vance's rejection of the subtreasury plan created a dilemma for local and state Alliance leaders. Many of them, including numerous legislative candidates, personally supported Vance, but they faced a rebellion among the rank and file over the subtreasury issue. One county leader warned the state Alliance president of the problem: "I have always been a great admirer of Senator Vance," said J. M. Mewboorne, but, "The boys are wrought up to such a high pitch that they will not hear me as they were wont to do."[30]

By midsummer Vance's own political confidants were alarmed. Josephus Daniels, then editor of the Raleigh *State Chronicle*, gave Vance this assessment of the situation: "I have been talking with some Alliancemen, and I will say to you what I would not admit to them: The sentiment for a man who favors [the] Sub. Treasury is greater than I thought, but there is great division on [it in] the Alliance. I have seen some letters that have *astonished me* and would astonish you—from men who have heretofore been enthusiastic for you . . . but they feel that the Sub-Treasury is above everything and everybody."[31] Despite the subtreasury controversy, a majority of Democratic nominees for the legislature, many of them Alliancemen, turned out to be Vance supporters, but the ground swell of discontent continued to rise in early autumn. State Democratic leaders began to fear that, unless Vance made concessions to the Alliance, agrarian anger might give the Republicans control of the legislature in November, a real possibility in North Carolina.[32]

That dire prediction did not come true, but most of the Democrats who went to Raleigh as legislators were members or supporters of the Alliance and faced extreme pressure to put a subtreasury advocate in the senate. Before the legislature convened, Vance accepted, in a vaguely worded statement, the legislature's right to instruct him on the subtreasury bill.[33] His response satisfied (and relieved) most Alliance leaders, but when the legislature, in fact, tried to instruct North Carolina's senators on the matter, Vance again balked, agreeing only to an even vaguer endorsement of Alliance principles. Even in North Carolina, an Alliance stronghold, the subtreasury did not provide a means of ousting entrenched Bourbon Democrats.

In 1890 some southern elections, including several congressional canvasses in Tennessee and Georgia, hinged on the subtreasury issue, but the Alliance was unable to get an endorsement written into the platform of a single state Democratic party, except in Florida, where the Democratic convention praised it obliquely. Supporters of the plan claimed, and rightly so, that they had insufficient time to educate Alliance voters on the matter before the campaign opened. As John H. Reagan observed in Texas, unswerving loyalty to the subtreasury required a rethinking of one's loyalty to the Democratic party. Few southern Alliancemen were yet prepared to entertain such thoughts.

Everywhere in the South, Alliancemen stressed state issues as well as the subtreasury, and in some states, the campaign focused largely on those issues. In Louisiana the Farmers' Union joined forces with the urban Anti-Lottery League in a drive to abolish the graft-ridden state lottery. In the process, the Union lost most of its independent political leverage. Members of the Union who opposed cooperation with the League threatened to bolt the Democracy and form an independent party.[34]

In Texas the "reform" wing of the Democratic party combined an appealing gubernatorial candidate, James S. Hogg, with a pledge to create a state railroad commission. The slogan of "Hogg and the Commission" proved irresistable to the state's farmers. In fact, the enthusiasm of the campaign helped revive the Alliance in its native state, but the same Democratic convention that nominated Hogg and endorsed the railroad commission denounced the subtreasury plan. Furthermore the editor of the *Southern Mercury*, Samuel Dixon, was a Hogg supporter, and he used the official organ of the Alliance to boost Hogg and the commission while ignoring the subtreasury issue. As in Louisiana, suppression of the subtreasury issue and the cooperation of Alliance leaders with mildly reformist Democrats pushed the left wing of the Alliance toward political insurgency. After the Texas Democratic convention rejected the subtreasury, William R. Lamb organized a lecturing campaign to explain the subtreasury to the local Alliances. In so doing, Lamb hoped to wean Alliancemen away from the Democracy.[35]

In Tennessee and South Carolina, as in Texas, Alliancemen expended considerable energy in electing "agrarian" governors whose candidacies and administrations, for all their apparent radicalism, posed no fundamental threat to existing political relationships. In Tennessee, while some local and congressional candidates were forced to stand up and be counted on the subtreasury issue, state Alliance president and Democratic gubernatorial candidate John P. Buchanan sidestepped the issue, saying that, although he personally supported the subtreasury, he would not endorse it because the state Democratic platform was silent on the matter. According to a recent study of Tennessee agrarianism, the most important factor in Buchanan's nomination and election was the persistence of ingrained voting habits rather than a unified Alliance effort.[36]

In South Carolina, where until 1891 the Alliance was virtually an adjunct of the Farmers' Association, most Alliancemen supported the successful gubernatorial candidacy of Ben Tillman in 1890. In addition, the state Alliance president, Eli T. Stackhouse was elected to

Congress that year, but neither his election nor that of Tillman signaled a radical break with traditional politics in the Palmetto state.[37]

In Mississippi the state Alliance endorsed the subtreasury in August 1890, but Macune's scheme did not dominate Alliance politics there until the following year. In 1890 small farmers from the hill counties, many of whom were Alliancemen, forced the calling of a state constitutional convention. They wanted to reapportion the state legislature so as to wrest power from the black-belt counties, which had become virtual rotten boroughs through planter manipulation of black votes. Some Alliance leaders, including the state president, Robert Patty, who chaired the committee on the franchise at the constitutional convention, supported the disfranchisement of blacks as a means of increasing the political power of the predominantly white hill counties.[38]

Who actually did what to whom in the convention remains unclear, but black-belt Bourbons apparently redirected the reapportionment-disfranchisement issue in a way that removed from the electorate not only most Mississippi blacks but many hill-county whites as well.[39]

In Missouri, where the Alliance and Wheel claimed a combined membership of over 150,000, opponents of the subtreasury, led by conservative Democrat Uriel S. Hall, defeated efforts at the meeting of the state Alliance to endorse the plan. Hall also dominated the state Democratic convention and helped write a party platform that conformed to the Alliance demands, minus the subtreasury. All of the successful congressional candidates and most who won seats in the legislature in 1890 endorsed the platform. Two of the three men elected to statewide office were members of the Alliance. Despite the apparent success of the Missouri Alliance within the Democratic party, advocates of the subtreasury supported independent tickets in several counties. Hall, who was elected president of the State Alliance in August, revoked the charters of at least twelve county Alliances for such actions. Nevertheless, Alliances in ten counties openly nominated independent slates for local and legislative offices.[40]

Involvement in southern politics had contradictory effects on the Alliance. To be sure, political enthusiasm created new interest in the order. The attention that candidates lavished on the movement and the political muscle that it seemed to exert held the interest of many old members and attracted new ones, at a time when the cooperative exchanges were proving to be a disappointment. On the other hand, the campaign of 1890 opened wounds within the Alliance which never healed. In Missouri, Mississippi, and Texas opponents of Macune tried to form a schismatic "antisubtreasury" Alliance.[41] In Georgia,

where factionalism had long plagued the order, the campaign set Allianceman against Allianceman. As early as the summer of 1889, two
leaders of the order, Leonidas F. Livingston and William J. Northen,
were seeking the Democratic nomination for governor. Livingston had
the support of the Alliance paper, the *Southern Alliance Farmer*, which
characterized Northen as "a politician of the Gordon type" who was in
league with the "silk-hat bosses."[42]

In June 1890 Livingston withdrew from the gubernatorial race to
run for Congress, but hostilities continued. Livingston and his supporters wanted to apply the "Alliance yardstick" to all prospective
officeholders, including John B. Gordon. When the legislature convened in November, Northen supported Gordon's candidacy for the
United States Senate, but Livingston opposed it, as did the *Southern
Alliance Farmer*. Livingston and his ally in Washington, Charles
Macune, endorsed the candidacy of Patrick Calhoun, an Atlanta attorney, whose law firm was general counsel for the Richmond Terminal
Company.[43] Calhoun had endorsed the subtreasury, but as a "railroad
lawyer," he was unacceptable to many Alliancemen.

Others of the brethren, including national President Leonidas L.
Polk, supported Thomas M. Norwood, a veteran opponent of the
Gordon-Colquitt-Brown triumvirate, who also supported the subtreasury. Gordon easily won the contest with the help of his "Alliance
friends" in the legislature, but the election further exacerbated relations within the Georgia and national Alliances. Some charged that
Livingston and Macune had been bribed to support Calhoun, and the
spectacle of Gordon's election to the Senate by an "Alliance" legislature enraged others.[44] The Georgia senatorial contest also illustrates
the difficulty of identifying "left" and "right" wings of the Alliance in
the Southeast, for the struggle between Calhoun and Norwood pitted
proponents of the subtreasury (and the editor of the *Atlanta Constitution*) against advocates of strong railroad regulation.

No such difficulty existed in the plains states, where in 1890
Alliance politics moved beyond pressure-group tactics to state-level
insurgency, the beginning of the People's party. Midwestern Populism had many founders, but as a grass-roots movement, it emerged
from local branches of the National Farmers' Alliance and Industrial
Union. The discussion that follows seeks to show how the Alliance
contributed to the rise of the People's party, without attempting to
provide a full account of Populism in the region.

Statewide insurgency in 1890 appeared first in South Dakota.
During the last years of the Dakota Territory, Alliancemen tried but
failed to win passage of effective regulatory legislation. Similarly, the

Alliance failed to dominate South Dakota's constitutional convention in 1889. As late as June 1889, President Henry L. Loucks persuaded the South Dakota Alliance to abjure a third party, but in succeeding months, GOP opposition to the Alliance hardened. Party officials, mainly townsmen and business leaders, shortsightedly tried to deny Alliance farmers any meaningful role in the party but instead damned them as cranks.[45]

Consequently, by early 1890, many Alliancemen were ready to join a new party. In South Dakota there would be little hairsplitting about whether the Alliance could openly support insurgency. By spring state business agent Alonzo Wardall, who was himself a Knight of Labor, was seeking labor support for a new party to be sponsored by the Alliance.[46] On 6 June 1890, at its meeting in Huron, the state Alliance voted overwhelmingly to form an Independent party. When the new party held its convention a month later, Loucks was nominated for governor, and the platform adopted was that of the Alliance. Local Alliances formed the nucleus of a statewide party structure that captured over 40 percent of the gubernatorial vote and sent almost seventy legislators to Pierre, enough to collaborate with Democrats in electing Alliance supporter James H. Kyle to the United States Senate in 1891.[47]

In North Dakota, where Alliancemen had enjoyed more success in Republican politics, the order's executive committee rejected the idea of independent political action in June, but by September sentiment for such a move had increased, and Alliance leaders joined Prohibitionists in forming an Independent party. Walter Muir, state Alliance president, was nominated for governor, but neither he nor the party made much headway against the Republicans. There were a number of reasons for the party's initial failure, one of which was the lack of support within the Alliance. Many of its leaders, personally involved in Republican politics, opposed insurgency. Similarly, the rank and file did not join the new party in large numbers. Muir received only about 5,000 out of 36,000 votes cast in the governor's race. After the election, an anti-third-party faction even won temporary control of the state Alliance.[48] In both Dakotas, the Alliance helped establish new parties, but in 1890 only South Dakota Alliancemen were united in the belief that such a step was necessary.

Alliance insurgency in Kansas came to fruition more rapidly than in the Dakotas, where the order had been active for six years. In Kansas, discounting the miniscule northern Alliance of the early 1880s, the progression from establishing a state Alliance to forming an Alliance-backed third party was telescoped into a period of nineteen months. Republican farmers, who were joining the Alliance by the tens of thousands in early 1890, faced a deepening economic depression. In the late 1880s, the efforts of farm spokesmen such as William A. Peffer to achieve reform through the GOP had failed miserably. Proponents of insurgency took pains to show Kansas farmers that similar Alliance efforts in the Dakota Territory had also failed.[49] Republican farmers, attracted to the Alliance by the cooperatives and by promises of vaguely defined political action, were ripe for insurgency by the end of 1889.

In addition to this army of disgruntled Republicans, the Alliance had among its leaders many veteran insurgents who saw in the order a means of promoting a new party, one which could attract far more than the 5 or 10 percent of Kansas voters who had supported the Greenback, Prohibition, and Union Labor parties. Armed with the Alliance's St. Louis demands of 1889, which gave them a litmus test with which to judge officeholders, these perennial insurgents worked diligently to wean Alliancemen away from the GOP. One of them, William F. Rightmire, would later claim that he and other Union Labor party activists introduced the southern Alliance in Kansas for the sole purpose of broadening the base of political insurgency.[50] Rightmire's claim is demonstrably in error. Alliance cooperatives were aiding Kansas farmers economically months before Rightmire claimed to have founded the order.[51]

To stress the importance of economic cooperation in the Kansas Alliance is not to suggest that cooperatives and political action were incompatible. Architects of Kansas insurgency such as Benjamin Clover, Alliance president, and Stephen McLallin, editor of the Topeka *Advocate*, strongly supported the state cooperative exchange. Indeed, the emergence of the state exchange in 1890 coincided with the movement of the Alliance toward independent political action. The records of county and subordinate Alliances substantiate this dual emphasis. During the spring and summer of 1890, local bodies simultaneously debated modes of economic cooperation and political action. In that period, for example, the Lone Tree Alliance discussed the subtreasury plan, a local arrangement for purchasing flour, the naming of an independent county ticket, subscription of stock in the state exchange, and the use of local Alliance funds for Populist expenses. The last proposal, as the secretary noted with diplomatic understatement, "made quite a controversy between Republican faction and people's party."[52]

As early as 1889, a few Alliances in eastern Kansas endorsed independent slates for local offices. Alliance support for those tickets was the deciding factor in their success. In Cowley County, birthplace of the order in Kansas, large-scale Alliance defections from the Republican party swept a "People's" ticket into office. The Republican paper in the county seat noted, "In every locality where the Alliance was strong, the People's ticket had large majorities, and in every township where there was no Alliance, the usual vote was cast." In Jefferson County, where the county Alliance did not endorse independent action, a similar slate was soundly defeated.[53] In these early forays into politics, insurgents within the order found a lever with which to pry Alliance farmers away from the GOP. County Alliances endorsed the national and state Alliance platforms and agreed to vote only for candidates who would support their demands. When local Republican candidates balked, independent tickets pledged to the Alliance platform took the field.[54]

In November, President Clover (of Cowley County) applied the same technique statewide by instructing the suballiances to petition Kansas congressmen and senators to support the Alliance demands. Of the entire congressional delegation, only Senator Preston B. Plumb responded affirmatively.[55] The lawmakers' negative reaction set Alliance "calamity howlers" to howling. Not all were willing to renounce the party of Lincoln, but county Alliances across the state began resolving to support no candidate who would not endorse the Alliance demands, which now included the St. Louis platform of the NFA&IU.[56]

On 25 March 1890, with grass-roots pressure growing for insurgency, Clover convened a conference of county Alliance presidents in Topeka. The assembled leaders discussed a wide range of topics, including plans for strengthening the state cooperative exchange, for they perceived that the expansion of cooperative efforts and successful recruitment for insurgency were inextricably linked. The political statement agreed upon at Topeka revealed the depth of anti-GOP sentiment within the Alliance. The county presidents, speaking for the state organization, declared that Republican patriarch John Ingalls should be retired from the United States Senate, called for labor organizations to join forces politically with the Alliance, and resolved "that we will no longer divide on party lines and will cast our votes for candidates of the people." To begin implementing these goals, President Clover was instructed to appoint Alliancemen from each congressional district to a "People's state central committee."[57]

The Topeka pronouncements touched off a sharp debate within the order. Some county Alliances, including those of Jackson, Haskell, Dickinson, and Pottowatomie counties, came to Senator Ingalls's defense, despite his refusal to support the Alliance demands, but the tide of Alliance sentiment was running the other way. In April and May, Alliancemen in county after county gathered to endorse the decisions reached in Topeka and, in many instances, to nominate independent slates for county offices. The work of organizing new Alliances continued, spurred by the prospect of Alliance-sponsored insurgency.[58]

On 12 June 1890, one week after South Dakota Alliancemen had launched an Independent party, the People's party of Kansas was formed in Topeka, at a convention chaired by Ben Clover and dominated by Alliancemen. Deferring to those who opposed transforming the Alliance bodily into a political party, the insurgents did not act in the name of the Alliance, but the new organization bore its stamp. As in South Dakota, its platform was that of the Alliance, and the party structure paralleled and sometimes supplanted the chain of local and county Alliances. When, in August, the People's party selected its slate for statewide offices, John F. Willits, president of the Jefferson County Alliance, was nominated for governor. The party nominated several other Alliance members, including Mrs. Fannie McCormick, who became the Populist candidate for superintendent of education. In succeeding years, the People's party came to include a broader segment of Kansas political life, but at its inception Kansas Populism was largely a creature of the Farmers' Alliance.[59]

The new party's achievements were phenomenal. In a state that two years earlier had given the Republican ticket a majority of 80,000, Populist Willits, unknown outside Alliance circles, missed the governor's chair by a tenth of that many votes. The Populists won five congressional seats (one going to Ben Clover) and elected enough legislators to replace John Ingalls with William Peffer, a late but enthusiastic convert to the new faith. The election was indeed "a Waterloo for the Republican party."[60]

The limited extant evidence suggests that after 1890 the *active* membership of the Alliance declined sharply in Kansas and the Dakotas. With a few exceptions, the cooperative agencies and stores in all three states suffered severe reversals in 1891. Politically, the order virtually lost its raison d'être when it became an adjunct of the People's party, although some sought to keep it alive as an "educational" agency. Farmers who remained loyal to the GOP understandably objected to the partisan endeavors of the Alliance. Populists, on the other hand, frequently found it convenient to reorganize themselves along more openly political lines. For example, the remaining Populist members of the Lone Tree Alliance ultimately disbanded their lodge and formed a People's party club.[61] The farmers' movement of which the Alliance was an institutional manifestation was still flourishing, but in Kansas and the Dakotas that movement was rapidly shifting to a new organizational base, the People's party.

Paradoxically, while the grass-roots base of the Alliance was being eroded in the plains states, midwestern leaders were gaining more influence in the national organization. Riding the crest of political successes in 1890 and heading what seemed on paper to be vigorous state Alliances, men like Ben Clover and Henry Loucks gained new stature in the predominantly southern NFA&IU. The westerners' influence at the top strengthened the position of the order's radicals. Some of the Kansans had been associated with the left wing of the Texas Alliance since 1888. By the end of 1890, many western Alliance leaders were pushing beyond the old Daws formula and seeking to make the Alliance an overt base for a new national party.

William Peffer, who knew something about the pain of severing old political ties, became a leading advocate of an Alliance-sponsored party that would unite South and West. In an editorial entitled "A Word to Our Southern Brethren," Peffer noted the sacrifice that Republican Alliancemen had already made in the Midwest. "We understand very well," wrote Peffer, "the force of the word 'Democrat' as applied to the South. . . . The sacrifice on your part is greater than on ours, but we are ready to assist you in carrying any new burdens you assume."[62]

The organization that Peffer hoped would usher in a new political era, the National Farmers' Alliance and Industrial Union, was now large enough and strong enough to attract nationwide attention. By the summer of 1890, the Alliance claimed over 1,200,000 members in twenty-seven states. The order had blanketed the South, having established an organization in virtually every county. Below Mason and Dixon's line, white Alliance membership approached that of Southern Baptist churches.[63] In Kansas and the Dakotas, the Alliance had mobilized far more farmers than had any previous agrarian organization and had aroused the kind of commitment that would reorder the politics of those states. By mid-1890 the Alliance was expanding beyond this southern and plains states base. In the older Midwest, it wooed farmers away from the conservative northern Alliance and mobilized rural people previously unreached by any agrarian organization. In California and the Pacific northwest, the "southern" Alliance combined cooperative enterprise and political activism to attract a substantial following. Through alignment with old Grange elements, the Alliance even established beachheads in the middle Atlantic states of Pennsylvania, New Jersey, and New York.[64]

At its annual meeting, held in Ocala, Florida, in December 1890, the Alliance seemed certain to expand its political efforts. The only question was how it would proceed. Unlike William Peffer and the mid-westerners, most southern leaders opposed endorsement of a third party. In the afterglow of the November elections, they believed they had captured much of the southern Democracy and thus saw no need to break with the old party.

The Supreme Council of the NFA&IU convened for a crucial session on 2 December in Ocala, a would-be metropolis in north central Florida whose boosters had lured the Alliance meeting away from Jacksonville. The session coincided with the opening of Ocala's Semi-Tropical Exposition, and many of the delegates, who came from as far away as California, North Dakota, and New York, spent their free hours strolling through the displays of Florida's agricultural products.[65] There was even a carnival, "for the children," exposition officials soberly explained. Local citizens provided free lodging, and delegates were treated to baskets of fruit and excursions to view the wonders of Florida. Their reception would have been a credit to latter-day Florida real estate agents.[66]

The carnival and the boosterism could not mask the political in-fighting that was going on in hotel lobbies and convention corridors. Because southerners still dominated the Supreme Council, the question of whether the Alliance should openly endorse the third party never came to a vote, but it profoundly influenced the actions of the delegates.[67] Proponents of a third party, acting independently of the Supreme Council, called a convention of all reform groups to meet in Cincinnati to form a national party. All who could endorse the St. Louis demands of 1889 would be welcome.[68] Few southern white Alliancemen signed the call for the Cincinnati convention, although leaders of the Colored Farmers' Alliance did so.

As an alternative to open endorsement of the People's party, the Supreme Council adopted Charles Macune's proposal that the Alliance enter a loose confederation with other "industrial" organizations. The confederation would coordinate political education during 1891 and hold a conference in February 1892 to decide on future actions.[69]

At Ocala the Supreme Council adopted a list of demands that differed only slightly from the St. Louis platform. The delegates added an appeal for direct election of senators, and over the objections of President Polk, they substituted government regulation for government ownership of railroads and telegraphs. At the urging of midwesterners, they added to the subtreasury plan a demand for government loans secured by real estate. The subtreasury-land-loan plank encountered small but spirited opposition, led by U. S. Hall, president of the Missouri Alliance. All other planks were adopted unanimously.[70]

Much of the publicity acquired by the Ocala platform in subsequent months derived from organizational changes agreed upon at Ocala which increased the Alliance's ability to disseminate political information to American farmers. At the request of President Polk, the council adopted a plan for putting full-time lecturers in the field to conduct an all-out educational campaign in 1891. At Macune's suggestion, the plan was amended to provide for paid lecturers in each congressional district, a system already in operation in several states. Polk also suggested that a national legislative council be established, composed of the national and state presidents, which would coordinate the political activities of the order between annual sessions of the Supreme Council—and would also replace Macune's legislative committee.[71]

The council further strengthened the cause of political militancy by electing Kansans to high office in the national organization. Ben Clover became vice-president, and John F. Willits assumed the strategic post of national lecturer, replacing Ben Terrell of Texas. Terrell, an ally of Macune, was a staunch supporter of the subtreasury but not yet a third-party advocate. Both Clover and Willits used their offices as platforms from which to support the People's party.[72] In addition, the reelection of Polk as president and the strengthening of his position relative to Macune insured that the Alliance would be led by a man who was at least sympathetic to the People's party and who quite possibly was already considering a campaign for national office under its banner.

Although the delegates to Ocala tried to unify the Alliance politically, the meeting revealed cleavages within the order, some of them personal and sectional as well as political. The controversy surrounding the Georgia senatorial contest gave Macune's critics an opening for attack. At the request of Macune, Polk, and Livingston, a committee investigated their involvement in that campaign. The committee exonerated all three of dishonesty but questioned the propriety of their conduct. U. S. Hall, a member of the investigating committee and a leader of the anti-Macune, antisubtreasury faction at Ocala, reportedly "produced a profound sensation in the convention hall" when he angrily dissented from the committee's findings. Macune, Hall revealed, had admitted to the committee that, while campaigning for Patrick Calhoun, he had borrowed $2,000 from the candidate.[73] The controversy left Macune's reputation under a cloud and also deepened the rift between him and Polk.

Another dispute, one that threatened the tenuous link between southern and midwestern Alliancemen, concerned the Lodge election bill. Alliance leaders in both regions had taken pains to prevent the polarizing symbols of the Civil War–Reconstruction era from blocking agrarian cooperation. In calling for (white) rural solidarity, William Peffer had recently pledged: "If the present Congress were made up of such men as the People's party in Kansas elected to Congress at the late election, no sectional force bill would have passed the House."[74] At Ocala the Supreme Council adopted a resolution offered by William S. McAllister of Mississippi which condemned the Lodge bill then pending in Congress, because it "involved a radical revolution in the elective machinery of this union . . . and its passage will be fatal to the autonomy of the states." A delegate from South Dakota later moved that McAllister's resolution be stricken from the minutes. Voting on the South Dakotan's motion divided along sectional lines, with only the Alabama and Texas delegations and one Floridian joining western Alliancemen in an unsuccessful attempt to strike the resolution.[75] The effort to form a coalition of "producers" which bridged the "bloody chasm" was already in jeopardy.

When the delegates ended their deliberations at Ocala, the Alliance entered a campaign of political education, this time on a national basis. The order was "going into politics" with a vengeance. In the North, the Alliance would be used openly as a vehicle for promoting insurgency. In the South, most Alliance efforts were still officially directed toward control of the Democratic party, but if that effort failed, the order's new political structure could form the nucleus of a new party.

CHAPTER 8

The Road to the People's Party

At the Ocala meeting, speaker after speaker predicted that 1891 would be crucial for the Farmers' Alliance. Their predictions were more than convention hyperbole. On three fronts, the Alliance faced challenges, the outcome of which would determine its institutional future and influence the course of American Populism. Within the national leadership, a power struggle raged which was both political (insurgents *vs.* old party loyalists) and personal (Polk *vs.* Macune). In the South, the order reached a critical juncture in its relationship with the Democratic party and with other powerful southern institutions. Southern Alliance leaders who insisted that support for the Ocala platform should be made a political test of faith were on a collision course with hostile Democratic leaders. At the same time, Alliance insurgents were seeking to extend the order beyond the southern and plains states to expand the base of the People's party. If they succeeded, the new party might soon become an important factor in the equation of national politics. Events on all three fronts helped push the Alliance *movement* toward insurgency while undermining the order's *institutional* viability.

The activities of Macune and Polk early in 1891 demonstrated the political drift of the Alliance and also laid bare the deepening conflict between the two leaders. In January representatives of the NFA&IU, Colored Alliance, Knights of Labor, and Citizens' Alliance met in Washington to implement Macune's proposal for a confederation of reform groups, to be called the Confederation of Industrial Organizations.[1] The representatives, including Macune, laid plans for political cooperation based on the St. Louis and Ocala demands. They reaffirmed the decision made at Ocala to hold a mass conference in February 1892 to adopt a plan of attack for the 1892 campaign.

The preliminary conference in Washington elected Ben Terrell of Texas as president of the Confederation. Effective control over the Confederation rested with a five-man committee in which Terrell and

Macune represented the NFA&IU; Richard M. Humphrey, the Colored Alliance; Terence Powderly, the Knights of Labor; and Ralph Beaumont, the Citizens' Alliance.[2]

On the face of it, the Confederation seemed capable of propelling the Alliance into the third party, as the kind of bridge between interest group and partisan organization envisioned in the old Daws formula. Two members of its executive committee, Beaumont and Humphrey, were already involved in insurgency. Even Macune said publicly that, should the major parties reject the Ocala platform, Alliance insurgency would be inevitable.[3] However, Macune, Terrell, and Powderly, a majority of the executive committee, wanted to prevent a stampede of farmers and laborers into the third party if at all possible. Macune, still loyal to the Democracy, and Powderly, now back in the Republican fold after flirting with insurgency, feared that the People's party would destroy the organizations around which their lives revolved, the Alliance and the Knights of Labor. Soon after the Ocala meeting, Macune requested that Powderly prepare articles for the *National Economist* dealing with a number of questions, one of which was: "must a leader of a great movement be conservative and if he is, what must he expect from the radicals among his following and from the opposition."[4] For both men the question was gratuitous.

To their chagrin, Populist leaders soon discovered that Macune was working to prevent the Conference from endorsing the People's party. Macune and Powderly reached an agreement (later overruled) that the February 1892 convention should be held in Washington, a site free from "sectional emotions," Macune said, and also too far from the centers of third-party strength for insurgents to pack the hall.[5] If the Confederation of Industrial Organizations were to become a vehicle for insurgency, it would be over the objections of Charles Macune.

In 1891 Macune was involved with another Alliance-related organization that, despite his intentions, aided the cause of insurgency, the National Reform Press Association (NRPA). In the summer of 1890, Macune and other Alliance leaders had considered forming a "newspaper Alliance" consisting of papers that supported the order's platform. At one point, they considered purchasing a national chain of papers. More realistically, the NRPA, established at Ocala, sought to insure that Alliance papers supported the Ocala demands and to provide them with appropriate boiler-plate material, including articles, editorials, and cartoons.[6]

Macune became the first president of the NRPA, but its other officers were men who supported the third party. Its secretary-treasurer was W. Scott Morgan, Arkansas Wheeler and insurgent publicist. The executive committee consisted of Cuthbert Vincent, Ralph Beaumont, and William R. Lamb. In 1891 the NRPA began forming state affiliates consisting of Alliance and reform editors. Over Macune's objections, this journalistic network provided an early focal point of insurgency within the Alliance, and it subsequently represented the radical, mid-road wing of the People's party.[7]

Clearly Macune was losing his dominant position in the agrarian movement. In 1891 his leadership of the Alliance was being challenged by Leonidas L. Polk. The infighting between their supporters at Ocala had been personal and intense. Macune's allies suspected Polk of siding with their enemies on the Georgia senatorial investigation. Macune's men had tried to discredit Polk's personal secretary and principal assistant, D. H. Rittenhouse, whose dislike for Macune was well known. Some of the charges against Rittenhouse were highly questionable, including one that he was conspiring with James G. Blaine to deliver Alliance votes to the Republicans in 1892, but evidence produced at Ocala of his intemperate political statements forced Polk to fire him.[8]

Upon his return to Washington from Florida, Polk removed his office from Macune's headquarters to a building on "D" Street. The distance between the two was far greater than a few city blocks. In March, Congressman Syd Alexander of North Carolina, a close friend of Polk, worried that Polk and Macune were about to have a "blow out." He wrote to Elias Carr that "Polk wont go about the Economist Crowd. He is running his machine his own way. He believes the Railroads have a grip on the Economist." Polk, Alexander warned, was "dickering with the third party too much. . . . I have heard him say several times that he was sitting with his hand on the brakes and [he] talked like he was watching his time to let go." Polk was then busily conferring with Kansas and Dakota Alliancemen about the upcoming Cincinnati meeting and was testing southern support for the People's party.[9]

Early in 1891 Polk dealt with his twin concerns, the elimination of Macune as a rival and the preparation of southern Alliancemen for insurgency, through the new Alliance agencies that he had helped create at Ocala, particularly the new Legislative Council. On 4 February Polk convened a meeting of that body, which consisted of the state Alliance presidents and himself. When the council assembled in Washington, they reaffirmed the Ocala platform but seemed to emphasize the free coinage of silver more than Macune's subtreasury plan. The group established a national lecture bureau that would act as a clearing-house for speakers and literature and authorized a network of legislative committees and paid lecturers in the counties and congressional districts. To finance these efforts the council established a "Propaganda Fund." The group also formed an Alliance Press Bureau, to be managed by Hal W. Ayre, Polk's new secretary.[10] Throughout 1891 Ayre provided weekly Washington newsletters to Alliance papers in the South and Midwest. His letters disseminated news of the national organization—from Polk's perspective—and vigorously supported the third-party movement well before Polk had announced his support for it.[11]

With Polk presiding, the Legislative Council meeting had a distinctly anti-Macune flavor. At least five of the thirteen members present, including U. S. Hall of Missouri, were openly hostile toward Macune. Hall, the arch-enemy of the subtreasury, was named to a national legislative committee, along with Polk and Arthur E. Cole, president of the Michigan Alliance and a committed third-party advocate. These three had only one apparent common interest, the overthrow of Macune. The Council exonerated William S. McAllister of disclosing Alliance secrets to the press at Ocala, although he had in fact published the details of the Macune investigation.[12] Polk seemed to be aligning himself with the more politically conservative element of the Alliance, but actually he was cooperating with men like Hall and McAllister only for the purpose of reducing Macune's power.

A St. Louis newspaper that was friendly to Hall entitled its account of the Washington meeting "Macune dethroned."[13] Macune denounced the Legislative Council for exceeding its authority and promised an investigation by the executive committee. Privately he complained that the Council had acted "purely in the interest of the ambition of the gentleman from North Carolina [Polk] for the express purpose of injuring . . . myself."[14] Macune was indeed losing influence. The embarrassment of the Georgia senatorial campaign, the growing prestige and organizational strength of Polk, and the shifting political mood within the order all undermined his position.

By 1891 Macune's nonpartisan stance found little support outside the South. The organizers who took the Alliance gospel beyond the southern and plains states were openly laying the foundation for insurgency, particularly in pivotal midwestern states like Indiana and Ohio. Working with organizers of the Citizens' Alliances and third-party journalists, representatives of the NFA&IU made full use of the new lecture bureau and propaganda fund to form or strengthen Alliance organizations sympathetic to Populism.

In Indiana, Ben Terrell had established an affiliate of the NFA& IU in the spring of 1890, and that fall Alliancemen, Greenbackers,

Grangers, and members of the FMBA established a new party that polled about seventeen thousand votes in November. The cause of Alliance insurgency was aided when Henry and Cuthbert Vincent moved their Populist newspaper from Kansas to Indianapolis. Their *American Nonconformist* absorbed the Indianapolis *Alliance Advocate* and became the order's official organ in Indiana. The Kansas gadflies helped launch a substantial movement of Hoosier farmers into the order. They hoped that the Indiana Alliance would recapitulate the Kansas experience and provide a host of converts for political independency.[15]

In December 1890 Kansas Populist George B. Long began recruiting Iowa farmers into the "southern" Alliance. In March 1891 President Polk and national lecturer John F. Willits met with Iowa Alliancemen to establish a state organization. Cooperating with the newly formed Citizens' Alliance and with veteran Iowa insurgents like James Baird Weaver, Alliancemen were soon busily organizing the nucleus of a third party.[16]

In California, where the NFA&IU established its strongest west coast affiliate, the Alliance was linked from its inception in the spring of 1889 to the third-party movement. Even before Alliance organizers appeared in California, urban supporters of Edward Bellamy's Nationalist movement declared their intention of promoting the Alliance as a means of broadening the base of political independency. By the end of 1891, the Alliance had won about thirty thousand converts, mostly in booming southern California. When a state People's party was organized in October 1891, most of its leaders were Alliancemen, many of them veterans of the Nationalist movement.[17]

Polk and Willits, along with other midwestern Alliance leaders, crisscrossed the northern and western states during 1891, organizing new Alliances, encouraging old ones, and, sometimes indirectly, laying the groundwork for Populist organizations. By the end of the year, they had established Alliances in Ohio, New York, Iowa, Delaware, Oregon, Washington, and New Jersey, bringing to thirty-two the number of states in which the NFA&IU had affiliates.[18] In none of those states, however, did the order achieve the popularity that it had won in the South and on the plains, nor was the Alliance highly successful in the areas where work had begun in 1890. However, this organizing campaign had substantial impact on the internal development of the NFA&IU. With the new state organizations committed to insurgency, the dominance of third-party advocates within the national organization was virtually assured.

Midwestern Populists like Willits did not restrict their efforts to the North. After the formation of the national People's party at Cincinnati in May 1891, Willits, Cuthbert Vincent, Jerry Simpson, and other like-minded westerners made repeated forays below Mason and Dixon's line to proselytize southern farmers and laborers for the new party.[19] Events in the South, political and economic, were creating a climate in which many southern Alliancemen could begin to consider such a move. Politically, this climate was produced by the failure of the order's interest-group tactics within the Democratic party. Economically, it was abetted by the decline of the cooperative movement. Institutionally, the spread of a more militant political sentiment was facilitated by the establishment of congressional district Alliances, which employed traveling lecturers to address local Alliances on the political objectives of the order. There was even a hint that for the first time black and white Alliancemen might work together politically.

Nowhere was the increasing militancy of Alliance politics more evident than in Mississippi, where in 1890 the subtreasury issue had been blunted by internal opposition and by the distraction of the constitutional convention. At the end of 1890, the aggressive state Alliance lecturer, Frank Burkitt, began organizing congressional district Alliances to solidify Alliance support for the subtreasury and to provide the machinery for imposing Alliance demands on political aspirants. Burkitt's organizing campaign tapped a powerful underground stream of animosity toward status quo politics in rural Mississippi. By February 1891, with district Alliances springing up across the state, the subtreasury threatened to become the central issue of legislative elections, for the upcoming legislature would fill both of Mississippi's United States Senate seats. The incumbents, James Z. George and Edward C. Walthall, denounced the plan as unconstitutional, and in July the state Democratic party similarly condemned it.[20]

Alliance leaders launched a full-scale attack against George, whose reelection was challenged by Ethelbert Barksdale, a longtime leader of agrarian Democrats in Mississippi. Outside speakers, including Alliance President Polk and national lecturer W. F. Willits, stumped the state encouraging the faithful to stand by the subtreasury and the Alliance. District and local lecturers took the same message to farmers at the forks of the creek. The state agent of the Colored Alliance, Joseph H. Powell, added his voice to the denunciation of George, calling him "the man who was foremost in the origination of the constitution that has disfranchised so much of the Alliance vote of the State of Mississippi."[21]

In the end, George's supporters in the legislature prevailed over Barksdale's by a margin of almost two to one. The full weight of the party machinery had been brought to bear against Barksdale, and partially as a result of that, the Alliance had not been able to maintain internal discipline in the attack on George. Several key Alliance leaders denounced the subtreasury and stood by George, among them J. H. Beeman, a congressman and member of the state executive committee; E. L. Martin, editor of the order's official paper; and William McAllister, assistant state lecturer. Martin and McAllister were read out of the order, but a significant minority of Alliancemen shared their political views. Had the campaign to educate farmers on the subtreasury and to unseat a popular incumbent not been telescoped into a few short months, more rural Mississippians would probably have been persuaded, but as it stood, only in the traditionally anti-Bourbon hill counties could the Alliance bring about the election of pro-Barksdale and prosubtreasury candidates to the legislature.[22]

The Alliance's interest-group approach was tested in legislative halls across the South in the spring of 1891, and in most instances, those who had looked to the order for substantial change were disappointed.

As in Mississippi, legislatures in Florida, Georgia, and North Carolina elected United States senators who opposed the subtreasury plan. The reelection of Zebulon B. Vance in North Carolina was particularly galling to many Alliancemen, because he had, under Alliance pressure, introduced the subtreasury bill in the Senate and then repudiated it.[23]

Not only did Alliance discipline break down in the election of senators, but state legislatures generally failed to enact the kind of laws that the Alliance was demanding. In Georgia, Florida, and Tennessee, legislators elected with Alliance support actually opposed measures to strengthen state regulation of railroads. Only in North Carolina and Texas was much of the Alliance platform enacted, although in several states, including Missouri and Mississippi, similar proposals had been adopted in the preceding decade.[24]

Some observers of the movement blamed these legislative failures on the inexperience of "farmer" representatives and on their wily opponents, but there was another cause, one that many Alliancemen sensed by the summer of 1891. Legislators elected with Alliance support in 1890 were for the most part veteran politicians whose primary loyalties were not to the Alliance. The order had failed to identify candidates who would put allegiance to the movement above loyalty to party; thus the Alliance's lobbying effort was in trouble before it began. The order could not enforce discipline because the Alliance "blocs" were in fact mixed collections of politicians ranging from independents to conservative Democrats, with the latter in the majority.[25]

In Georgia, for example, the *Atlanta Constitution* reported that all but a handful of the state representatives were *members* of the Alliance,[26] but this statement is exaggerated. Probably fewer than 100 of the 164 representatives belonged to the order. Alliance candidates had been defeated in urban and coastal counties. In some rural counties having two representatives, the Alliance had followed tradition and endorsed one townsman. The so-called Alliance legislature also included long-time officeholders who had joined the order to insure their reelection. In some respects, legislators who were members of the Alliance had more reason to uphold tradition than did their colleagues. They were older, and substantially more of them were Confederate veterans.[27] Although less wealthy and less well educated than their non-Alliance colleagues in the Georgia House, nearly half of the Alliance legislators had previously held local office, and perhaps one-third of them were professional men (ministers, physicians, teachers) or merchants. In short, their collective experience did not make them likely candidates to lead the revolution in Georgia. And they did not.[28]

By the summer of 1891, leading southern Democrats had launched a counterattack against the Alliance. In some instances, their strategy was one of appeasement—giving in on some issues while trying to steer the order away from electoral politics. Elsewhere Democratic leaders openly denounced the order, sometimes reviving the tactics employed against radical Republicans and political independents in the 1870s and 1880s.

One attempt to appease and manipulate the Alliance is revealed in a letter to a northern Alabama congressman from his chief political advisor. The congressman was Joseph Wheeler, General "Fighting Joe" Wheeler of Civil War fame. His confidant was Robert Barnwell Rhett, Jr., secessionist editor of the Charleston *Mercury*, Alabama planter, railroad promoter, and member of the Farmers' Alliance. In a letter that ended with an admonition to "Burn this when you read it," Rhett warned that the Alliance, "a great and growing power," was controlled by "demagogues and office-seekers who are trying to use the honest and ignorant people for their own promotion." Noting that the current leaders of the order were advocating a third party, Rhett outlined a course of action:

I deem it of the utmost importance, that strong and substantial Democrats throughout this District should enter the order and control it, as they can readily do, if they choose and will go to the trouble. . . . You know the most influential men in the District and can *quietly* urge them to go into the Alliance without delay. An ounce of prevention is worth a pound of cure. Hence I would suggest, that the grass be not allowed to grow under our feet, lest a crop of weeds and tares overwhelm us. As it now stands, the Alliance is surely after your scalp. But with judicious effort, the intemperate brothers may be checkmated.[29]

Wheeler must have taken Rhett's advice, for the general himself soon joined the Alliance. In Georgia and Florida, Senators John B. Gordon and Wilkinson Call joined the procession into the order, reinforcing that segment of the Alliance's leadership which sought to hold the order within the tradition of noncontroversial agricultural societies.[30]

Elsewhere in the South, Democratic leaders launched a frontal attack against what they considered the most vulnerable and yet potentially most dangerous point of the Alliance's program, the subtreasury. In Texas, Mississippi, and Tennessee, state Democratic leaders attempted to make opposition to the scheme a test of admission to the party, claiming—often with good reason—that its promoters were using it to weaken the faith of good Democrats.[31]

The Democracy had been caught off guard by the well-organized Alliance in 1890. Now its leaders fought back through what Alliancemen called the "subsidized press" and through the organization of local Democratic clubs, as advocated by the Democratic national committee. Democratic regulars sought to turn the subtreasury issue upon its supporters and woo Alliancemen away from those who fostered "dangerous heresies and condemnable ideas."[32]

Some Democrats feared that such tactics would play into the hands of Alliance radicals. In Alabama one such leader cautioned the chairman of the state Democratic committee against making opposition to the subtreasury a test of faith: "The people in the Alliance are in earnest . . . and they cannot be driven from the error of their ways," warned Robert McKee. "They are Democrats, working inside the party, and are indispensable to the maintainance of white rule in the State."[33]

Robert McKee's fears were soon borne out. For a growing number of southern Alliancemen, the political lesson of 1891 was obvious. To insure the enactment of their demands, they must work within a party that was committed to the Ocala platform. The Democracy was not that party. Many began to take seriously the advice of one insurgent: "Take the Ocala Demands to each aspirant for office, from constable to president; if he refuses to endorse them over his signature, let him severely alone; he is too far behind progressive reform for us to camp and wait for him."[34]

Also contributing to unrest among farmers in the South was a growing awareness that cooperative enterprise was not solving their basic economic problems. The cooperatives *had* saved Alliancemen money on specific items, primarily fertilizer and cotton bagging, but given the prevailing credit and marketing structure of the South, they could not make the difference between bankruptcy and survival for the mass of small farmers, no matter how ingenious the plan of operation or how sound the management.

Furthermore, the cooperatives, and the Alliance itself, seemed able to function only when the income of their potential patrons fell within a rather narrow range. If most farmers were prospering, they saw no need for the cooperatives, but if most were abjectly poor, they could not provide the operating capital that cooperatives required, capital that had to come from patrons before the time when federal funds would keep farmers' cooperatives afloat.[35]

By 1891 a growing number of Alliancemen were slipping out of the range in which they could support or benefit from the cooperatives. As economic conditions worsened across much of the South, more and more Alliancemen could not even pay their dues, which in most instances were only forty cents per year. The financial dilemma of the Alliance and of the cooperatives was expressed by the president of a suballiance in North Carolina who wrote to Elias Carr: "I wish to kno whot to do with my alianc. The members is all so pore that the[y] cant pay thare duse. if I drop them my alianc will hav to go down. I dont suppose there is 3 members out of 18 that can get seed corn or seed cotton to plant."[36]

Confronted with these problems, southern cooperatives ceased to play a meaningful role in the lives of most Alliance members, although a handful remained financially solvent by retrenching and adopting more conservative credit policies. When the cooperatives died, the Alliance began to die. In July 1891 S. D. A. Duncan resigned as head of the struggling commercial agency in Texas, complaining of "the impossibility to enlist a sufficient number of Alliance men in the business enterprise . . . to make it a success." In North Carolina local cooperative stores that had sprung up in 1888 and 1889 perished one by one, and the state business agency had to be reorganized to keep it from going under.[37] In 1890 and 1891, the Georgia exchange was beset by scandals, first when its president, Felix Corput, was charged with price fixing, and later when its principal agent, J. O. Wynn, admitted embezzling between $15,000 and $20,000. The state Alliance exonerated Corput, and bondsmen made good on Wynn's defalcation, but the confidence of Georgia farmers in the exchange, already beginning to waver, was badly shaken. The southern cooperatives were not alone in their distress. By 1891 the exchanges in Kansas and the Dakotas were also folding.[38]

Another indication that the cooperative experiment had failed was the retreat in several states to the Rochdale system, in which only those with ready cash could participate. The career of cooperative enterprise in Virginia illustrates this trend and also shows the continuing importance of the cooperatives, however weakened, in the internal politics of the order.

The Alliance got a late start in Virginia and in fact never gained massive support there, but by late 1890 the order was operating numerous cooperatives, some of them resurrected Grange ventures, including stores, tobacco warehouses, a state business agency, and even manufacturing plants for farm implements and fertilizer. The state agency, under the direction of A. R. Venable, was unsuccessful in coordinating local cooperative efforts, and although it did business of $135,000 in the year following August 1890, it failed to meet expenses.[39]

In May 1891 county business agents met in Richmond to revise the cooperative system. Many of the agents opposed Venable's leadership because he sold goods directly to local Alliancemen, thus bypassing them (Alliance middlemen!). One of the most influential local agents was Charles H. Pierson, whose prosperous exchange at Fredericksburg operated on the Rochdale plan. Under Pierson's leadership, the agents devised a new plan whereby the state agency would act only as a wholesale outlet for a network of district exchanges. The exchanges would follow the Rochdale system, whereby goods would be sold at prevailing retail prices for cash and profits divided among stockholders.[40]

From the perspective of the local business agents, the new system had two advantages. It put the cooperative system on a sounder financial footing, and it gave the agents more autonomy within the system. They were able to carry out the suggestion of the Richmond exchange manager in regard to the state agent: "Let us so muzzle him, if possible, that he will not swallow us," but to the mass of Virginia farmers who could not pay cash for their supplies, particularly those in the impoverished tobacco region of the the Southside, the system was of no use. Alliance membership in the state dwindled.[41]

Another sign of the cooperatives' declining vitality in the South and the Midwest was the development of a grandiose scheme to bring all Alliance stores under the control of a central agency, the National Union Company (NUC) and operate them on the Rochdale plan. Proposals for unifying the cooperative effort had been made repeatedly by Alliance leaders, but the NUC represented, at best, a last-ditch effort

to preserve the dying system and, at worst, a plan to hasten the cooperatives' demise.

Oswald Wilson, business agent of the Florida exchange, had led
early efforts to combine all the state Alliance agencies. When those
efforts failed, he continued to dream of building a national exchange.
To that end, Wilson opened a branch of the Florida exchange in New
York in 1889. He began by selling Florida citrus fruit but was soon
issuing market reports to southern Alliance newspapers and acting as
purchasing agent for several southern exchanges and stores.[42]

While in New York, Wilson contacted representatives of the
National Cordage Company, which reportedly controlled all but one
of the firms comprising the Alliance's old enemy, the jute-bagging
trust. Out of those discussions came an amazing proposal. The Cordage Company offered to supply jute bagging to the Alliance at prices
that had prevailed before the increase in 1888. Furthermore, the
company proposed to finance a national wholesale agency that would
supply Alliance exchanges with everything from "a knitting needle to
an elephant."[43]

Wilson submitted the plan to Polk and the national executive
committee at Ocala and won their approval, but not an official endorsement. Wilson worked out details of the plan in the spring of
1891, in meetings involving Charles Macune and several state business
agents from both the southern and plains states. What emerged was
the National Union Company, headed by Wilson and apparently
financed by the National Cordage Company. The new company proposed to take over the purchasing activities of the Alliance exchanges
by acquiring stores in trading centers across the country (four thousand of them, according to one report), placing local Alliancemen in
charge, and operating them on the Rochdale plan, dividing profits
between the NUC and patrons of the stores. According to the plan,
local owners of the cooperatives would turn over operational control of
the stores to the NUC, in return for which they would receive first
debenture bonds of the company, making the arrangement a veritable
Alliance trust![44]

Proponents of the NUC had trouble convincing state Alliance
leaders. The plan was adopted in South Dakota and Kansas, where
officials of the state cooperative exchanges signed on as agents. The
North Carolina business agency approved the plan, despite the objections of Syd Alexander, but there is no evidence that the company
ever operated in the state. Alliances in Illinois, Georgia, and Virginia
rejected the plan outright. By February 1892 the company had reportedly opened some forty stores, most of them in the Midwest.[45]

The National Union Company had little direct impact on Alliance cooperatives in the South, beyond the selling of some cotton bagging in 1891. Advertisement of the company's scheme did elicit charges that the nefarious bagging trust was conspiring to take over the cooperative system and even the Alliance itself.[46] The controversy within the Alliance over the NUC had political overtones, its principal backers in both the South and the Midwest being opponents of the People's party and the most outspoken criticism of it coming from insurgents, who claimed that Wilson and Macune were conspiring with the forces of evil to destroy the newly radicalized farmers' movement.[47] Whatever the merits of such a devil theory—and they seem dubious—the fact that pioneers of the cooperative movement could condone such a plan showed the extent to which cooperative enterprise had fallen on hard times.

Confronted by the decline of the cooperatives and the thwarting of its political efforts, the Alliance experienced a precipitous decline in its southern membership. In Missouri, South Carolina, Tennessee, and Virginia, the dues-paying membership had dropped 10 to 25 percent by the summer of 1891. Reports from the hinterlands of North Carolina indicated a similar decline there during the last three months of that year, with some of the strongest Alliance counties in the state losing one-fourth to one-third of their members in that quarter alone. By summer the active membership in Georgia had fallen by two-thirds, and within another year, before the People's party had completed its first campaign in the state, it had dropped by more than half again, to around 16,000.[48] In Alabama and Texas, the order probably held its own or even made slight gains during 1891, but in the South as a whole the trend was unmistakably downward.

Although the number of active southern Alliancemen declined in 1891, the movement's potential for spearheading political insurgency did not. The departure of many staunch Democrats left the order largely in the hands of men who were unmoved by appeals to party loyalty and were, in some instances, already committed to third-party action. Furthermore, the active membership of the Alliance represented only the tip of the iceberg, the vanguard of a host of rural southerners who were embittered by the experiences of the recent past and "educated" by prior membership in or exposure to the Alliance. To be sure, some of those who dropped out of the Alliance (or who never joined) had despaired of political solutions and settled into the lethargy of the impoverished, while others had been disfranchised by the roadblocks already being thrown up by some southern states in the path of would-be troublemakers, black and white.[49] But many of those disorganized rural southerners were potential recruits for the army that insurgent strategists planned on leading into battle, an army whose cadre could come from the radicalized Farmers' Alliance.

Institutionally, the Alliance encouraged the expression of political discontent and the mobilization of disorganized farmers by establishing a new stratum of Alliance organization at the congressional district level. These district Alliances employed traveling lecturers to explain the political objectives of the order to members and to the general public. From the days of its resurgence in Parker County, Texas, the Alliance had relied on traveling lecturers who went from one suballiance to the next informing the brethren of Alliance programs, reviving the fainthearted, and making new converts. The traveling lecturers differed from both the early Alliance organizers and the elected lecturers of subordinate and county Alliances. Unlike the organizers, they primarily visited established suballiances. Unlike the local lecturers, they were paid, either by the state Alliance or by the cooperative exchanges and Alliance newspapers for which they often solicited.[50]

By 1890 Alliances in Texas, Alabama, and North Carolina had formed teams of congressional district lecturers. Their responsibilities varied. Dr. Dennis Reid Parker of North Carolina reported, after making the rounds of suballiances in his district, that his mission had been: "(1) to look after the membership, (2) to circulate our literature, and (3) to raise stock for the State agency fund." The district-lecturer system and district Alliances that emerged in Alabama early in 1890 had political organization as their objective.[51]

The Texas Alliance first adopted a district lecturing system in 1888 to reactivate dormant lodges and advance the interests of the state exchange. The system was revived and expanded in 1890, when the state organization authorized the formation of district Alliances "for the purpose of holding farmers' encampments, where a general consultation and social reunion may be had." The "general consultations" were to be political. The district system was the creation of the order's left wing, including W. R. Lamb, J. M. Perdue, and Milton Park, the new editor of the *Southern Mercury*.[52] In the fifth congressional district, Lamb formed an Alliance that endorsed the subtreasury, provided political liaison with the local Knights of Labor assembly, and chose a district lecturer who was instructed to canvass the district, organizing suballiances and explaining the subtreasury plan. As 1890 came to a close, district Alliances were springing up all over Texas, for the most part controlled by political insurgents, and district lecturers were educating farmers in the intricacies of the subtreasury, which the state Democratic party had already denounced.[53]

Most of the men who became district lecturers were veteran Alliance organizers and speakers. In North Carolina their number included Dr. D. Reid Parker of Trinity College and the Reverend Pleasant H. Massey of Durham, both of whom had been local Alliance leaders from the beginning.[54] As had been the case with the early organizers, many of the district and county lecturers were ministers, physicians, and teachers, but in recruiting district lecturers, the Alliance was less dependent upon entrenched local elites than it had been in its initial recruitment of organizers. The district lecturers tended to be insurgents or were moving in that direction. In Texas, J. M. Perdue, "Stump" Ashby, and Evan Jones, all third-party advocates of long standing, became district lecturers. In almost every southern state, the district Alliances and lecturers facilitated the leftward movement of the Alliance because they were more responsive to the increasing militancy of the movement than many of the established county and state Alliance leaders.[55] As one district lecturer in eastern North Carolina, who had helped organize the People's party in his district, told his constituents: "We must have more lecturing and by active men. If one would not suit, he would be required to stand aside."[56]

Across the South, district and county lecturers explained the Ocala demands to farmers gathered in their suballiances and addressed public rallies that, as 1891 wore on, began to resemble the mass meetings out of which political institutions are born. This was what the Alliance meant by "education." Alliancemen were convinced that if they could confront the voters of the rural South with their program of relief they would rise up and demand its enactment. Farmers who had "never heard the aims and principles of the Alliance . . . explained" listened to discourses on the subtreasury and other features of the Ocala demands. In 1891 and 1892, the district lecturers made enough converts to provide a committed base of support for the People's party in the South.[57]

While district lecturers were mobilizing white southerners for political action, Alliance leaders were seeking to combine the voting strength of black and white farmers through cooperation with the Colored Farmers' Alliance. Before 1891 political contacts between the two groups had been limited to Macune's appeal for black support of the subtreasury bill and scattered attempts to gain black support in local Democratic campaigns. Early in 1891 officials of the national Alliance urged southern leaders to cultivate friendly relations with black Alliancemen and to support their recruiting efforts with an eye toward political cooperation. Even some white Alliancemen who opposed insurgency argued for political cooperation with black farmers.

After the Colored Alliance of South Carolina endorsed Ben Tillman's gubernatorial candidacy, Eli T. Stackhouse, former state president of the white Alliance and a Tillman lieutenant, advised white Alliance-men to seek black support within the Democratic party. (Stackhouse himself won a congressional seat in 1890.) Addressing a conference of politically minded Alliancemen in Texas, Stackhouse pointed out "the necessity and importance of cultivating the closest possible fraternal relations with our brethren of the Colored Alliance."[58]

In North Carolina the "closest possible fraternal relations" involved white subsidies for a Colored Alliance organizing campaign. President Elias Carr of the white state Alliance provided financial assistance to W. A. Patillo, lecturer of the state Colored Alliance. Patillo spent the spring and summer of 1891 working with local Alliance leaders, black and white, trying to recruit more blacks into the Colored Alliance.[59] Patillo, a black Baptist minister from Oxford, North Carolina, accepted a small stipend from Carr but urged him not to publicize their arrangement, fearing that if blacks knew "one cent had been given to aid me in this work, they would not follow me though they knew I was working for their good."[60]

When Carr set out to contact leaders of the Colored Alliance in his own state, he had to enquire of National Superintendent R. M. Humphrey who those leaders were. Humphrey passed Carr's enquiry on to Patillo and to J. J. Rogers, the white superintendent of the Colored Alliances in Virginia and North Carolina. Rogers recommended Patillo as being *perfectly reliable.*"[61] Rogers, a North Carolina native who managed the Colored Alliance's cooperative exchange in Norfolk, further advised Carr: "I will give as my experience with the Col. Alliance that you need not expect to organize the Negro to-day and expect him to vote with us tomorrow. But first organize them because their interest and ours as farmers and laborers are the same and *teach* them. They will then if called on vote with us for our good and theirs." It is impossible to gauge the impact of Patillo's work on biracial politics in North Carolina, but when the People's party sprang up in the Tarheel state the following year, Patillo was an early and active supporter.[62]

In Georgia there was virtually no contact between the two Alliances before 1891, despite the apparent success of the Colored Alliance in mobilizing black farmers. In July 1891 Lon Livingston, president of the white Alliance, and W. L. Peek, head of the state cooperative exchange, offered the facilities of the state exchange to black Alliancemen, in return for which blacks were tacitly expected to follow the political lead of the white Alliance. After hearing the proposals of Livingston and Peek, delegates to the Colored Alliance's state convention appointed a committee to confer with a corresponding white group "in reference to the third party."[63]

A political union of white and black Alliancemen failed to materialize in Georgia during 1891–92 for reasons that prevented similar cooperation in most of the South. Most white Alliancemen were ambivalent about organizing black farmers and farm workers. On occasion they objected strenuously to policies of the Colored Alliance which were antithetical to their own economic interests, as when R. M. Humphrey tried to organize a southwide cotton pickers' strike in September 1891.[64]

Conversely, most blacks mistrusted the white Alliance. Many had long feared that the Alliance movement, representing the interests of white farm owners, would speed the economic subjugation of black people, a view that had some validity. Politically, as well as economically, there was a wide gap between white Alliancemen and blacks. Most politically active blacks retained a reflexive suspicion of the Democratic party, and for them biracial cooperation within the party of white supremacy was unthinkable. Their skepticism was well founded. In 1890 Georgia and Louisiana legislators backed by the Alliance had supported bills that further circumscribed the civil rights of blacks, and with Alliance support, the Tennessee legislature had established de facto disfranchisement in 1889.[65]

The recruitment of blacks into the Colored Alliance and cooperation between white and black Alliancemen largely failed to promote biracial insurgency in the South. One astute black Populist, J. B. Raynor of Texas, argued that the Knights of Labor would be a more effective vehicle for achieving that purpose.[66] Again, evidence is lacking to measure the success of such efforts, but in some parts of the South, the Knights had for almost a decade recruited blacks into an organization that was free of association with the Democratic party and more attuned to the interests of black laborers and farm workers than the Alliance movement, white or black.

Despite the failure to unite white and black farmers under the third party banner in 1891 the southern Farmers' Alliance moved closer to a break with the Democratic party. Throughout the spring and summer, local and state Alliances voted to stand by the Ocala platform, including the subtreasury plan, despite the mounting opposition of Democratic leaders. In South Carolina, Governor Ben Tillman and Ben Terrell debated the merits of the platform before the state Alliance, and despite Tillman's opposition, the delegates endorsed it overwhelmingly. In Mississippi the order not only pledged to support the subtreasury but impeached the assistant state lecturer, W. S. McAllister, who had opposed it. The Virginia state Alliance, which had previously refrained from taking a stand on the subtreasury, voted to support it. In August, President Polk enthusiastically reported : "13 States [state Alliance meetings] heard from and in *all the 13 only* ONE man voted *against* the Ocala Demands!"[67]

Opposition to the subtreasury and its political ramifications continued within the order, but on a reduced scale. In Texas opponents of the plan made a feeble effort to organize a rival antisubtreasury Alliance but only succeeded in arousing more support for the plan. In Georgia the conflict between Governor Northen and Lon Livingston continued, focusing in part on Northen's failure to support the subtreasury, but Georgia Alliancemen were beginning to consider Livingston too conservative because he refused to countenance a third party through which to implement the demands.[68]

Talking about independent political action was one thing, but mobilizing the host of southern Alliancemen to leave the Democratic party was something else. C. Vann Woodward best described the implications of such a switch: "Changing one's party in the South of the nineties involved more than changing one's mind. It might involve a falling-off of clients, the loss of a job, of credit at the store, or of one's welcome at church. It could split families, it might even call into question one's loyalty to his race and his people."[69]

The first southern step toward Alliance involvement in the third party came in April 1891 at Waco, Texas. The occasion was a conference of Alliance lecturers from across the state, called to discuss the political issues confronting the order and to perfect the new district lecturing system. Leaders of the National Citizens' Alliance and the National Reform Press Association, both of which were by then auxiliaries of the People's party, also attended the meeting and pressed for direct political action. National and southern Alliance leaders who opposed the third party were present as well, notably Macune and Congressman Eli Stackhouse, but their pleas for restraint were drowned out by the chorus of insurgent-minded Texans. Alonzo Wardall of South Dakota reported from Waco to Alliancemen in his state who were already committed to the third party that "If a Dakota man had been suddenly transferred to the meeting he could have sworn it was a South Dakota Alliance convention."[70]

Out of the Waco meeting came the beginning of the People's party in Texas. Its founders, including W. R. Lamb, "Stump" Ashby, and other veterans of the Alliance's left wing, did not involve the Alliance directly in the formation of the new party but persuaded the Waco conferees to elect delegates to the third-party convention in Cincinnati and to form Texas affiliates of the Reform Press Association and the Citizens' Alliance. The latter group was headed by William E. Farmer, labor leader; Thomas Gaines, longtime Allianceman and insurgent; W. R. Lamb; and "Stump" Ashby. The Waco conferees pledged to support only candidates who endorsed the Ocala platform and set in motion an intensive Alliance propaganda campaign.[71]

As the Alliance's Year of Education progressed, the third-party spirit evidenced at Waco increasingly dominated the order. State Alliances in Kansas and the Dakotas had long since become adjuncts of the People's party. Now Alliance affiliates in the older midwestern states were following that pattern. In Texas third-party advocates controlled the Alliance's state organization and were attracting strong grass-roots support. Even in the Southeast, a growing minority of Alliancemen supported insurgency.[72]

In May 1891 Alliancemen, most of them westerners, played an important part in the Cincinnati conference that created the national People's party.[73] W. F. Rightmire, Kansas Allianceman and insurgent, gaveled the meeting to order. Alliancemen dominated the large delegations from Kansas and other western states, but of the more than 1,400 delegates fewer than 40 were from the South. Macune and Livingston both attended, the former in conjunction with a meeting of the NRPA, the latter to lobby against establishment of a third party. Polk did not go to Cincinnati, but in a letter to the delegates, he advised against the immediate formation of a third party. The recommendation, coolly received by the convention, represented no more than a tactical hesitancy on Polk's part, for he was already personally committed to the cause of national insurgency.[74] A handful of insurgent southern Alliancemen did attend the conference, among them Hardy Brian of Louisiana, W. R. Lamb of Texas, and George F. Gaither, manager of the Alabama Alliance exchange. Lamb and Gaither were named to the national executive committee of the new party.[75]

Brian, Gaither, and Lamb all established nuclei of the People's party in their home states during the summer and fall of 1891, operating largely through the Alliance. Several southern Alliance papers editorially praised the Cincinnati meeting and came close to acknowledging the inevitability of a third party. Hal W. Ayer, manager of Polk's Reform Press Bureau, was more explicit. Noting that the Populist executive committee elected at Cincinnati planned to consult with the Confederation of Industrial Organizations in February he wrote: "[In] that conference the Alliance and other organizations will take the People's party by the hand and their five millions of members can and will say through their representatives: 'Your principles are our principles, your platform is our platform, we . . . will stand by you to the end.' "[76]

When the NFA&IU held its annual meeting at Indianapolis in November 1891, proponents of the third party held the upper hand. The largest state delegation was from Kansas, and Polk, whose third-party leanings were by then well known, was elected to a third term as president. The Supreme Council readopted the Ocala platform, including the subtreasury plan, which delegate James Baird Weaver endorsed in an impromptu address. Looking toward the upcoming session of Congress, the Council demanded that "Alliance" congressmen enter no party caucus unless endorsement of the Ocala platform were made a test of admission to it.[77]

The third-party issue was not formally debated at Indianapolis, but it was uppermost in the minds of the delegates. There were signs of growing support for insurgency among the strategically important southern delegates. C. H. Ellington, a Georgian and an ally of Tom Watson, told a reporter that, if the Supreme Council endorsed the third party, his state would "be red hot for it."[78]

In his presidential address, Polk left no doubt about his own political views. He called financial reform (including free silver and the subtreasury) "the supreme issue before the American people" and charged that "it is the deliberate purpose of the two great parties of the country to avoid, evade, and ignore this great issue in their platforms and campaigns."[79]

Despite his veiled endorsement of the People's party, Polk perceived himself to be pursuing a middle course between the militant insurgents and old-party loyalists in the Alliance. After the Council adjourned, he told Elias Carr, "My Message was most heartily and warmly received by the level headed and conservative, while the radical element was disarmed. Tremendous effort was made by outside influences to create dissension and division but they failed utterly." Polk contested every effort to bring the Alliance into open union with the People's party. He was already leaning toward the position later taken by the more conservative wing of the People's party of emphasizing free silver while soft-pedaling more divisive issues.[80] Nothing in Polk's background marked him as a thoroughgoing radical; indeed, he was more at ease with some traditional Democratic leaders than with barn-burners like the Vincent brothers and William Lamb. Like Macune, Polk thought of himself as a centrist, one whose task included keeping the farmers' movement from becoming too radical, but in Polk's estimation, the center of the movement was further to the left than Macune imagined.

At Indianapolis the most effective argument against immediate endorsement of the People's party was that partisan action should more properly be discussed at the upcoming Conference of Industrial Organizations. That long-awaited meeting commenced in St. Louis on 22 February 1892. Macune had arranged for the conference to be held in Washington but third-party advocates including H. E. Taubeneck and Robert Schilling, chairman and secretary, respectively, of the Populist national committee, had insisted on moving it to St. Louis, which was more accessible to western third-party men.[81]

The conference was a magnet for reformers of all stripes. Well-known leaders of the antimonopoly, soft-money, labor, and prohibition movements were there, including Ignatius Donnelly, James Baird Weaver, Terence V. Powderly, and Francis Willard, along with hundreds of lesser spokesmen for a score of organizations, some of which existed largely in the minds of their "representatives" at St. Louis. The NFA&IU dominated the meeting, having almost one-third of the 764 delegates, but its southern representatives were divided on strategy, with the delegations from Georgia, Alabama, Tennessee, and Missouri particularly split. Some were ready for insurgency, although part of that group, including Polk, did not want to endorse the People's party openly. Others, led by Lon Livingston, opposed any effort to lead Alliancemen out of the Democracy. A substantial number, chief among whom was Charles Macune, had fought to prevent a third party in the South but by February 1892 could be swept up in the rising tide of southern Populism.[82]

The "convention" was in fact a noisy mass meeting. Officers of the People's party and Citizens' Alliance suspected that some southern Alliancemen, led by Terrell, Macune, and Livingston, would take advantage of the confusion to deflate the third-party balloon. The Populists lobbied vigorously to prevent Terrell from doing more than calling the meeting to order. They battled for two days in the credentials committee to insure the inclusion of delegates friendly to their cause.[83]

The beleagured credentials committee finally accredited almost anyone who claimed to represent a reform organization. Polk was elected permanent chairman over Terrell on the basis of his support for Populism. The delegates did not formally endorse the People's party (which had a conference committee on hand), but the St. Louis Conference, like the People's party, adopted a platform based on the demands of the NFA&IU. The platform began with a stirring preamble written by Ignatius Donnelly which announced, "We meet in the midst of a nation brought to the verge of moral, political and material ruin."[84]

Just as Polk was declaring the conference adjourned, Charles Macune took the floor. In a dramatic reversal, he urged the delegates to form a mass meeting and join with the representatives of the People's party in calling a national nominating convention. Macune pushed James Baird Weaver to the front as "chairman" of the mass meeting, and between them they were able to delay the Populist nominating convention until July, later than the conventions of both the Democratic and Republican parties. In part Macune was trying to give the Democratic party one last chance to redeem itself, but despite his public statements to the contrary, Macune must have known that the national Democratic convention would not adopt the platform written in St. Louis. Macune had watched the Alliance evolve from frontier protective association to an agency for economic cooperation and then to a political pressure group. His own position had usually been a reliable indicator of the center of the movement. Macune's startling reversal at St. Louis demonstrated that the center had shifted once again. The order and the good doctor were ready to support a third party.

A committee elected by the mass meeting, including Macune, Polk, Terrell, and Alliance lecturer John F. Willits, conferred with the executive committee of the People's party and announced that a national convention would be held in Omaha on 4 July which would be open to all who endorsed the platform just adopted at St. Louis. The joint committee further stated: "We urge that all citizens who support these demands shall meet on the last Saturday in March next, in their respective towns and villages, and hold public meetings and ratify these demands and take steps to organize preparatory to electing delegates to a National Convention."[85]

Thus, by an old and familiar formula, the Alliance was to be brought to the support of the People's party.

CHAPTER 9

The Demise of the Farmers' Alliance

Following the tumultuous meeting in St. Louis, Nelson A. Dunning, a leading reform publicist, wrote that the conference had begun to separate the true reformers from the hangers-on: "The die has been cast, the shibboleth has gone forth, and the alignment will soon begin. . . . Let no one be discouraged when some trusted leader or friend gathers up his arms and joins the other side, since it were better so."[1] Within the NFA&IU, only Alliances in the southern states had yet to undergo such a rending. Elsewhere the decision had long since been made to support insurgency, and the focal point of agrarian protest had shifted away from the Alliance to the new party. It remained to be seen whether southern insurgents could use the shibboleth of the St. Louis platform to transform the once-powerful Alliance into a viable third party below Mason and Dixon's line.

The St. Louis conference and the mass meeting that followed forced many southern Alliancemen to choose between the Alliance and the Democratic party, even though the action called for—endorsement of the St. Louis demands by local Alliances and the formation of separate People's party organizations—theoretically preserved the Alliance as a nonpartisan institution.[2] Within a month after the St. Louis conference, grass-roots Populist organizations were springing up from Alliance seedbeds across the South. In Georgia the DeKalb County Alliance, which had previously opposed any political action, met to endorse the St. Louis demands. Later the same day, Alliancemen and other DeKalb County citizens held a mass meeting to organize the People's party. The Clay County, Alabama, Alliance ratified the demands, and two days later, many of its members helped establish a local Populist group at a mass meeting attended by four or five hundred men. In Chatham County, North Carolina, the Democratic newspaper was dismayed when the county Alliance adopted the St. Louis platform by a six-to-one margin, despite the opposition of "prominent and intelligent alliancemen."[3]

Opponents of the third party recognized the importance of the movement to ratify the St. Louis demands and responded accordingly. In Georgia, Lon Livingston, still president of the state Alliance, tried to rescind the charters of suballiances that endorsed the demands on the grounds that to do so was an overt political act and thus violated the Alliance constitution. Democrats raised the specter of race by dwelling on the participation of blacks in the St. Louis meeting and on the threat to white solidarity created by the People's party. At Scotland Neck, North Carolina, William Hodge Kitchin, country squire, Democratic leader, and member of the Farmer's Alliance, persuaded all but a handful of whites to walk out of an integrated public meeting called by the Alliance to consider the St. Louis platform.[4]

The Alliance, which had heretofore functioned within the bounds of southern respectability, was now coming under heavy attack from spokesmen of the region's leading institutions. The alienation of many Alliancemen from their culture can be seen in the rift between them and leaders of southern white Protestantism. By the 1890s denominational leaders and editors of the religious press were predominately urban- or town-oriented. Most gave at least tacit approval to New South industrialism and to the hegemony of the Bourbon Democracy. On the other hand, the membership of most southern Protestant denominations was still largely rural, and many rural church members were not able to affirm the cultural myths that denominational leaders espoused, myths that implied that commercial and industrial endeavors centered in the region's towns and cities would rejuvenate the southern economy and that the forging of a politically solid (white) South, presided over by the lords of factory, firm, and plantation, would restore a Golden Age of southern politics.[5] With relations in many churches already strained, the agrarian revolt precipitated serious cleavages within the major denominations, essentially along the same town-country lines that were demarcating the larger society.[6]

When the Alliance first appeared, the religious press either ignored or faintly praised it, but as Populism gathered momentum in 1892, church papers across the South joined their secular Democratic counterparts in denouncing the third party and the Alliance's role in it. The Raleigh *Christian Advocate* lamented, "There are plenty of professing Christians in North Carolina who just now are much more concerned about the 'Sub Treasury' or the 'Third Party' or the St. Louis Platform or the Democratic platform or the Republican party than they are about the conversion of the world to Christ."[7]

Alliance spokesmen were interpreting the gospel differently than were most church leaders. As Alliancemen strove to divide the world into supporters and opponents of their programs, some began to number ministers among the unsaved. In an article entitled "Which Side Will the Clergy Take?" a Virginia Allianceman warned of the coming struggle that would divide the nation into two camps: "Many who are trying to follow Christ will be found on the Lord's side and some who are vainly trying to serve God and gold will sooner or later be found on the other side. The Lord's side is the side of the oppressed; the other side is the side of the oppressor." Noting that Christ had thrown money changers out of the temple, the *Choctaw Alliance* of Butler, Alabama, wondered "what the [Democratic] preachers are doing about this Wall street business? We believe they are all agents without credentials properly signed."[8]

In rural communities, the presence of the Alliance apparently did little to disturb churches until the order aligned itself with the People's party, but the violent campaign of 1892 split many local congregations. A Baptist minister from Bullock County, Alabama, reported at the close of the state campaign in August, "Families have been divided, communities have been rent by contention and churches have been torn by unholy political strife." A Georgia Baptist noted similar conditions in his state and added that voting for delegates to local Baptist associations was dividing along Populist-Democrat lines. He saw in the conflict a more generalized cleavage: "And so its town and city against country, and *vice versa*. When will it end?"[9]

The focal point of many local clashes was a minister who took a strong stand for or against the third party. Baptist ministers in several states were forced from their pulpits by hostile church members. A Presbyterian minister in Warsaw, North Carolina, who was an active Populist, resigned while under fire from the officers of his church, most of whom were Alliancemen but not Populists.[10]

Itinerant Methodist ministers, appointed by a conference rather than a local congregation, were less susceptible to such pressures. Nevertheless, several Methodist Alliancemen encountered opposition to their political activities, the most prominent of whom was "Stump" Ashby, whose ministerial career is described above.[11] In 1890 the Arkansas Conference of the Methodist Church censured the Reverend T. M. C. Birmingham who had run for state superintendent of public instruction on an Independent-Republican ticket. In his own defense, Birmingham pointed out that Methodist ministers had previously held the post that he sought, but as Democrats, and that the bishop presiding over the conference had held a similar position in California, also as a Democrat.[12] An Alabama Methodist minister who was located (removed from the itinerant ministry) for his support of Reuben

Kolb's gubernatorial candidacy returned to his former church and "preached against sin in high as well as low places." His condemnation of "political fraud, theft, robbery, and ballot box stuffing" brought down the wrath of the local Democratic editor but won praises from a Baptist minister, also an Allianceman, who claimed his own career had been wrecked by Democrats.[13]

One of the sharpest verbal exchanges between southern churchmen and Alliance leaders came in the summer and early fall of 1895, by which time the Alliance was totally identified with Populism. In an impromptu speech at an Alliance-Populist rally in Cary, North Carolina, Cyrus Thompson, president of the state Alliance and a locally prominent Methodist layman, charged, "The church today stands where it has always stood—on the side of human slavery—and not on the side of liberty," but, added Thompson, when the church fully understood its own mission, its ministers would flock to the support of the Alliance.[14]

The most critical response to Thompson's charges came from the Democratic Raleigh *News and Observer*. Editor Josephus Daniels not only expressed his own (Methodist) righteous indignation but also invited clergymen to respond. President John Carlisle Kilgo of Trinity College was surprisingly conciliatory in his reply, but the Reverend Edwin A. Yates, presiding elder of the Methodist's Raleigh district, warned that unless Thompson got rid of his strange notion "it will haunt his mind in the dark hours of affliction, and trouble his soul in the dying hour."[15]

The Reverend Dr. Yates's criticism revealed more about his understanding of the relationship between church and society than about Thompson's heresy. He explained that in times of unrest there is a natural tendency to "strike at sacred things." He defended the church's support of the political status quo by saying that it had to stand against "anarchy" and "nihilism": "It can but align itself with the powers that be, for 'they are ordained of God,' whether the government be Populist, Democrat, Republican . . . or whatever," but, he added, "[T]he business of the church is to save souls, and not to rectify governments and make civil laws."[16]

Thompson replied to his critics in a lengthy article that revealed the great gap between his view of Christian responsibility and that of Dr. Yates. Referring to the Alliance he said: "The genius of the order, therefore, is Christianity, manifest not only in feeling good, but in doing good to his creatures here. Therefore, I thought, the Alliance challenged the active countenance and support of the church and its membership. In the place of it, however, while the membership of this order consists of sterling Christian men and women, it has received little encouragement and positive opposition at the hands of the church."[17]

A few clergymen supported Thompson. D. H. Tuttle defended him from his Methodist pulpit in Raleigh and, in a letter to Thompson, conceded that the church was dominated by its wealthy and politically powerful members: "It would take an arch-angel from heaven with a search warrant, backed by a $1,000 reward, to find a preacher with grace and grit enough to turn a rich man out of the church."[18] Yates's view was closer, however, to that of most southern Protestant leaders than was Tuttle's.

Relations between the Farmers' Alliance and the churches of the South, particularly their clashes in the 1890s, reveal something about both. The deep involvement of Alliancemen in southern white Protestantism, culturally and institutionally, suggests that Alliancemen were well integrated into southern society, but the town-country cleavages within the churches during the Populist upheaval indicate the limits of that integration. At no point was the Alliance's effort to force clear-cut responses to issues more pronounced than in its use of evangelical rhetoric and its dealings with the church. The language of politics is often conciliatory, but the language of Zion, as used by the Alliance, was divisive. "He that is not for us is against us," proclaimed the Alliance orators. What they were about was not an exercise in paranoia but a struggle for control of culturally sanctioned symbols and values. In quarreling with ministers (or Democratic politicians) over the meaning of Scripture and the mission of the church, Alliancemen were seeking to buttress their cause with the one-value system that was almost universally accepted in the South.

As for the church, its relations with the Alliance and the People's party reveal the divided mind of southern white Protestantism. The quarrel with agrarian spokesmen showed the extent to which the churches were committed, at the level of denominational leadership, to supporting existing political and economic institutions, but political controversies within the denominations revealed substantial grassroots disagreement with that stand.

A leading student of American Christianity has found the immediate cause of the social gospel movement in the labor conflicts that erupted in the two decades after 1876. Confronted by violent strikes born of economic despair, churchmen in the North and Midwest began reassessing their view of the church's role in industrial society.[19] For a brief period in the years around 1890, southern church leaders faced a similar situation. A host of southerners demonstrated their lack of faith in the social and economic status quo and called upon church-men to address the problems of society. From Alliance leaders like Cyrus Thompson and "Stump" Ashby, the call for a southern social gospel was clear, but the reply of denominational leaders was that of the Reverend Dr. Yates. The church "can but align itself with the powers that be." Its "business [an instructive term] is to save souls, and not to rectify governments and make civil laws." The priority of individual salvation and personal piety was too firmly established, and the threat to the churches' internal stability too costly, to permit any other response. Equally important, the agrarian critique of southern churches was coupled with an all-out attack on the Democratic party and an implied threat to white solidarity. Church leaders were too deeply committed to both to countenance such attacks.[20]

Considering the social strain that the third-party movement gen-erated, as evidenced by church controversies, the campaign to ratify the St. Louis demands was remarkably effective in winning Alliance support for the People's party. By the end of March, two-thirds of Georgia's suballiances had reportedly endorsed the demands, and that state was developing one of the strongest Populist organizations in the South.[21] The vigorous People's parties in Texas, Alabama, and North Carolina were also based on powerful Alliance organizations. How-ever, the presence of a strong Alliance was no guarantee that Populism would flourish, as was demonstrated in Tennessee and Mississippi.

In most southern states, the initial leadership of the People's party came from the Alliance and included many longtime political insurgents. In Texas, W. R. Lamb and other Alliancemen organized the People's party along with officers of the state Federation of Labor and some black leaders. In Louisiana leaders of the order's left wing, including former Greenbacker Benjamin Brian and business agent T. J. Guice, broke with the state Alliance president in the summer of 1891 and formed a third party rather than cooperate with urban Democrats in the antilottery campaign. Elsewhere in the South, Alli-ancemen formed the nucleus of most state Populist organizations that were formed in 1892. One exception was in Tennessee, where former leaders of the Union Labor party who were not Alliancemen orga-nized the People's party. Even there, by May 1892, Alliance leaders had assumed important positions in the new party.[22]

In several states, leaders of the Farmers' Alliance helped organize Citizens' Alliances in an effort to broaden the political base of insur-gency. In Texas, William R. Lamb and his associates performed that task, and in Georgia, C. H. Ellington, an ally of Tom Watson, was influential in the town-oriented Populist organization. In Alabama, however, the leadership of the Citizens' Alliance came primarily from urban supporters of Reuben F. Kolb.[23]

Most Alliance leaders, Populists as well as Democrats, hoped that the Alliance organization could avoid being swallowed up by the third party, but amid the political revolution of 1892 this proved impossible. The complicated relationship of the Alliance to politics in Leonidas Polk's native state illustrates the kind of institutional problems that the order faced elsewhere in the south. In the spring of 1892, Polk was being widely mentioned as a nominee for president or vice-president on the Populist ticket. In North Carolina, Polk's identification with Populism and the *Progressive Farmer*'s support of the new party led to criticism of the paper by the Alliance executive committee, which was dominated by Democrats. Polk promptly tendered the resignation of his paper as the official organ of the state Alliance. In a letter written soon thereafter, Polk's son-in-law, the business manager of the paper, expressed the dilemma facing the *Progressive Farmer* and the Alliance as a whole: "I must confess I think we had better held on to the Alliance, kept the Progressive Farmer in the middle of the road and started another organ of the Party and kept the Alliance, as far as possible, free as an educational institution. . . . Still I hardly see how that can be done."[24]

Even after the St. Louis conference, relatively few North Carolina Alliancemen favored a complete break with the Democrats. State president Marion Butler, a rising young politician, advocated cooperation with Democrats in state politics and support for the People's party at the national level, a course that Polk supported. Butler called a conference of "one true representative Allianceman or more from each county" to meet in Raleigh just prior to the Democratic state convention. His idea was to gain control of the convention, nominate state candidates friendly to the Alliance, and, some believed, send delegates to the Populists' national convention.[25]

The Alliance caucus could not commit the Democratic convention to the St. Louis platform, nor did Alliancemen attempt to elect delegates to Omaha. The gubernatorial candidate selected by the Democratic convention was Elias Carr, former president of the state Alliance but an opponent of the St. Louis demands. The failure of the Alliance caucus to dominate the state Democratic convention and the exclusion of Alliancemen from some county Democratic meetings contributed to a ground swell of Alliance support for the People's party, particularly in the heavily Democratic eastern part of the state, despite the continued opposition of Butler and other state leaders.[26] Tensions multiplied within the state leadership, with Democrats charging that Alliance lecturers were organizing Populist clubs, and populists accusing Butler of using Alliance funds to support the Democratic campaign. Both charges seem to have been true.[27]

Despite the divisiveness of the third-party issue in the South, the Alliance held its own during the early months of 1892 and in some states even gained strength. This temporary reversal of the order's decline was encouraged both by Populists' use of the Alliance as a recruiting tool and by Democrats' efforts to retain control of the order, thus keeping it from endorsing the third party. As late as the fall of 1892, a local Alliance leader in North Carolina urged Democratic members to "Stay with us until after the January meeting [of the county Alliance] or until we go down in the muddy waters of the St. Louis Platform."[28]

But by summer Alliance membership was declining once again. In every southern state, the order was being pulled in opposite directions. District lecturers became Populist organizers and suballiances were converted to People's party clubs. Many Democratic Alliancemen who objected resigned from the order, but where Democrats prevailed, Populist members complained. Alliancemen of all persuasions simply shifted their attention away from the Alliance to direct partisan activities. By election time, the order was all but defunct.[29]

In May officials of the NFA&IU met with presidents of the southern state Alliances in an effort to prevent just such a disintegration. According to the Democratic press, the conferees narrowly rejected an open endorsement of the People's party. After a tense session, the presidents announced that Alliancemen should support the principles of the order at the ballot box but declared that "this order as such, or any of its branches has no right to take any partisan political or sectarian or religious actions."[30] Such pronouncements, however, could not halt the partisan political actions that were already being undertaken in the name of the Alliance.

On 11 June, Leonidas L. Polk, who had suffered periodically for several years from hemorrhaging of the bladder, died suddenly in Washington.[31] Many Populists in the West as well as in his native region were supporting him for the Populist presidential nomination. His death denied the People's party an attractive candidate and also deprived the Alliance of an effective leader who was widely respected both in the South and in the Midwest.[32] Alliance Vice-President Henry L. Loucks of South Dakota, who became president upon Polk's death, was the first nonsoutherner to hold that office. He was not well known in the South and soon proved unwilling to continue Polk's work for sectional reconciliation within the Alliance.

An event that influenced the southern agrarian movement in another way was the nomination of Grover Cleveland for president by the Democrats on 22 June. The nomination of the "gold bug" Cleveland and the failure of the Democratic national convention to adopt the St. Louis platform started a stampede of southerners into the People's party. The disaffection would have been even greater had the Populists found a more appealing presidential candidate than James B. Weaver, who among other things, was a former Union general.[33]

The reaction of one Virginia Allianceman was typical of many Democrats to whom the nomination of Cleveland was intolerable. Edmund R. Cocke was a scion of a powerful Virginia family and a large landowner but was finding agriculture to be an unprofitable enterprise. Although active in the Alliance, Cocke at first opposed the third-party movement. In July 1892 he wrote to his cousin, Democratic Congressman Henry St. George Tucker, to explain why he had changed his mind. For Cocke "the money question" was the great issue before the nation. He denounced Cleveland for supporting the "monstrous combination of capital" that controlled the volume of money. "A very short duration of existing conditions will reduce all Virginia farmers to serfdom," Cocke prophesied. Leaving the Democratic party required him to separate himself "from many near and dear to me," but there was no choice: "On the 23d June at 2 P.M. I recd the papers giving me the [Democratic] platform and the nomination of Cleveland. In one hour I was en route to the People's Party Convention in Richmond."[34]

The rush of Alliancemen into the People's party pulled along many of their leaders. In North Carolina, Marion Butler joined the insurgents just in time to organize the People's party in his native Sampson County and accept a Populist nomination for state senator. In Mississippi, Frank Burkitt, by then president of the state Alliance, withdrew from the Democratic electoral slate and became a Populist. What another Mississippi Allianceman said about Burkitt's change could be applied to more than one leader: "Mr. Burkitt had gotten to the point where he could hardly do otherwise. The people to whom he has been a political Moses for twenty years had passed him on the road, and he was being [led] by the very men to whom he had been a leader so long."[35]

Among those who were swept into the third-party movement after Cleveland's nomination was Charles Macune. After the mass meeting at St. Louis, Macune had retreated from his support of insurgency. He reminded Alliancemen that the order had not tied itself to the People's party and suggested that the old parties had one last chance to accept the demands of the order, but as results came in from state Democratic conventions in the South, Macune's paper edged closer to an endorsement of Populism. After the nomination of Cleveland, the *National Economist* proclaimed: "The die is cast. The spell is broken. . . . The Economist recognizes the fact that no longer can any man claim devotion to the Demands of the Alliance and consistently affiliate with the Democratic or the Republican parties." From then until October, Macune's paper strongly supported Weaver and the People's party.[36] Other officials of the NFA&IU took an even more active role in the Populist campaign. President Loucks and lecturer John F. Willits spent much of the summer and fall campaigning for the third party, both in the South and in the Midwest.

In July and August, Populist influence was evident at the various state Alliance meetings. In almost every instance, state Alliances adopted the St. Louis–Omaha platform and elected Populists to leadership. Even in South Carolina, where the Tillman organization had largely co-opted the Alliance, third-party men controlled the state meeting of the order.[37] In most states, the Alliance had now become an adjunct of the People's party.

Southern Populism as a whole was most nearly radical when it first emerged from the Alliance. In 1892 it was based on a genuine grass-roots movement of substantial, if as yet undetermined, proportions. It was overwhelmingly committed to the entire St. Louis–Omaha platform, which, although not a revolutionary document, proposed changes far more sweeping than anything accepted by either major party. Most of the original converts to Populism favored a root-and-branch separation from the old parties. Outside of Louisiana and North Carolina, there was little support for fusion with either Democrats or Republicans. Early Populist leaders were for the most part Alliancemen with a longstanding commitment to insurgency. In 1892 many of the nimble politicians who ultimately attached themselves to the People's party were still safe in the bosom of the Democracy.[38] In short, southern Populism at its inception was dominated by the "mid-road" mentality, which, by 1896, would reflect only a minority view.[39]

For a brief moment in 1892, it seemed as if the Alliance-Populist movement might alter the shape of southern politics. Western Populists, in particular, awaited with keen anticipation the outcome of elections in Dixie, for they believed that the NFA&IU still commanded the allegiance of a great host of southern voters, most of whom would turn instinctively to the People's party on election day. In August, however, third-party candidates for state office were overwhelmed in Alabama and Georgia, both strongholds of the movement. In October the Populist gubernatorial candidate in Florida, a leading Alliance-man, was defeated by a margin of almost four to one.[40] In November state and federal candidates were similarly defeated across the South. Only in Alabama did Populist presidential candidate James Baird Weaver receive more than 25 percent of the vote. To be sure, there were scattered victories, and more would come in 1894, but, all in all, southern Populists mobilized slightly less opposition to the Democrats than had Independents and Republicans in the 1880s.[41]

Why did southern Populism not fare better in 1892 and succeed-ing years? The party's presidential nominee, a former Union general, was an easy target for rebel flag-waving Democrats. Economic and social intimidation prevented many voters from breaking ranks, and election fraud negated the votes of others who did. (In Alabama the Populist gubernatorial candidate, Reuben F. Kolb, was apparently counted out.) In addition, six southern states—Arkansas, Florida, Georgia, Mississippi, South Carolina, and Tennessee—had adopted effective, if sometimes informal, means of disfranchising most blacks and many poor whites by 1894. Of the six, only Georgia developed a viable Populist movement, and even Georgia Populists failed miser-ably in 1892.[42] Such techniques as multiple ballot-box laws, periodic registration, and poll-tax requirements had disfranchised much of Pop-ulism's potential constituency before the crusade was even launched.

If the conclusions reached in this study concerning Alliance membership are correct—that the lowest stratum of rural white south-erners were underrepresented in the order—then the beginnings of disfranchisement, significant as they were for Populism as a whole, did not drastically reduce the Alliance's electoral potential. To be sure, some Alliancemen were among the impoverished southerners, black and white, who were denied the right to vote, but developments within the Farmers' Alliance contributed heavily to the initial failure of southern Populism.

The Alliance's campaign of political education did not bring into the third-party fold the great mass of southern farmers who had joined the order between 1888 and 1890. In only five southern states did the total Populist presidential vote in 1892 amount to more than one-half of the Alliance's potential voting strength at its peak, those states being Alabama, Georgia, Louisiana, North Carolina, and Texas.[43] In some states, particularly Mississippi and Tennessee, Alliance leaders who opposed the third-party movement blocked efforts to focus attention on the St. Louis platform or delayed such efforts until campaigns were underway.[44] More importantly, the Alliance had lost much of its grass-roots support before the Populists ever fielded a candidate in the South.

Despite the efforts of third-party Alliancemen, the sharp drop in membership experienced in 1891 was not substantially reversed. While the third-party debate caused considerable tension within the Alliance in 1892, the collapse of the cooperative system and the consequent decay of the order's grass-roots organization had already rendered the Alliance incapable of launching a successful third-party movement.[45]

In August 1892, after the Populist defeats in Alabama and Georgia, Charles Macune sensed that the People's party would be routed throughout the South, and he tried frantically to disassociate the Alliance from Populism. On the eve of the federal elections, the *National Economist* warned, "It is no use now to calculate and discuss whether it was a mistake for the People's party to make a start this year, or not. . . . [T]he Alliance is not responsible for the starting or success of the People's party."[46]

With such statements issuing from Macune's headquarters, third-party men charged that he had sold out to the enemy and was in the employ of the Democratic national committee. The plausibility of such charges increased when, just before the federal election, southern Alliancemen began receiving campaign literature, some of it arriving with copies of the *National Economist*, which was directed to "straying Democratic members of the Farmers Alliance and the laboring classes." The Democratic literature was accompanied by a letter from J. F. Tillman of Tennessee, member of the NFA&IU's executive committee and director of the lecture bureau. The circular bore the letterhead of the executive committee, whose other members were Macune and Alonzo Wardall. According to Tillman, the material was being distributed to local Alliance secretaries in areas where Populism posed a major threat and was designed to reclaim Alliancemen "whose feelings have been DEMOCRATIC from CHILDHOOD UP."[47]

Macune denied any knowledge of Tillman's actions, and Tillman denied having consulted with Macune before publishing the circulars.[48] Yet Macune did retreat from his announced support for the People's party. It is possible, but unlikely, that he helped circulate the campaign literature, either out of loyalty to the Democratic party or for cash. Macune's chief interest was the Alliance, not partisan politics. Through it he had risen from obscurity and personal defeat to a position of national prominence. In the latter stages of the campaign, he observed, correctly, that the Alliance was being destroyed. Faced with a choice between trying to preserve the Alliance in the South and participating in a long-range struggle to build a new party—a struggle that others were leading—Macune opted for the Alliance.

During the campaign, southern Democrats accused Populists of conspiring with northern Republicans to disrupt the Solid South. Officials of the Republican party did try to win support from southern Populists in 1892, although Populist-Republican fusion was effected only in Louisiana.[49] Alliance-Populist leaders were generally unresponsive to Republican overtures in 1892, but there is some evidence that the head of the Knights of Labor, Terence Powderly, helped implement the Republicans' southern strategy. Powderly gave nominal support to the Populist presidential nominee (having earlier opposed Weaver because of the "odor of defeat" that lingered around the former Greenback standard bearer), but he refused to join the Populists in his own state of Pennsylvania. Instead he privately supported local GOP candidates.[50]

Throughout the campaign, Powderly was in contact with leading Republicans, including President Benjamin Harrison, Senator Matthew Quay of Pennsylvania, and officials of the Republican national committee. It appears that, with their encouragement and financial aid, he channeled K. of L. and Republican speakers into the South, particularly Louisiana, to support the Populists' national ticket.[51] Political conspiracies were no doubt afoot in 1892 as Macune's critics charged, but they were not all of Democratic making.

The bitter campaign of 1892, which split communities, churches, and even families in the South, put an end to the Farmers' Alliance as a viable institution. The decline in membership accelerated during the summer and fall. Democrats left in droves, and Populists simply ignored the order during the political season. No accurate membership figures are available for 1892, but Alliance spokesmen across the South admitted to a precipitous decline. Students of the movement in Georgia and Virginia estimate that the Alliance had lost up to 80 percent of its members by the end of 1892.[52] Similarly, the newer Alliance organizations in the Midwest and elsewhere faded as rapidly as they had sprung up. The once-powerful organizations in Kansas and the Dakotas, which had reached their peak in 1890, continued to dwindle, despite efforts to revive them as agencies for "political education."[53]

The 1892 meeting of the Supreme Council, held in Memphis just after the elections, demonstrated the weakened condition of the order and also contributed to its further decline. In his presidential address, Henry L. Loucks reopened sectional wounds by blaming southerners for the failure of the People's party. In fact, Loucks was merely repeating charges leveled by many Western Populists against southern Alliancemen. Believing that the Alliance was strong enough to dominate elections in most southern states, the westerners concluded that their southern compatriots had simply broken faith with them.[54]

A conflict with both political and sectional overtones developed at Memphis when Loucks and Charles Macune contested the presidency of the Alliance. According to Macune's supporters, H. E. Taubeneck and other officials of the People's party lobbied vigorously against Macune, whom they charged with conspiring against the third party. In the climactic session of the convention, both men were nominated for president, but immediately thereafter Macune left the hall to caucus with his supporters. Macune realized that he had lost the battle for the presidency and the war for control of the Alliance. He announced his resignation from all offices in the Alliance and condemned the outside forces that he claimed were manipulating the convention. Twenty-three delegates, all but three of them southerners, supported a resolution denouncing the attacks upon the South and the high-handed opposition to Macune.[55] The Council elected Loucks to a full term as president and named Marion Butler as vice-president. Ben Terrell, still a supporter of Macune, became lecturer once again. News of the divisive Memphis meeting could not have helped the Alliance in the South at a time when it was struggling to rebuild. Alliance papers hastened to deny that there had been a split in the order or that Macune had withdrawn from office.[56]

The attack on Macune continued with a drive to remove the *National Economist* as official organ of the Alliance. At Memphis the Supreme Council authorized an investigation of the paper by the order's executive committee. The committee, along with President Loucks, questioned the *Economist*'s official status and charged that the paper was being subsidized by the Democratic National Committee, a charge in which several southern mid-road Populists concurred.[57]

Macune replied that Loucks and other Populists were persecuting him, and he used the *National Economist* as a platform from which to warn the brethren of their invidious plot against the order. He subsequently backed down and agreed to let a representative of the executive committee screen the paper's editorials. Despite this concession, in February 1893 the committee declared that Macune's paper was no longer the voice of the NFA&IU. Circulation of the *Economist* was already declining, and this action compounded its problems. Sometime during the summer of 1893, the paper went under.[58]

After the *National Economist* folded, Macune returned to Texas. According to one report, he tried to publish a paper at Cameron but failed. In 1900 the Methodist church appointed him as a "supply preacher," and, like his father before him, he served as a lay minister for a number of years. Later he reopened his medical practice, doing volunteer work among the poor with one of his sons, the Reverend Dennis Macune. He subsequently moved to Fort Worth, where he died in 1940 at the age of eighty-nine.[59]

More than any other Alliance leader of national standing, Macune remains an enigma. He left no personal papers, and the brief history of the Alliance that he wrote in 1920, like most of his public utterances, reveals little about Macune himself, except by inference. He rose out of obscurity to take charge of the Alliance movement and returned to obscurity when he lost power in it. Macune was the organization man par excellence. He lacked the charismatic appeal of Polk and he was not an adroit business manager, either as head of the Texas exchange or as editor of the *National Economist*, but his knowledge of how the Alliance organization functioned, his knack for occupying the center ground, and his ability to work with or coerce those to the right and left of him enabled Macune to dominate the order between 1887 and 1891.

The Alliance never recovered its momentum after a drive to rebuild the order in 1893 brought nothing more than limited and temporary success. Only pockets of die-hard Alliancemen kept the order alive until the close of the century and beyond. Leaders of the People's party realized that the Alliance could no longer provide a mass base of support for them. Recognizing the need for ongoing political education, Populist leaders formed the Industrial Legion during the Memphis meeting of the NFA&IU. Patterned after the Grand Army of the Republic and "commanded" by Paul H. VanDervoort of Nebraska, a leader of the G.A.R., the Industrial Legion was designed to generate grass-roots support for the People's party. Spokesmen for the Legion claimed that it would not conflict with the work of other "industrial organizations," including the Alliance, but it was clearly supposed to function as the Alliance had relative to the People's party.[60]

The Legion was never very successful, particularly in the South. It may have been true of VanDervoort, as one northern Populist said, that "The G.A.R. boys will follow him *anywhere*," but his appeal was understandably limited in the former Confederacy. Nevertheless, some Alliance leaders and Populists in the South endorsed the legion, among them Frank Burkitt in Mississippi and Charles H. Pierson of Virginia.[61]

Remnants of the Alliance's cooperative empire survived after 1892. At the Memphis meeting, southern Alliancemen who had worked for years to regulate the marketing of cotton made one last effort in that direction. Members from five southern states organized a Cotton Cooperative Bureau that developed an elaborate plan for reducing cotton acreage and regulating marketing practices. Backers of the plan were unable to engender much public support for it, and they also failed to win the endorsement of the national Alliance. In April 1893 R. J. Sledge, president of the Cooperative Bureau, announced that his organization was giving up the fight. The dream of increasing cotton prices by reducing production would remain unfulfilled until help came from an unwanted source, the boll weevil.[62]

From time to time, suggestions had been made to add life and property insurance programs to the cooperative agencies of the Alliance. In 1891 the Supreme Council, hoping to revive the cooperative features of the Alliance, authorized Alonzo Wardall to extend to the order as a whole the mutual insurance program that he had pioneered in South Dakota. Wardall organized an "Alliance Aid Degree," and during 1892 and 1893, he appointed as agents well-known Alliance leaders in the South and Midwest, but the insurance program did not survive the general decline of the order. By the end of 1893, it, like the rest of the Alliance, had virtually collapsed.[63]

A few of the thousands of local cooperatives survived for several more years. Most of the remaining cooperatives were grain mills, cotton gins, or cotton and tobacco warehouses, which once in operation were less dependent upon capital reserves than were retail stores. Politics and deepening depression took their toll of the few remaining ventures. As a Populist trustee of an exchange in Virginia reported, "The Democratic brothers seem to think if they did not vote with us, they would not deal with us.[64]

One by one, the state exchanges also went under. The Kansas and Dakota exchanges were defunct by 1892; the Georgia exchange folded in 1895, as did its South Carolina counterpart in 1899. Only in North Carolina did a state agency survive into the twentieth century, and then on a very limited scale. In the Tarheel State, Democratic and Populist Alliancemen cooperated to preserve the business agency, and its capital reserve of over $30,000 remained largely intact. The agency survived an attack upon it by the Democratic legislature in 1893 and continued to operate from its office in Raleigh. In 1892 and 1893, its volume of business declined, but not sharply.[65]

In 1893 the agency began marketing eggs as a service to the growing egg and poultry industry in North Carolina, but falling egg prices soon forced the abandonment of the project. Meanwhile the deepening depression caused the overall business of the agency to dwindle. In 1895, in an effort to revive interest in the order, the Alliance invested in tanning and shoe-manufacturing equipment and opened a shoe factory at Hillsboro. The project was a complete failure. Not only did the venture weaken confidence in the struggling business agency, but the order was forced to liquidate about $15,000 worth of bonds to cover the loss.[66] The agency continued to operate on a limited basis into the twentieth century, but it had long since ceased to be the heart of a vital Alliance organization.

The national Alliance continued to hold annual meetings for several years, but after 1892 it was virtually a paper organization. In the spring of 1893, the bankrupt Alliance had to close its Washington office. In February 1894 the NFA&IU met in Topeka and elected Marion Butler of North Carolina as president. The delegates did little more than reaffirm the St. Louis–Omaha platform. Meeting one year later in Raleigh, the Supreme Council endorsed its old platform but also agreed that "no other reform is possible until the destructive policy of contracting our money volume is overthrown and the banks of the country be forced to retire from government business."[67]

At its next meeting, the Alliance dropped the subtreasury plan from its platform, which drew from one determined Alliance in Texas a resolution condemning "all efforts of demagogues and political tricksters to modify or eliminate any part of the Ocala demands." In February 1897 President Mann Page of Virginia presided over what was apparently the last meeting of the NFA&IU. The handful of delegates who gathered in a Washington hotel conducted no business except to reelect their officers and endorse a plan to establish cooperative agencies.[68]

No doubt many of those veteran Alliance leaders who watched the national organization die could agree with the lament of Nelson A. Dunning who in 1892 had written the stirring call to arms quoted above. In 1895 Dunning wrote to Marion Butler, now senator from North Carolina, explaining that his newspaper, the St. Louis *National Watchman*, was bankrupt: "Now Senator, what shall I do? I am 53 years old, have spent 17 years in this fight, 7 years that you know of. I am getting worn out and must begin to look for something for old age. I want to get out of the business of reforming and that as soon as possible."[69]

At the state and local level, the Alliance in the South dwindled and disappeared in the latter half of the nineties. In most cases, local Alliances simply ceased to meet, although in some instances they formally merged with local Populist organizations. As late as 1894, a remnant of the organization survived in Kansas. State Alliances hung on until 1896 in Alabama and Georgia. In Louisiana the Farmers' Union folded in 1897, despite the efforts of its founder J. A. Tetts, to revive it. In South Carolina a remnant of the state Alliance continued to function until 1901.[70]

By the turn of the century, the Alliance had disappeared in Texas, the state of its birth, but some of the earliest members were among the last to leave. A. P. Hungate, S. O. Daws, and Evan Jones all tried their hands at rekindling the old fire. Hungate, lecturer of the first Alliance in Lampasas, urged the brethren to hold firm in the faith: "The purposes for which we labor cannot be finished; they must be to us as a life work, and then be handed down to our children as unfinished business."[71]

In 1902 the Texas Alliance experienced something of a rebirth under a new name. That year Newton Gresham, one of the Alliance organizers who had traversed the South in 1887, founded the Farmers' Union, which he patterned after the defunct Alliance. Emphasizing economic cooperation, the new organization caught fire in the burned-over district of West Texas, and many former Alliancemen joined its ranks.[72]

The Union, like the Alliance before it, soon spread across the South and into the Midwest. The Union gained particular strength on the Oklahoma–Indian Territory frontier. At the same time, large numbers of farmers were being pushed by the boll weevil into Oklahoma from those sections of West Texas where the Alliance had been strongest and most radical. Many of the Oklahoma farmers who joined the Union and who helped form an indigenous base for that state's strong Socialist party were in fact transplanted Texas Alliancemen and Populists. In 1896 A. P. Hungate, who by then was a self-styled Socialist, migrated to Oklahoma. "Stump" Ashby moved to Oklahoma in 1900 and subsequently became president of a local Farmers' Union there. S. O. Daws, the indefatigable organizer, became the first president of the "Indiahoma" State Farmers' Union in 1905 and immediately began full-time work as an organizer.[73]

The Farmers' Alliance made its last stand in North Carolina, at the opposite edge of the South from the land of its birth. There a remnant of the faithful, along with their sons and daughters, continued to hold annual meetings until 1941. By the turn of the century, their organization had no political or economic leverage, but the Business Agency Fund still contained over $20,000. Preservation of the fund and the miniscule business agency provided a reason for the remaining members to keep on meeting. Every year they gathered at State College in Raleigh or at the coastal resort of Morehead City, where they reminisced, heard financial reports, passed innocuous resolutions, and honored the brethren and sisters who had gone to their reward during the preceding year. After the annual meeting in August 1941, the passing of the old guard and the difficulty of wartime travel apparently put an end to the last of the state Alliances.[74]

In 1926 a rural sociologist at North Carolina State College, Carl Cleveland Taylor, joined the Alliance. Taylor had a professional interest in developing effective rural organizations. As a student of the agrarian movement and the son of an Allianceman, he viewed critically and yet with sympathy that handful of old men who gathered each year in the name of the once-powerful Alliance. What he remembered about their meeting in 1928 reveals not only the irony of that tiny band but also something of the importance that the Alliance once held for many thousands of American farmers.

Almost all of the thirty-odd delegates were elderly, the oldest of them over eighty. The president opened the meeting according to the time-honored ritual, but at the point where the ritual called for those present to recite the oath and give the appropriate signs, Taylor found himself in an embarrassing situation: "As the oath was repeated, I, not knowing the signs, spent my time observing the audience and discovered that less than one half the persons there went through with the signs. The chairman overlooked the fact that the meeting was supposed to be opened with prayer, but the chaplain, one of the oldest members present, reminded him of the slip. All during the meeting there were many promptings from the older members, who apparently remembered the ritualistic way in which Alliance meetings had been conducted thirty or forty years ago."[75]

The only substantive business before the Alliance that year was a proposal, supported by Taylor and a few of the younger members, to modernize the organization and establish ties with the newly revived Grange. The issue was debated during three business sessions, consuming eight hours, but the outcome was never in doubt: "We [the proponents of merger] were overwhelmingly outvoted on the basis of arguments presented on both the sacred name 'Alliance' and the ancient traditions which would be sacrificed if any change in the purpose and name of the organization was made."[76] When Taylor joined the order, the Alliance prairie fire that once swept across the South and Midwest had long since turned to ashes, but the movement had so effected the lives of many rural Americans that the last spark would not be snuffed out until all were dead.

CHAPTER 10

The Alliance Movement in Retrospect

Between 1888 and 1892, the National Farmers' Alliance and Industrial Union profoundly influenced political, economic, and social relationships in the American South and Midwest. By 1890 over one million southerners belonged to the Alliance, four times the number who had joined the Grange in the mid-1870s and probably twice as many as belonged to the Farmers' Union after the turn of the century. In Kansas and the Dakotas, two out of every five farmers belonged to the order. Rural people in smaller numbers joined affiliates of the NFA&IU from New York to California. The National Farmers' Alliance and Industrial Union was, until the mushrooming of the American Farm Bureau Federation, the largest and most influential farmers' organization in the history of the United States.

The historian of Georgia Populism was only partially correct in suggesting that the Alliance was "Like Topsy, it 'just grew'!"[1] True enough, the Alliance flourished amid a ground swell of agrarian discontent, but it was also rooted in a complex institutional structure. It drew on the organizational patterns of voluntary associations, secular and sectarian, to which Americans had traditionally looked in time of need, while at the same time employing programs and techniques attuned to new economic and political realities. The order's cooperative experiment was unprecedented in conception and scope. Its lobbying and educational campaign, although hampered by disagreement among the membership, often showed a keen awareness of power relationships in state capitols and in Washington.

The fundamental source of the Alliance's popularity, both in the South and the plains states, was its cooperative program. The promise of direct economic relief attracted farmers to the Alliance by the hundreds of thousands, but for reasons largely beyond the control of the cooperatives' managers and patrons, that promise could not be fulfilled. The tasks that the cooperatives undertook, a reordering of the credit, marketing, and mercantile systems of the American South and

West, were beyond the purview of *any* private group, much less an undercapitalized farmers' organization. The success of cooperatives in the twentieth century has demonstrated that, given the financial and managerial resources that the Alliance lacked, cooperation in marketing and purchasing can do much to alleviate rural poverty.[2]

The promise of economic cooperation does not fully explain the rise of the Alliance, however.[3] The Alliance's program was made meaningful to rural people within the congregation of the suballiances and in other congenial social settings. The sense of community that was engendered there became in itself a powerful stimulus to the growth of the movement.

When the Alliance began shifting its emphasis from business to politics, it became apparent that the movement was far from monolithic. It was in fact a coalition of rural interest groups that had found a common ground under the banner of "Cooperation." This pluralism was most pronounced in the Southeast but was also evident in Texas and in the Midwest, particularly in North Dakota. In the South, the Alliance was superimposed on a going "farmers' movement" that included such diverse elements as the genteel agricultural societies and the radical Agricultural Wheel. From that base, the Alliance mushroomed until the rural white population of the region seemed to be supporting it en masse, with the exceptions of most farm laborers and some tenants, on the one hand, and many large planters, on the other. Actually the Alliance had only papered over the tensions that plagued rural southern society. When southern Alliancemen had to choose between participating in traditional friends-and-neighbors politics and supporting specific, controversial proposals, the order's internal conflicts burst into the open. The struggle to define political goals amid such diversity marked a recurring theme in the career of the Alliance. As the movement's popularity increased, the problem of defining objectives and distinguishing true believers from hangers-on became even more acute.

The Alliance shared the fragility of associations organized for specific purposes. When the Alliance proved unable to make good on the pledge of salvation through cooperation, it began to die. When its efforts as a political pressure group failed, the Alliance proved structurally incapable of transforming itself into a political party. Amid the internecine struggles of 1892, the Alliance could not retain its vitality while providing recruits for the People's party. The agrarian movement shifted to the new party, leaving the Alliance an empty shell.

Although the Alliance appeared to be a disciplined national movement, it was in fact a rather loose confederation of state organizations, which in turn consisted of independent-minded local Alliances.[4] Because the locus of power was in the state and even local Alliances, the national organization never acquired the authority or financial resources to mold the Alliance into a united political force. Only the personal influence of strong leaders like Polk and Macune gave the national organization what little cohesion it did possess. When the Alliance declined, the national structure was the first to become moribund. It should be noted in comparison, however, that there were few truly national organizations in late nineteenth-century America. In the 1880s and 1890s, for example, the two major political parties were similarly fragmented.[5] What is remarkable under the circumstances is that the order developed as much national cohesion as it did.

In some respects, the policies that the Alliance adopted were myopic. The Alliance, a rigidly segregated institution in the South, never fully appreciated the need for cooperation between black and white farmers. Similarly, despite its talk about the unity of all producers, the Alliance appealed largely to farm operators. With some notable exceptions, largely in the Southwest and Midwest, its program did not provide a basis for political cooperation with labor, urban or rural, after the decline of the Knights of Labor in 1887.

Few Alliancemen sensed the importance of overproduction as a possible cause of agricultural distress. Most leaders of the national organization, including Polk and Macune, rejected the idea that overproduction was contributing to agricultural depression. Acreage reduction played only a miniscule role in the order's program of relief. Those limited efforts to curtail the production of cotton failed, not only because of rigid credit and marketing structures, but also because many small farmers suspected that the plan would reduce their output so that the big planters could increase their profits.[6]

Nevertheless, given the diversity of the Alliance movement and the limited options available, the progression of economic and political steps that the Alliance took was, on balance, reasonable. The cooperatives *did* in many instances provide short-term relief. With better financing, they might have altered significantly the conditions about which farmers were distressed. The Alliance's demands for enactment of the subtreasury plan and monetary reform were logical outgrowths of the cooperative movement. To a farmer who had invested capital, energy, and faith in one of the cooperatives, only to see it founder on the rock of credit, Macune's characterization of the subtreasury as the "Solution of the Industrial Problem of the Age" could make a great deal of sense.[7] The experiences that farmers shared within the social

setting of the Alliance—the failure of the cooperatives and the unresponsiveness of the major political parties—had by 1890 and 1892
brought many of them to a point of anger and frustration, which,
when viewed without reference to the development of issues over
time, seems irrational.

The argument that the Alliance destroyed itself by shifting from
economic cooperation to radical political action is not supported by
the evidence, particularly in the South.[8] It is true that, in Kansas and
some other western states, the Alliance was caught up in the third-
party movement before the cooperatives had a chance to prove themselves, but even in Kansas, it is unlikely that the state exchange and
local cooperatives could have enjoyed long-term success in any event.
The Kansas marketing agency folded in 1891 for nonpolitical reasons.
In the south, the cooperative experiment had clearly failed and Alliance membership had plummeted before the People's party appeared.
In the crippling depression of the mid-1890s, the southern exchanges
would have gone under, dragging the Alliance down with them, even
if there had been no Populist movement.

The development of a relatively cohesive structure at the heart of
the agrarian movement before 1892 has been largely overlooked in
recent discussions of Populist ideology,[9] but the ideas that the People's party advanced in the 1890s had been incubated within the
Farmers' Alliance, as well as in the antimonopoly and soft-money
campaigns. The shared experience of almost a million and a half rural
Americans helped give those ideas power in the Populist crusade. Except in Nebraska, every vigorous Populist organization sprang from a
state affiliate of the NFA&IU.

In part the Alliance was able to mobilize rural support in the
southern and plains states because those regions were economically
and socially underdeveloped. It is instructive to view the efforts of the
Alliance in the underdeveloped South and West as an organizing process as well as a struggle against entrenched interests. The Alliance
was most successful in areas where economic institutions—banks,
marketing outlets, and mercantile establishments—were inadequate
or nonexistent. Similarly, the Alliance was often strong where political and social institutions were relatively unstable. Like the Methodist
circuit riders of the early nineteenth century, Alliance lecturers helped
bring order to a disorganized region. The zeal for economic reform
which they imparted can be likened to the spiritual awakening that
followed in the train of the evangelists.[10]

Much of the recent literature on Populism has been influenced by
theories of collective action which originated in the social and behav-

ioral sciences. How well do these theories comport with that part of the agrarian movement encompassed by the Farmers' Alliance? Richard Hofstadter's widely read work, *The Age of Reform*, was influenced by the kind of structural-functionalism advocated by sociologists Talcott Parsons and Seymour Martin Lipset. Recently Sheldon Hackney has suggested that the complex structuralist model developed by Neil J. Smelser might also be applied profitably to the study of Populism.[11] Structuralist theory in general and Smelser's model in particular are of some use in explaining the rise of the agrarian movement. The concepts of structural strain and status anxiety certainly identify one source of rebellion among farmers, and Smelser's application of the economists' value-added theory to collective behavior provides a helpful framework for analyzing the process of rural mobilization.

As a general theory with which to assess the Farmers' Alliance, however, structural-functionalism is unacceptable on at least two counts. First, there is implicit in the structuralist model the assumption that the normal state of society, like that of an organism, is stability and structural compatibility. At least in its application to the Populist movement, the further assumption has been made that protest movements, which challenge the stability of social organism, are inherently dysfunctional, so the enquiry has often focused on what is wrong with the farmers to the exclusion of what might be wrong with the society about which they were protesting.[12] Even though evidence presented in this study shows that factors other than rational economic self-interest made the Alliance attractive to rural Americans, the Farmer's Alliance was, on balance, a reasonable movement of people who had legitimate grievances about the exercise of economic and political power in the United States.

Secondly, functionalism is inadequate for studying the Alliance because it ignores the development over time of the institutions spawned by protest movements.[13] Without question the course of the farmers' movement in the years around 1890 was influenced by the organizational needs of the Alliance and its leaders. Struggles for control of the Alliance not only reflected the interests of contending factions in the agrarian movement but also helped define what those factions would be.

One of the earliest and most vociferous critics of structural-functionalism as applied by Hofstadter was Norman Pollack. First in a free-swinging critique of *The Age of Reform*, then in a book-length study, *The Populist Response to Industrial America*, Pollack attempted to replace Hofstadter's strain theory with an interest theory that approximated Marxism. "In a word," Pollack suggested, "Populism regarded itself as a class movement."[14]

Pollack, like Hofstadter, was not describing the Alliance movement alone, but in his discussion of midwestern Populism, particularly of the Kansas variety, he did deal with the "southern" Alliance. Pollack's description of Populism as a class movement, one that offered a radical critique of industrial America, does not square with the Alliance experience, nor does it help explain what happened to former Alliancemen after the organization folded. The Alliance did make some efforts to join forces with labor, and some of its leaders even appealed to farmers as an oppressed class, but, particularly in the South, the Alliance was woven too deeply into the social fabric, and its rank and file were too consciously farm *owners* for it to become the near-proletarian movement that Pollack describes. To be sure, the Alliance movement drifted steadily to the left, but for every Allianceman who became a mid-road Populist or a socialist, many others dropped out of the agrarian crusade altogether.

Another interest-group theory, less sweeping than the one suggested in Pollack's work, seems more helpful in analyzing the Alliance than the models of either Pollack or Hofstadter. Mancur Olson, Jr., has outlined a theory of group behavior that challenges both the Marxist class theory and the group theories of political scientists Arthur B. Bentley and David Truman.[15] Olson rejects the notion that groups will necessarily act in support of their mutual political interests. "Indeed," Olson contends, "unless the number of individuals in a group is quite small, or unless there is coercion or some other specific device to make individuals act in their common interest, *rational, self-interested individuals* will not act to achieve their common or group interests."[16]

As groups become larger, the incentives diminish for an individual to invest his resources in the struggle to achieve collective benefits. Consequently, most powerful lobbying groups—labor unions, farm groups, and professional organizations—gain the support necessary to influence government policy by performing functions other than lobbying. Their effectiveness in government is in fact a "by-product" of those other functions.[17] Labor unions, for example, have at hand the weapon of the union shop, and farm organizations, by which Olson means primarily the American Farm Bureau Federation, can recruit members through agricultural cooperatives and through their connections with government agencies which dispense technical assistance and farm subsidies.

Stated in this blunt and oversimplified fashion, Olson's model is not flexible enough to account for the varying motivations of individual Alliancemen, but in the aggregate, the Alliance experience seems to support his general scheme. Before the rise of the Alliance, farmers in the South and the plains states had not united to further their political interests, despite a demonstrable common need and despite the recruiting efforts of a plethora of agricultural organizations, but the Alliance, with its concrete, proximate program of relief through cooperation, attracted southern and midwestern farmers in droves. As long as immediate economic assistance through the cooperatives was a real possibility, the movement flourished and its political stock rose, but as soon as the cooperative empire crumbled, the Alliance began to fall, even though the order had developed an elaborate political apparatus. Without the promise of direct, individual benefit through the cooperatives, most Alliance farmers would not, except for a relatively brief time, commit themselves to working for generalized political objectives.

What are we to say, finally, of these earnest, God-fearing Alliancemen? Most of them were neither socialists seeking to usher in the revolution nor reactionary yeomen searching for a lost Arcadia, but rather they were actors in the marketplace with their backs to the wall. Their vision of what ailed American farmers was incomplete, but not irrational. Their cooperative efforts failed because of the enormity of the problems, and their very failure pushed a great many mild-mannered Democrats and Republicans a long way toward a break with their political and cultural heritage.

Appendixes
Notes
Bibliography
Index

Appendix A
PROFILE OF ALLIANCE LEADERSHIP IN THE SOUTH

The following tables represent biographical information concerning ninety-five officers of national and state Alliances. They include four presidents and five secretaries of the national Alliance, and twenty-six presidents, nine business managers, and eight lecturers of state Alliances. The geographical distribution is as follows: Texas, 21; Georgia, 14; North Carolina, 11; Tennessee, 7; South Carolina, 7; Alabama, 7; Louisiana, 6; Missouri, 6; Mississippi, 5; Arkansas, 4; Kentucky, 3; Virginia, 3; Florida, 1.

Certain characteristics of the data limit their usefulness. The leaders, all but one of whom were men, represent those for whom information was available rather than a controlled sample. However, all of the southern presidents of the NFA&IU and most presidents of state Alliances are included. Most of the information came from biographical sketches written or authorized by the leaders themselves and published through Alliance channels. Most identified themselves as farmers, although some had dubious claims to that calling. Some may have suppressed information concerning their business or professional dealings to avoid embarrassing questions about their eligibility for membership in the Alliance.

Because of these limitations on the data and with little comparative information available about similar elites, this profile is not presented in an effort to explain the motivation of Alliance leaders (a risky venture under the best of circumstances) but rather to describe what some of them were like.

TABLE 1 PLACE OF BIRTH

Place of Birth*	South as a Whole (n = 95)	Southwest† (n = 31)
State in which they represented Alliance	47.37%	12.90%
Another state	40.00	70.96
Foreign country	6.31	12.90

*The percentages given are of the whole population (i.e., 95 or 31 people), rather than of those for whom data were available on a specific item. For that reason columns will not necessarily total 100 percent.

†Includes leaders from Texas, Louisiana, and Arkansas.

TABLE 2 MEDIAN AGE IN 1890

South as a Whole (n = 95)	Southwest (n = 31)
47	44

TABLE 3 EDUCATION

Education	South as a Whole (n = 95)	Southwest (n = 31)
Common School	12.63%*	12.90%
Academy or secondary school	8.42	6.45
Professional reading†	5.26	9.67
Attended college or university	5.26	—
Graduated from college or university	17.89	12.90

*Presumably most of those for whom no data were available had only minimal exposure to formal education.

†Denotes those who read law or medicine but had no academic training in those fields.

TABLE 4 CIVIL WAR EXPERIENCE

Civil War Experience	South as a Whole (n = 95)	Southwest (n = 31)
Confederate enlisted*	20.00%	22.58%
Confederate officer	24.21	22.58
Union	2.10	3.22
Under age 18 in 1865	26.31	25.80

*Includes those designated merely as "Confederate."

TABLE 5 OCCUPATION

Occupation*	South as a Whole (n = 95)	Southwest (n = 31)
"Farmer" (undifferentiated)	35.78%	29.03%
Small farmer†	8.42	19.35
Planter‡	23.15	25.80
Businessman	5.26	3.22
Teacher	14.73	12.90
Minister	8.42	9.67
Physician	6.31	6.45
Editor	13.68	3.22
Officeholder/politician§	16.84	—
Laborer/craftsman	2.10	3.22

*Several were engaged in more than one occupation during the Alliance period. These figures do not include earlier occupational experiences.

†Denotes those who were identified as operating small farms or, where the size of their holdings was available, farmed less than 200 acres.

‡Denotes those who were identified as large farmers or planters or, where the size of their holdings was available, owned more than 500 acres.

§Denotes those who, during most of the Alliance period, held or were seeking office.

TABLE 6 AGRICULTURAL SOCIETIES AND FRATERNAL ORDERS

Agricultural Societies and Fraternal Orders	South as a Whole (n = 95)	Southwest (n = 31)
Grange*	14.73	9.67
State agricultural societies	9.47	3.22
Agricultural Wheel	3.15	9.67
Masons or I.O.O.F.	10.52	—

*None appear to have been active in the Grange during the Alliance period.

Appendix B

ALLIANCE MEMBERSHIP
IN PERSPECTIVE

The following graph shows the approximate membership of the Alliance in the seventeen states where it was most successful. Almost 90 percent of all Alliancemen lived in those states. Alliance membership is compared with that of the Grange and with the first major Populist vote in each state. (For the South and California, that figure is the Populist presidential vote in 1892. In Kansas and the Dakotas, it is the gubernatorial vote of 1890.) A fourth line on the graph shows potential Alliance voting strength by removing from the state totals the estimated number of women and young men under twenty-one who belonged to the order. The figures in parentheses represent the approximate percentage of eligible people who joined in each state.

The Alliance membership figures, although clearly inflated in a few instances, reflect fairly accurately the number of people who had joined by June 1890, which was several months before the movement peaked. Probably the only significant distortion in the graph is in the comparison with southern Populist votes. In 1892 a large but undeterminable number of Populists were either prevented from voting or had their ballots thrown out.

Except as otherwise noted, data for the graph are taken from the following sources: Grange membership from Solon J. Buck, *The Granger Movement: A Study of Agricultural Organization and Its Political, Economic and Social Manifestations, 1870–1880* (Cambridge: Harvard University Press, 1913), following p. 58; Alliance membership from *Appleton's Annual Cyclopedia and Register of Important Events of the Year 1890*, n.s., vol. 15 (New York: D. Appleton and Company, 1891), p. 301; Populist vote from Arthur M. Schlesinger, Jr., ed., *History of American Presidential Elections, 1789–1968*, 4 vols. (New York: Chelsea House Publishers and McGraw-Hill Book Company, 1971), 2:1784; total number of eligible people from *Eleventh Census of the United States, Report on Population of the United States*, pt. 2 (Washington: Government Printing Office, 1897), p. 343. The table used to determine the percentage of those eligible who joined lists the total number of white persons ten years of age and over who were engaged in agriculture, fisheries, and mining.

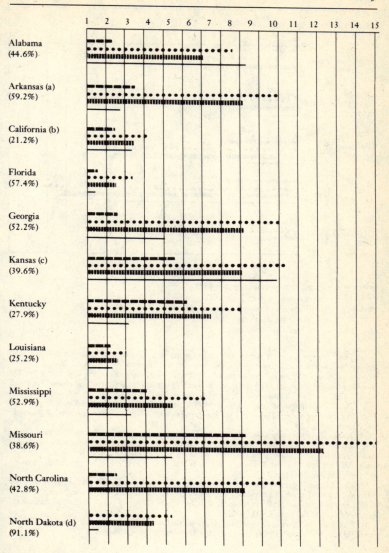

Alabama
(44.6%)

Arkansas (a)
(59.2%)

California (b)
(21.2%)

Florida
(57.4%)

Georgia
(52.2%)

Kansas (c)
(39.6%)

Kentucky
(27.9%)

Louisiana
(25.2%)

Mississippi
(52.9%)

Missouri
(38.6%)

North Carolina
(42.8%)

North Dakota (d)
(91.1%)

(continued on page 166)

(continued from page 165)

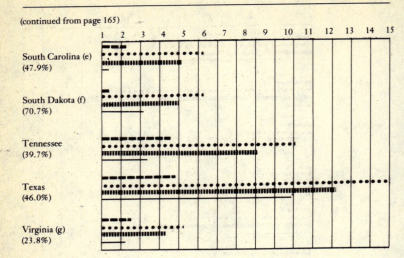

South Carolina (e) (47.9%)

South Dakota (f) (70.7%)

Tennessee (39.7%)

Texas (46.0%)

Virginia (g) (23.8%)

▬▬▬▬ = Grange membership, October 1875
●●●●● = Alliance membership, June 1890
▮▮▮▮▮ = Potential voters among Alliance membership, June 1890
───── = First major Populist vote, 1890 or 1892
One unit = 10,000 members or voters

(a) The Alliance figure for Arkansas includes many members of the Agricultural Wheel who dropped out of the organization after it merged with the Alliance.

(b) The Alliance figure is from Donald E. Walters, "The Period of the Populist Party," in *The Rumble of California Politics, 1884–1970*, ed. Royce D. Dalmatier *et al.* (New York: John Wiley and Sons, 1970), p. 104. This figure is for membership in 1891.

(c) The Kansas Populist vote (1890) is from Peter H. Argersinger, "Road to a Republican Waterloo: The Farmers' Alliance and the Election of 1890 in Kansas," *Kansas Historical Quarterly* 33 (Winter 1967): 468.

(d) Total Grange membership for Dakota Territory is shown in the South Dakota column. The Alliance figure for North Dakota is higher than nonquantitative information about the Alliance there would indicate. The Populist vote (1890) is from Glenn Lowell Brudvig, "The Farmers' Alliance and Populist Movement in North Dakota (1884–1896)" (M.A. thesis, University of North Dakota, 1956), p. 143.

(e) The Alliance figure for South Carolina probably includes many who belonged to both the Alliance and the Farmers' Association and whose primary allegiance was to the latter.

(f) The Populist vote (1890) is from Herbert S. Schell, *History of South Dakota* (Lincoln: University of Nebraska Press, 1961), p. 228.

(g) The Alliance figure is from William DuBose Sheldon, *Populism in the Old Dominion: Virginia Farm Politics, 1885–1900* (Princeton: Princeton University Press, 1935), p. 32.

Notes

INTRODUCTION

1. Galveston *Daily News*, 13 September 1891; Lampasas (Tex.) *People's Journal*, 30 December 1892; [James P. Cole], "The Lampasas Farmers' Alliance," MS in Lampasas County file, Texas State Historical Commission, Austin.

CHAPTER 1

1. Rupert N. Richardson, *Texas, the Lone Star State*, p. 242; Samuel Lee Evans, "Texas Agriculture, 1880–1930" (Ph.D. diss., University of Texas, 1960), map 1.

2. Rupert N. Richardson, *The Frontier of Northwest Texas, 1846 to 1876*, pp. 287–92; Charles L. Sonnichsen, *Ten Texas Feuds*, p. 6. The term "West Texas" was, and is, applied to the west-central region of the state which for many years marked the edge of Anglo settlement.

3. John D. Hicks, *The Populist Revolt*, p. 104; Ralph Smith, "The Farmers' Alliance in Texas, 1875–1900: A Revolt against Bourbon Bourgeois Democracy," *Southwestern Historical Quarterly* 48 (January 1945): 348; Lee Benson, *Merchants, Farmers and Railroads*, p. 277, fn 55.

4. William L. Garvin, *History of he Grand State Farmers' Alliance of Texas*, p. 5; William L. Garvin and S. O. Daws, *History of the National Farmers' Alliance and Co-operative Union of America*, p. 14; Farmers' State Alliance of Texas, *Proceedings . . . 1888*, pp. 26, 27. Baggett's testimony on the date of origin is suspect, since he was not a charter member of the Lampasas group. He was teaching in neighboring Coryell County when the order began and probably joined it in 1878. Garvin and Daws, *National Farmers' Alliance*, p. 125; Lampasas (Tex.) *People's Journal*, 30 December 1892.

5. Galveston *Daily News*, 13 September 1891; Lampasas *People's Journal*, 30 December 1892; Adolphus Philoneous Hungate Memoir-Notebook, sec. 2, pp. 9–13, in possession of James P. Cole, Austin, Texas; FSAT, *Proceedings . . . 1888*, p. 26; Dallas *Southern Mercury*, 31 August 1893. The Lampasas tradition, like the Garvin-Baggett tradition, is suspect. Although several individuals repeated it in substantial detail, it did not appear in print until 1891, six years after publication of the Bagget account.

6. Hungate Memoir-Notebook, sec. 2, p. 5.

7. Lampasas (Tex.) *Dispatch*, 9 August 1877.

8. Ibid., 16 August, 13 September 1877; Hungate Memoir-Notebook, sec. 2, p. 10; Lampasas *People's Journal*, 16 August 1895; Lawrence C. Goodwyn, "The Origin and Development of American Populism" (Ph.D. diss., University of Texas at Austin, 1971), p. 29; *Tenth Census*, Agricultural Schedule, Justice Precinct 1, Lampasas County, Texas, Reel 275 (microfilmed copy at University of North Carolina Library, Chapel Hill).

9. Hungate Memoir-Notebook, sec. 2, pp. 24, 26; *Tenth Census*, Agricultural Schedule, Justice Precinct 5, Lampasas County, Texas, Reel 275. The Patrons of Husbandry (Grange) reached its peak in Texas in 1877 with a membership of forty-five thousand. Although the Grange had local lodges as far west as Lampasas, its strength lay in the fertile blackland prairie of central Texas. The Grange initiated a wide range of cooperative enterprises but, as Hungate suggested, that order was more closely linked to the tradition of agricultural self-help than was the Alliance. Robert A. Calvert, "The Southern Grange: The Farmers' Search for Identity in the Gilded Age" (Ph.D. diss., University of Texas, Austin, 1968).

10. Allen and Hungate later disputed the source of the new name. Hungate claimed that Chavose had heard of a group by that name in New York and suggested it for the Lampasas club. Allen contended that the name was of local origin. Lampasas *People's Journal*, 16 August 1895; Dallas *Southern Mercury*, 12 September 1895; Galveston *Daily News*, 13 September 1891; Nelson A. Dunning, ed., *Farmers' Alliance History and Agricultural Digest*, pp. 16–18.

11. The following generalizations are based on material from manuscript agricultural and population schedules of the tenth census (1880). Records were located for twelve of the thirteen men identified by Allen or Hungate as early members of the Pleasant Valley Alliance.

12. Thomas J. Pressley and William H. Scofield, eds., *Farm Real Estate Values in the United States by Counties, 1850–1959*, p. 60.

13. Unless otherwise noted, biographical material on Allen and Hungate is taken from [James P. Cole], "The Lampasas Farmers' Alliance," MS in Lampasas County file, Texas State Historical Commission, Austin.

14. *Tenth Census*, Agricultural Schedule, Justice Precinct 2, Lampasas County, Texas, Reel 275.

15. Ibid., Justice Precinct 5. Cf., lecture in defense of socialism and a poem by Hungate entitled "The Red Flag" in the Hungate Memoir-Notebook.

16. Lampasas *People's Journal*, 30 December 1892; Hungate Memoir-Notebook, sec. 2, p. 13.

17. Galveston *Daily News*, 5 August 1886.

18. *Dallas Mercury*, 5 August 1886.

19. Alwyn Barr, *Reconstruction to Reform*, p. 44; Lampasas *Dispatch*, 28 February 1878.

20. Galveston *Daily News*, 13 September 1891; Hungate Memoir-Notebook, sec. 2, pp. 12, 21, 26. It should be noted that Hungate, although supposedly basing his account on documents dating from 1877 and 1878, was writing in 1895, after the Alliance had been torn apart through identification with the People's party and was attempting to rebuild itself as an "educational" organization.

21. Hungate Memoir-Notebook, sec. 2, pp. 18–20.

22. Lampasas *People's Journal*, 15 August 1895; D. C. Thomas Diary, cited in Goodwyn, "American Populism," p. 33.

23. Hungate blamed Chavose for the Alliance's "early decline in the land of its nativity" but does not fix the date. Lampasas *People's Journal*, 6 August 1895. William T. Baggett later claimed that the Alliance disbanded in 1879, but the presence of a strong Greenback party in 1880 whose slate included men prominently identified with the Alliance suggests that it may have hung on until 1880. Garvin and Daws, *National Farmers' Alliance*, p. 14.

24. Garvin and Daws, *National Farmers' Alliance*, p. 14; Dunning, ed., *Farmers' Alliance History*, p. 16; Jacksboro (Tex.) *Rural Citizen*, 15 May 1884; W. Scott Morgan, *History of the Wheel and Alliance, and the Impending Revolution*, p. 281.

25. G. A. Holland, *History of Parker County and the Double Log Cabin*, p. 119; Garvin, *Grand State Farmers' Alliance*, p. 6.

26. John S. Spratt, *The Road to Spindletop*, p. 119.

27. Interview with Fred R. Cotten, 2 August 1971, Weatherford, Texas; *Paradise* (Tex.) *Messenger*, 23 July 1880; Fort Worth *Democrat*, 14 June 1881.

28. *Tenth Census*, Population Schedule, Precinct 3, Parker County, Texas, Reel 1323; Garvin and Daws, *National Farmers' Alliance*, pp. 30, 125; Garvin, *Grand State Farmers' Alliance*, pp. 6, 28; FSAT, *Proceedings . . . 1888*, p. 27.

29. Thomas F. Horton, *History of Jack County*, p. 151; Garvin and Daws, *National Farmers' Alliance*, p. 127; *Tenth Census*, Agricultural Schedule, Precinct 4, Parker County, Texas, Reel 274. According to inscriptions on his tombstone in Poolville, Montgomery was also a Mason.

30. Garvin, *Grand State Farmers' Alliance*, p. 29; Jacksboro *Rural Citizen*, 17 March 1881, 6 August 1884; Charles W. Macune, "The Farmers' Alliance," 1920, typescript, University of Texas Archives, Austin, p. 4; *Paradise Messenger*, 22 April 1881.

31. [Fred G. Blood, ed.], *Hand Book and History of the National Farmers' Alliance and Industrial Union*, pp. 35, 36; Richard Maxwell Brown, "The American Vigilante Tradition," in *Violence in America*, ed. by Hugh Davis Graham and Ted Robert Gurr, 1:126; Patrick Bates Nolan, "Vigilantes on the Middle Border: A Study of Self-Appointed Law Enforcement in the

States of the Upper Mississippi from 1840 to 1880" (Ph.D. diss., University of Minnesota, 1971); Elizabeth N. Barr, "The Populist Revolt," in *History of Kansas*, comp. by William E. Connelley, 1:9. Both Blood and Mrs. Barr suggest that members of the Kansas organization had a hand in creating the Texas Alliance. No evidence from Texas sources corroborates their suggestion, however.

32. Jacksboro *Rural Citizen*, 15 May 1884; Dunning, ed., *Farmers' Alliance History*, p. 16; Brown, "Vigilante Tradition," in *Violence in America*, ed. Graham and Gurr, 1:127.

33. Spratt, *Road to Spindletop*, pp. 123–25.

34. Barr, *Reconstruction to Reform*, p. 81.

35. Ida Lasater Huckabay, *Ninety-Four Years in Jack County*, p. 261; Jacksboro *Rural Citizen*, 7 February 1884.

36. Fort Worth *Democrat*, 12 July 1881; Garvin, *Grand State Alliance*, pp. 12, 13; Garvin and Daws, *National Farmers' Alliance*, pp. 24–28. Garvin and Daws, both of whom participated in the meeting, refer to Lanham as "Congressman." In fact he was then "candidate" Lanham. He won a seat in Congress in 1882 only after a tough four-man race with two other Democrats and an independent. Barr, *Reconstruction to Reform*, p. 66.

37. *Paradise Messenger*, 19 August 1881.

38. Arthur M. Schlesinger, "Biography of a Nation of Joiners," *American Historical Review* 50 (October 1944): 11, 19, 20; Noel P. Gist, *Secret Societies*, chap. 7.

39. Garvin, *Grand State Farmers' Alliance*, pp. 29, 31, 40.

40. Jacksboro *Rural Citizen*, 6 October 1881; 17 June 1883.

41. Ibid., 13 July 1883; 3 September 1885; 21 January 1886; Dunning, ed., *Farmers' Alliance History*, p. 37.

42. Garvin and Daws, *National Farmers' Alliance*, p. 132; *Paradise Messenger*, 4 June, 14 December 1880. In 1880 Peterson's ninety-seven acre farm was valued at $2,000 and produced seven bales of cotton. *Tenth Census*, Agricultural Schedule, Precinct 4, Wise County, Texas, Reel 281.

43. Morgan, *Wheel and Alliance*, pp. 364, 365; *Paradise Messenger*, 18 November 1881.

44. *The National Economist Almanac, 1890*, p. 73; Morgan, *Wheel and Alliance*, pp. 364, 365; U.S. Census Office, *Tenth Census*, Agricultural Schedule, Precinct 4, Wise County, Texas, Reel 281; Dallas *Southern Mercury*, 2 January, 10 September 1896. Daws's local paper identified him as a Methodist minister, but according to another account, he was a Baptist. *Alvord* (Tex.) *Messenger*, 25 July 1884; Galveston *Daily News*, 28 September 1894.

45. Garvin, *Grand State Farmers' Alliance*, pp. 36, 39, 46, 47; Fort Worth *Democrat-Advance*, 21 March 1882.

46. Horton, *Jack County*, p. 147; Jacksboro *Rural Citizen*, 4 June 1880, 17 March 1881; Garvin, *Grand State Farmers' Alliance*, pp. 46, 47; *Dallas Mercury*, 13 August 1886.

47. Jacksboro *Rural Citizen*, 31 March, 29 September, 10 February 1881. Cf., *Alvord* (Tex.) *Messenger*, 26 October 1883. These passing references constitute the only evidence found by the author of contact between George and the Texas Alliance before the mid-1880s. See inf., chap. 6.

48. Despite the existence of a "state" Alliance at Lampasas, a strong central organization seems to have emerged only in the second growth of the order.

49. Garvin and Daws, *National Farmers' Alliance*, pp. 128, 129; Garvin, *Grand State Farmers' Alliance*, pp. 35, 36.

50. Jacksboro *Rural Citizen*, 17 March 1881. Solon J. Buck correctly noted that the Declaration of Purposes appended to the Alliance constitution was "but a crude paraphrase of the Grange's Declaration of Purposes." Solon Justus Buck, *The Granger Movement*, p. 303. But the language of the document as a whole, similar in all but detail to the constitutions of other secret societies, and the varied organizational experiences of the men who drew it up suggest a more eclectic origin.

51. Jacksboro *Rural Citizen*, 24 March 1881; Garvin and Daws, *National Farmers' Alliance*, p. 35.

52. Dunning, ed., *Farmers' Alliance History*, pp. 24, 29; Horton, *Jack County*, p. 151; Garvin and Daws, *National Farmers' Alliance*, pp. 127, 134; Jacksboro *Rural Citizen*, 24 February,

23 June, 1881; U.S. Census Office, *Tenth Census*, Agricultural Schedule, Precinct 1, Jack County, Texas, Reel 274.

    53. Garvin and Daws, *National Farmers' Alliance*, p. 134; Jacksboro *Rural Citizen*, 10 February 1881; Huckaby, *Ninety-Four Years in Jack County*, p. 491; Jacksboro *Rural Citizen*, 24 February 1881.

    54. Jacksboro *Rural Citizen*, 9 June 1881.

    55. Garvin and Daws, *National Farmers' Alliance*, pp. 37, 38; Dunning, ed., *Farmers' Alliance History*, p. 37. In 1882 the Greenback party in Wise County nominated a full slate and supported a congressional candidate in opposition to S. W. T. Lanham. No specific evidence has survived on the role of the Alliance in that campaign. *Dallas Herald*, 24 August, 21 September 1882.

CHAPTER 2

    1. William L. Garvin, *History of the Grand State Farmers' Alliance of Texas*, p. 68; Jacksboro (Tex.) *Rural Citizen*, 21 February 1884; *Alvord* (Tex,) *Messenger*, 8 February 1884.

    2. Jacksboro *Rural Citizen*, 21 February 1884.

    3. Ibid., 27 February, 6 March, 20 March 1884.

    4. Louis Tuffley Ellis, "The Revolutionization of the Texas Cotton Trade, 1865–1884," *Southwestern Historical Quarterly* 73 (April 1970): 506; Jacksboro *Rural Citizen*, 6 August 1880; Fort Worth *Democrat-Advance*, 26 March 1882; Weatherford (Tex.) *Weekly Exponent*, 31 January 1880.

    5. John S. Spratt, *The Road to Spindletop*, chap. 6; Charles W. Macune, "The Farmers' Alliance," 1920, typescript, University of Texas Archives, Austin, pp. 5, 6.

    6. Garvin, *Grand State Farmers' Alliance*, pp. 47, 51; Ralph Smith, "The Farmers' Alliance in Texas, 1875–1900: A Revolt against Bourbon and Bourgeois Democracy," *Southwestern Historical Quarterly* 48 (January 1954): 350, 351.

    7. Macune, "Farmers' Alliance," pp. 11–13; Decatur (Tex.) *Wise County Messenger*, 1 August 1884; *Dallas Mercury*, 22 October 1886. The practice worked only temporarily in most instances. Cf., Nelson A. Dunning, ed., *Farmers' Alliance History and Agricultural Digest*, p. 38.

    8. Garvin, *Grand State Farmers' Alliance*, p. 67; Jacksboro *Rural Citizen*, 20 August, 5 November 1885. The Erath model was widely copied by other county Alliances.

    9. Jacksboro *Rural Citizen*, 6 August 1880; Garvin, *Grand State Farmers' Alliance*, p. 16.

    10. *Alvord* (Tex.) *Messenger*, 17, 31 October 1884.

    11. Decatur *Wise County Messenger*, 1 August, 26 September, 17 October 1885. Use of the -yard was not restricted to members of the Alliance.

    12. Garvin, *Grand State Farmers' Alliance*, p. 16; Jacksboro *Rural Citizen*, 3 September 1885; *Dallas Mercury*, 17 September 1886; Decatur *Wise County Messenger*, 29 August 1885.

    13. *Dallas Mercury*, 4 March 1887; Denton (Tex.) *Record-Chronicle*, 21 February 1956.

    14. *Alvord* (Tex.) *Messenger*, 14 March 1884; Dunning, ed., *Farmers' Alliance History*, p. 37. The order's line of advance often retraced the path that had led men to the frontier. Among the targets of the organizing campaign were Montague and Denton counties, from which many Parker County settlers had migrated. Interview with Fred R. Cotten, 2 August 1971, Weatherford, Texas.

    15. *Dallas Mercury*, 21 May 1886.

    16. Decatur *Wise County Messenger*, 8 August 1885; Jacksboro *Rural Citizen*, 17 September 1884; *Dallas Mercury*, 30 April 1886; Dunning, ed., *Farmers' Alliance History*, p. 41; William L. Garvin and S. O. Daws, *History of the National Farmers' Alliance and Co-operative Union of America*, p. 39.

    17. Jacksboro *Rural Citizen*, 24 March 1881; A. J. Rose to T. A. Patillo, 31 August 1886, Patrons of Husbandry Records, University of Texas Archives, Austin; Garvin, *Grand State Farmers' Alliance*, p. 46. Grange dues were ten cents per month plus an initiation fee of $5.00 for men and $3.00 for women. Robert A. Calvert, "The Southern Grange: The Farmers' Search for Identity in the Gilded Age" (Ph.D. diss., University of Texas at Austin, 1968), p. 23.

    18. Jacksboro *Rural Citizen*, 24 March 1881; Garvin and Daws, *National Farmers' Alliance*, p. 36. The Grange had seven degrees. The three highest degrees were open only to masters of local, state, and national Granges and their wives. Calvert, "Southern Grange," pp. 23, 24. Cf.,

D. Sven Nordin, *Rich Harvest: A History of the Grange, 1867–1900* (Jackson: University Press of Mississippi, 1974), chap. 6. For additional information on Alliance ritualism see inf., chap. 5.

19. James L. Ray to R. T. Kennedy, 7 June 1886; A. J. Rose to N. G, Williams, 29 May 1886; Rose to John Trimble, 6 September 1886, all in Patrons of Husbandry Records.

20. Rose to J. J. J. Whitman, 31 July 1899, Patrons of Husbandry Records.

21. Spratt, *Road to Spindletop*, pp. 141–46; Ida Lasater Huckabay, *Ninety-Four Years in Jack County*, pp. 272, 273.

22. Spratt, *Road to Spindletop*, p. 145. The following year the state legislature authorized expenditure of $100,000 for relief, but by then it was too late for many farmers.

23. Huckabay, *Ninety-Fours Years in Jack County*, pp. 273–75; Austin *Firm Foundation*, September, 1886; A. J. Rose to D. L. Deaton, 30 August 1886, Patrons of Husbandry Records; *Dallas Mercury*, 10 September 1886.

24. *Dallas Mercury*, 2 July, 13 August, 10 September 1886; Macum Phelan, *A History of the Expansion of Methodism in Texas, 1867–1902*, p. 269.

25. Jacksboro *Rural Citizen*, 24 January, 10 April, 22 May, 6 June 1884. The successful third party movement in frontier Comanche County in 1886 had overtones of the farmer-cattleman conflict. Billy Bob Lightfoot, "From Frontier to Farmland: Highlights of the History of Comanche County," *West Texas Historical Association Year Book* 32 (October 1956): 37.

26. Alwyn Barr, *Reconstruction to Reform*, pp. 88–92; Robert C. McMath, Jr., "The Godly Populists: Protestantism in the Farmers' Alliance and People's Party of Texas" (M.A. thesis, North Texas State University, 1968), pp. 56–61.

27. Ernest William Winkler, ed., *Platforms of Political Parties in Texas*, pp. 244–46; *Dallas News*, 9 September 1886.

28. Garvin, *Grand State Farmers' Alliance*, p. 78; *Dallas Mercury*, 19 June 1885; 22 January 1886. On the persistence of prohibition as a reform issue in Texas, see Lewis L. Gould, *Progressives and Prohibitionists*.

29. Lawrence C. Goodwyn, "The Origin and Development of American Populism" (Ph.D. diss., University of Texas at Austin, 1971), pp. 58–106. I am indebted to Professor Goodwyn's perceptive account of Alliance-labor politics during 1885–86.

30. Spratt, *Road to Spindletop*, p. 241; Ruth A. Allen, *The Great Southwest Strike*, p. 33.

31. Garvin, *Grand State Farmers' Alliance*, pp. 77, 78; *Dallas Mercury*, 19 February 1886; *Palo Pinto County* (Tex.) *Star*, 29 January 1886.

32. Jacksboro *Rural Citizen*, 25 February 1886; *Dallas Mercury*, 26 February 1886; Weatherford (Tex.) *Times*, 22 March 1886.

33. Jacksboro *Rural Citizen*, 11 March 1886. Lamb earlier sought arrangements with manufacturers which would have enabled Alliancemen to buy implements directly from them, but he was rebuffed.

34. Weatherford *Times*, 22 March 1886; Decatur (Tex.) *Tribune*, cited in Jacksboro *Rural Citizen*, 25 March 1886.

35. The most complete account of the strike is found in Allen, *Great Southwest Strike*.

36. Goodwyn, "American Populism," p. 87; Allen, *Great Southwest Strike*, pp. 86, 87; Clarksville (Tex.) *Standard*, 30 April 1886.

37. Jacksboro *Rural Citizen*, 26 May 1886; Goodwyn, "American Populism," pp. 96–99; Decatur *Wise County Messenger*, 29 August 1885.

38. Decatur *Wise County Messenger*, 10 July 1886; *Palo Pinto County* (Tex.) *Star*, 9 April 1886. Italics added.

39. Billy Bob Lightfoot, "The Human Party: Populism in Comanche County, 1886," *West Texas Historical Association Year Book* 31 (October 1955): 28–33; Comanche (Tex.) *Town and Country*, 5 August, 8 July 1886; Decatur *Wise County Messenger*, 7 August 1886.

40. *Dallas Mercury*, 21 May, 9 July, 12 November 1886. For further examples of Alliance–Knights of Labor rallies, some of them involving Prohibitionists, see *Dallas Mercury*, 9 June 1886; Comanche *Town and Country*, 1 July 1886. In a foretaste of things to come, an Alliance-Knights attempt to control the Democratic party in Red River County was co-opted by conservative Democratic regulars. Clarksville *Standard*, 4, 11, 15 June 1886.

41. For a different view on this point see Theodore Saloutos, *Farmer Movements in the South, 1865–1933*, pp. 72, 73.

42. The demands are printed in full in Dunning, ed., *Farmers' Alliance History*, pp. 41–43; Decatur *Wise County Messenger*, 10, 24 July 1886.

43. For antecedents of many of these demands see Allen Weinstein, *Prelude to Populism*, pp. 354–68; James C. Malin, *A Concern about Humanity*, pp. 24, 25.

44. *Constitution and By-Laws of the Farmers' State Alliance of Texas* (Dallas: Dallas Printing Company, 1886), p. 1; *Dallas Mercury*, 20 October 1886; Dunning, ed., *Farmers' Alliance History*, p. 47. Dunning incorrectly states that the addition was made at a called meeting of the state Alliance in January 1887. The change was proposed at Cleburne by Charles W. Macune, serving as a delegate from Milam County.

45. Goodwyn, "American Populism," p. 126.

46. *Dallas Mercury*, 19 November 1886; Dunning, ed., *Farmers' Alliance History*, p. 45; *Dallas Mercury*, 29 October 1886.

47. The breakaway group had previously announced a convention to be held in Waco on that date. Leaders of the state Grange tried unsuccessfully to use the occasion to bring that faction of the Alliance into the Grange. *Dallas Mercury*, 5 November 1886; A. J. Rose to James L. Ray, 25 October 1886; Rose to James Armour, 25 October 1886, both in Patrons of Husbandry Records.

48. One executive committee member, Evan Jones, balked at the compromise. Jones, who had masterminded a successful independent political campaign in Erath County, denounced the report of the Conference Committee as "inconsistent, unjust, and antagonistic" to the agreements reached at Cleburne. *Dallas Mercury*, 10 December 1886.

49. Macune, "Farmers' Alliance," pp. 15, 16; *Dallas Mercury*, 26 November 1886.

50. *Dallas Mercury*, 24, 31 December 1886. Perhaps smarting from Evan Jones's denunciation of the Waco compromise, Jackson explained that he had signed the conference resolutions to scotch rumors that the Knights had ramrodded passage of the demands.

51. *Dallas Mercury*, 14 January 1887; 17 December 1886; Gillespie County Farmers' Alliance Minute Book, 31 December 1886, University of Texas Archives, Austin.

52. W. Scott Morgan, *History of the Wheel and Alliance, and the Impending Revolution*, pp. 354–56; *Dallas Mercury*, 29 October 1886. For a biographical sketch of this fascinating and crucially important leader see Theodore Saloutos, "Charles W. Macune: Large Scale Cooperative Advocate," in *Great American Cooperators*, by Joseph G. Knapp and associates, pp. 9–12.

53. *Dallas Mercury*, 5 November 1886.

54. See inf., chap. 3.

55. *Dallas Mercury*, 21 January 1887. The following day, when Macune resigned from the executive committee to become president of the national Alliance, John H. Harrison, formerly president of the breakaway Alliance, was restored to a seat on the committee. Waco (Tex.) *Daily Examiner*, 22 January 1887.

56. Dunning, ed., *Farmers' Alliance History*, pp. 53–55; *Dallas Mercury*, 28 January 1887.

57. Waco (Tex.) *Daily Examiner*, 22 January 1887; *Dallas Mercury*, 28 January, 25 February 1887.

58. *Dallas Mercury*, 4 March 1877; Macune, "Farmers' Alliance," pp. 18–26.

59. Ralph Smith, " 'Macuneism,' or the Farmers of Texas in Business," *Journal of Southern History* 13 (May 1947): 230, 231.

60. Clarence N. Ousley, "A Lesson in Cooperation," *Popular Science Monthly* 36 (April 1890): 823, 824.

61. Dallas *Southern Mercury*, 2 October 1888; Farmers' State Alliance of Texas, *Proceedings . . . 1888*, pp. 20–24; Ousley, "Lesson in Cooperation," p. 825.

62. Goodwyn, "American Populism," pp. 167–72; Dallas *Southern Mercury*, 13 November 1888; 3 January 1889; Ousley, "Lesson in Cooperation," pp. 826, 827; Decatur *Wise County Messenger*, 23 June 1888. Following the demise of the exchange, members of the Alliance launched a less ambitious Commercial Agency that acted as a commission agency for cotton sales and sold supplies on a cash basis.

63. FSAT, *Proceedings . . . 1890*, p. 33; Goodwyn, "American Populism," pp. 223, 224.

64. Centennial Farmers' Alliance Minute Book, 2 and 23 March 1889, University of Texas Archives, Austin.

CHAPTER 3

1. *Dallas Mercury*, 24 December 1886; [Fred G. Blood, ed.], *Hand Book and History of the National Farmers' Alliance and Industrial Union*, p. 45; Dallas *Southern Mercury*, 29 April 1887; Nelson A. Dunning, ed., *Farmers' Alliance History and Agricultural Digest*, p. 241. DeSpain, who had been organizing in east Texas, was sent to Louisiana by the state Alliance after T. J. Guice of DeSoto Parish read about the Alliance in an agricultural journal and requested an organizer.

2. Nashville *Weekly Toiler*, 10 April 1889; *Dallas Mercury*, 24 September, 17 December 1886. Alliances may have also been organized in Mississippi during 1886.

3. Tetts was a native of South Carolina who had homesteaded in Louisiana in the 1870s. He had been a Granger and in 1881 helped establish the Lincoln Parish Farmers' Club, from which the Union developed. In 1880 his 160-acre farm was valued at $625. William I. Hair, *Bourbonism and Agrarian Protest*, pp. 142–48.

4. *Dallas Mercury*, 31 December 1886; Charles W. Macune, "The Farmers' Alliance," 1920, typescript, University of Texas Archives, Austin, p. 16; Dunning, ed., *Farmers' Alliance History*, p. 221; Hair, *Bourbonism and Agrarian Protest*, pp. 150, 151.

5. Choudrant (La.) *Farmers' Union*, quoted in *Dallas Mercury*, 4 March 1887.

6. *Dallas Mercury*, 28 January 1887; Waco (Tex.) *Daily Examiner*, 20 January 1887. At the meeting of the national Alliance in December 1887, Tetts was listed as "first vice-president," but neither the minutes of the Waco meeting nor Tetts's report of it indicate that he was so designated at the beginning.

7. *Dallas Mercury*, 21 January, 11 March 1887; Dallas *Southern Mercury*, 22 April 1887.

8. C. Vann Woodward, *Origins of the New South, 1877–1913*, chap. 7; Theodore Saloutos, *Farmer Movements in the South, 1865–1933*, chap. 1; Harold D. Woodman, *King Cotton and His Retainers*, chaps. 24–27. Economic historians are now measuring more precisely the impact of commercialization on southern farmers in the late nineteenth century. Their findings are not yet conclusive enough to rewrite the standard generalizations concerning economic conditions in the South. Cf., William E. Laird and James R. Rinehart, "Deflation, Agriculture, and Southern Development," *Agricultural History* 42 (April 1968): 115–24; Roger L. Ranson and Richard Sutch, "Debt Peonage in the Cotton South after the Civil War," *Journal of Economic History* 32 (September 1972): 641–69; Stephen DeCanio, "Cotton 'Overproduction' in Late Nineteenth-Century Southern Agriculture," *Journal of Economic History* 33 (September 1973): 608–33.

9. Robert M. Saunders, "Progressive Historians and the Late Nineteenth-Century Agrarian Revolt: Virginia as a Historical Test Case," *Virginia Magazine of History and Biography* 79 (October 1971): 485; H. Wayne Morgan, *From Hayes to McKinley*, p. 384.

10. Margaret Pace Farmer, "Furnishing Merchants and Sharecroppers in Pike County, Alabama," *Alabama Review* 23 (April 1970): 147; Ben Robertson, *Red Hills and Cotton*, p. 82. As Thomas D. Clark and others have pointed out, the furnishing merchants were merely the most visible representatives of a complex economic system. Their visibility in a system that was unfair to the farm operator, not their personal dishonesty or greed, made them the symbols of all that was wrong to impoverished farmers. Thomas D. Clark, "The Furnishing and Supply System in Southern Agriculture since 1865," *Journal of Southern History* 12 (February 1946): 24–44.

11. Lewis C. Gray, *History of Agriculture in the Southern United States to 1860*, 1: 924, 925; William Warren Rogers, *The One-Gallused Rebellion*, pp. 102–4; Willard Range, *A Century of Georgia Agriculture, 1850–1950*, pp. 123, 124; Stuart Noblin, *Leonidas LaFayette Polk, Agrarian Crusader*, pp. 176, 177; Hair, *Bourbonism and Agrarian Protest*, pp. 163–5; Saloutos, *Farmer Movements in the South*, pp. 57–60.

12. J. T. Henderson to Leonidas L. Polk, 10 June 1887; "Proceedings of Preliminary Conference on Interstate Convention," 15 April 1887, both in Leonidas LaFayette Polk Papers, Southern Historical Collection, University of North Carolina, Chapel Hill.

13. Inter-State Convention of Farmers, *Proceedings . . . 1887*, pp. 11–13; George Allen to L. L. Polk, 8 July 1887, Polk Papers. One Texas delegate reported: "I have had an audience with a number of gentlemen here who have told me they are running from 100 to 800 or 1,000 people upon their lands. I am supporting nearly 100 upon mine." I-SCF, *Proceedings . . . 1887*, p. 24.

14. I-SCF, *Proceedings . . . 1887*, pp. 92–96.

15. Ibid., p. 32.

16. W. Scott Morgan, *History of the Wheel and Alliance, and the Impending Revolution*, pp. 119–26; Rogers, *One-Gallused Rebellion*, pp. 121–27; Homer Clevenger, "The Farmers' Alliance in Missouri," *Missouri Historical Review* 39 (October 1944): 27; James S. Ferguson, "Agrarianism in Mississippi, 1871–1900: A Study in Nonconformity" (Ph.D. diss., University of North Carolina, 1952), pp. 92–99; F. Clark Elkins, "The Agricultural Wheel: County Politics and Consolidation, 1884–1885," *Arkansas Historical Quarterly* 29 (Summer 1970): 164–66.

17. *Dallas Mercury*, 28 January, 4 March 1887.

18. Ferguson, "Agrarianism in Mississippi," pp. 90–97; Putnam Darden to A. J. Rose, 25 June 1888, Archibald Johnson Rose Papers, University of Texas Archives, Austin.

19. Morgan, *History of the Wheel and Alliance*, pp. 293–95; *Dallas Mercury*, 24 March 1887.

20. J. K. P. Wallace to L. L. Polk, 8 June 1886; A. P. Butler to L. L. Polk, 24 March 1886; Benjamin R. Tillman to Polk, 17 May 1886, all in Polk Papers.

21. Noblin, *Leonidas LaFayette Polk*, pp. 163–82.

22. Melton A. McLaurin, "The Knights of Labor in North Carolina Politics," *North Carolina Historical Review* 49 (July 1972): 298–315.

23. Thaddeus Ivey to L. L. Polk, 1 July 1887, Polk Papers; Raleigh *Progressive Farmer*, 30 June 1887; Laurinburg (N.C.) *Exchange*, cited in Raleigh *Progressive Farmer*, 30 June 1887; Adolph Jenkins Honeycutt, "The Farmers' Alliance in North Carolina" (M.S. thesis, North Carolina State College of Agriculture and Engineering, 1925), p. 4.

24. James Buckner Barry, *A Texas Ranger and Frontiersman*.

25. Raleigh *Progressive Farmer*, 18 August 1887; Dallas *Southern Mercury*, 19 September 1887. According to an Alliance leader who followed Barry in Wake County, the Texan was not overly cautious about whether his "ripe fruit" paid their initiation fees or were even eligible for membership in the Alliance. J. P. Meacham to Elias Carr, 15 December 1889, Elias Carr Papers, Archives Department, East Carolina University, Greenville, N.C. The Carr Papers have only recently been acquired by East Carolina University and are now being edited for publication by Professor Lala C. Steelman. They constitute the richest extant archival source for the Farmers' Alliance in the South.

26. S. B. Alexander to L. L. Polk, 9 June 1886; Elias Carr to Polk, 2 July 1887, both in Polk Papers; Noblin, *Leonidas LaFayette Polk*, p. 205; Raleigh *Progressive Farmer*, 23 March, 12 May, 8 September 1887; Alexander McIver to Elias Carr, 13 November 1888, Carr Papers.

27. North Carolina Farmers' State Alliance Minute Book, 4 October 1887, Farmers' Alliance Papers, North Carolina Archives and History Division, Raleigh. On the elite status of early Alliance leaders in North Carolina, see Phillip R. Muller, "New South Populism: North Carolina" (Ph.D. diss., University of North Carolina, 1971), chap. 1.

28. Polk, who received an annual salary of $1,200, devoted most of his time to the secretaryship. Noblin, *Leonidas LaFayette Polk*, pp. 210, 211.

29. [Blood, ed.], *Hand Book and History*, p. 56; Joseph Church, "The Farmers' Alliance and the Populist Movement in South Carolina (1887–1896)" (M.A. thesis, University of South Carolina, 1953), pp. 19, 20; Raleigh *Progressive Farmer*, 2, 24 July 1888.

30. Rogers, *One-Gallused Rebellion*, pp. 121–24. Professor Rogers characterizes the Wheel as "more militant and class conscious" than the Alliance.

31. Dunning, ed., *Farmers' Alliance History*, p. 237; *Montgomery Advertiser*, 14, 25 July 1887.

32. Dallas *Southern Mercury*, 6 May 1887; Dunning, ed., *Farmers' Alliance History*, p. 237; Rogers, *One-Gallused Rebellion*, p. 134. Adams, who received little more than a grammar school education, served as pastor of a succession of Baptist churches in central Alabama beginning in 1881. He apparently had no political experience before entering the Alliance, but he subsequently served in the legislature and was a county probate judge. Thomas M. Owen, *History of Alabama and Dictionary of Alabama Biography*, 3:13.

33. Rogers, *One-Gallused Rebellion*, pp. 109, 110; John B. Clark, *Populism in Alabama*, pp. 65, 66.

34. Carrollton (Ga.) *Carroll Free Press*, 26 August 1887, 11 May 1888; Clarksville (Tex.) *Standard*, 4, 11, 15 June 1886.

35. *Atlanta Constitution*, 9 March 1888; Carrollton *Carroll Free Press*, 19 August 1887, 27 January 1888. Wilkes's first deputy, J. H. Turner, was a Troup County school teacher and

farmer who had attended the University of Georgia. Like Wilkes, he had lived for several years in Texas. In 1889 he became secretary of the National Farmers' Alliance and Industrial Union. Morgan, *History of the Wheel and Alliance*, pp. 291, 292.

36. The first president of the Carroll County Alliance was a county commissioner, and its first lecturer was a physician and prominent Methodist layman. Carrollton *Carroll Free Press*, 30 September 1887.

37. Ibid., 21 October, 18 November 1887.

38. Macon *Weekly Telegraph*, 18 September 1888.

39. Wilson was born in Grooville, Georgia, in 1860. He moved to Springtown, Texas, at about the time the Alliance was being established less than ten miles away in Parker County. He soon joined the Alliance, and when the order expanded outside the state he accepted an organizer's commission. *The National Economist Almanac, 1890*, p. 71; Macune, "Farmers' Alliance," p. 33.

40. Atlanta *Southern Cultivator* 45 (October 1887): 475.

41. Robert H. Jackson was a Baptist minister from Heard County who had been a county judge and had served in both houses of the Georgia legislature. In 1889 he resigned from the Alliance presidency under fire and was replaced by Leonidas F. Livingston. Carrollton *Carroll Free Press*, 27 January 1888; Atlanta *Southern Cultivator* 46 (December 1888): 567.

42. Atlanta *Southern Cultivator* 46 (March 1888): 125.

43. Savannah *News*, cited in Sandersville (Ga.) *Middle Georgia Progress*, 12 February 1889; *Atlanta Constitution*, 9 December 1888.

44. Range, *Georgia Agriculture*, pp. 141, 142; *Atlanta Constitution*, 17 March 1889; Sandersville *Middle Georgia Progress*, 7 January 1890.

45. *Atlanta Constitution*, 9 October 1888. Cf., Atlanta *Southern Cultivator* 46 (October 1888): 468; Ellaville (Ga.) *Schley County News*, 4 July 1889.

46. Valdosta (Ga.) *Times* (weekly), 28 January 1888; Sandersville *Middle Georgia Progress*, 27 May 1890; Atlanta *Southern Alliance Farmer*, cited in Valdosta *Times* (weekly), 1 February 1890; *Atlanta Constitution*, 23 December 1888.

47. Dunning, ed., *Farmers' Alliance History*, pp. 237–48; National Farmers' Alliance and Co-operative Union, *Proceedings . . . 1887*, p. 1.

48. *Eleventh Census, Report on Population*, 2:343; Morgan, *History of the Wheel and Alliance*, p. 81; Lloyd Walter Corey, "The Florida Farmers' Alliance, 1887–1892" (M.S. thesis, Florida State University, 1963), p. 26.

49. McLaurin, "Knights of Labor," pp. 308–14; Robert C. McMath, Jr., "Southern White Farmers and the Organization of Black Farm Workers: A North Carolina Document," forthcoming in *Labor History*.

50. *Dallas Mercury*, 22 October 1886; Bernice R. Fine, "Agrarian Reform and the Negro Farmer in Texas, 1886–1896" (M.A. thesis, North Texas State University, 1971), pp. 81, 82.

51. Atlanta *Southern Cultivator* 45 (December 1887): 557; Dallas *Southern Mercury*, 26 September 1889; Washington *National Economist* 2 (25 January 1890): 292; Fine, "Agrarian Reform and the Negro Farmer," p. 101.

52. Theodore Saloutos's suggestion that the Colored Alliance "got its start as a result of the liberal charter-issuing policies of the Northern Alliance" (*Farmer Movements in the South*, pp. 69, 70) is not supported by the evidence. See inf., chap. 6.

53. Saloutos, *Farmer Movements in the South*, pp. 79, 80; Richard M. Humphrey, "History of the Colored Farmers' National Alliance and Co-operative Union," in *Farmers' Alliance History*, ed. Dunning, pp. 288, 289; Church, "Farmers' Alliance and the Populist Movement in South Carolina," p. 31; Floyd J. Miller, "Black Protest and White Leadership: A Note on the Colored Farmers' Alliance," *Phylon* 33 (June 1972): 169–74; John D. Hicks, *The Populist Revolt*, pp. 114, 115.

54. Humphrey, "Colored Farmers' National Alliance," pp. 289, 290; Washington *National Economist* 1 (7 September 1889): 329; Nashville *Weekly Toiler*, 19 June 1890. Humphrey's claims appear to be highly inflated. A membership of 1,200,000 would have included three out of every four southern blacks who were engaged in agriculture, mining, and fishing in 1890. *Eleventh Census, Report on Population*, 2:343.

55. William Warren Rogers, "The Negro Alliance in Alabama," *Journal of Negro History* 45 (January 1960): 41; Washington *National Economist* 2 (16 November 1889): 137; Hair, *Bourbonism and Agrarian Protest*, p. 196.

56. Nashville *Weekly Toiler*, 27 June 1888, 27 February 1889; Rogers, *One-Gallused Rebellion*, p. 142; Raleigh *Progressive Farmer*, 26 August 1890; Jack Abramowitz, "The Negro in the Populist Movement," *Journal of Negro History* 38 (July 1953): 259; Moses W. Williams and George W. Watkins, *Who's Who among North Carolina Negro Baptists: With a Brief History of Negro Baptist Organizations* (n.p., 1940), pp. 34, 35; Thomasville (Ga.) *Times*, 25 August 1888; Thomasville *Times-Enterprise*, 2 August 1890, 1 October and 19 November 1892. In the absence of documentary evidence on the black Alliance, accounts of it have necessarily depended on Humphrey's historical sketch and on excerpts from his paper, the Houston *National Alliance*, which appeared in the white press.

57. Raleigh *Progressive Farmer*, 18 December 1888. Five months earlier, under a headline reading "A Nigger in the Woodpile," the *Progressive Farmer* had reported on efforts in eastern North Carolina to establish black Alliances. The editor wished the movement success "if it shall make them more industrious, more frugal, [and] more reliable." (10 July 1888).

58. National Farmers' Alliance and Co-operative Union, *Proceedings . . . 1888*, p. 45; Washington *National Economist* 2 (25 January 1890): 295; Nashville *Weekly Toiler*, 24 October 1888; Rogers, *One-Gallused Rebellion*, pp. 142–44. Cf., inf., chap. 4.

59. Dallas *Southern Mercury*, 26 September 1889.

60. NFA&CU, *Proceedings . . . 1888*, pp. 14, 15, 20. The official membership figure of 411,340 may be close to the actual strength of the order. The figure seems to include about 150,000 members in Texas, well below the 250,000 claimed before the exchange debacle. Elsewhere, the statistics probably reflect accurately the number of people initiated into the order, and attrition had not yet reduced that number substantially. Figures for other leading Alliance states included Georgia, 75,000; North Carolina, 52,000; and Mississippi, 50,000. Cf., inf., app. B.

61. See inf., chap. 4.

62. NFA&CU, *Proceedings . . . 1888*, pp. 10, 11, 30, 31.

CHAPTER 4

1. Joseph Church, "The Farmers' Alliance and the Populist Movement in South Carolina (1887–1896)" (M.A. thesis, University of South Carolina, 1953), pp. 27, 28. On the operation of local cooperatives see Robert C. McMath, Jr., "Agrarian Protest at the Forks of the Creek: Three Subordinate Farmers' Alliances in North Carolina," *North Carolina Historical Review* 51 (Winter 1974): 48–53.

2. Webbie Jackson Lever, "The Agrarian Movement in Noxumbee County" (M.S. thesis, Mississippi State College, 1952), p. 48; James S. Ferguson, "Agrarianism in Mississippi, 1871–1900: A Study in Nonconformity" (Ph.D. diss., University of North Carolina, 1952), p. 144.

3. Ferguson, "Agrarianism in Mississippi," pp. 145–50; Washington *National Economist* 1 (14 March 1889): 5.

4. Washington *National Economist* 1 (14 March 1889): 5, and 2 (14 December 1889): 198; Atlanta *Southern Cultivator* 46 (December 1888): 567, 568; William Jonathan Northen, ed., *Men of Mark in Georgia*, 4: 334-36. The Alabama exchange was structurally similar to the one in Georgia. It made more ambitious plans but was less successful than the Georgia exchange. William Warren Rogers, *One-Gallused Rebellion*, pp. 154–57.

5. Atlanta *Southern Cultivator* 46 (August 1888): 372; *Atlanta Constitution*, 10 March 1889.

6. Washington *National Economist* 1 (20 April 1888): 75, 76; *Atlanta Constitution*, 26 January 1890; Atlanta *Southern Cultivator* 47 (March 1889): 144. President Jackson opposed the leadership of Felix Corput in the exchange, while vice-president Lon Livingston supported him. Their dispute also had political overtones. Jackson, unlike Livingston, supported vigorous legislation to regulate railroads. Nashville *Weekly Toiler*, 10 April 1889; Evan P. Howell to Rebecca L. Felton, 13 August 1889, Rebecca Latimer Felton Papers, University of Georgia, Athens.

7. Athens (Ga.) *Weekly Banner*, 14 January 1890; *Atlanta Constitution*, 20 December 1889.

Macon, Columbus, and Rome had also competed for location of the exchange but had lost out to Atlanta. Not to be outdone by the *Constitution*, the *Atlanta Journal* contributed $1,000 to the capital fund of the exchange through its owner, Hoke Smith. Atlanta *Georgia Alliance Quarterly* 2 (September 1890): 29.

8. *Atlanta Journal*, cited in Athens *Weekly Banner*, 14 January 1890; Atlanta *Southern Alliance Farmer*, 23 September 1890; Washington *National Economist* 2 (14 December 1889): 198. Apparently the exchange restricted its activities to merchandising, with fertilizer sales representing a large percentage of the total. Commercial fertilizer was essential for cotton production in much of the state. In south Georgia and in overworked areas it made barren soil productive, and in the cooler north it shortened the growing season so as to make cotton production possible. Willard Range, *A Century of Georgia Agriculture, 1850–1950*, p. 101.

9. Atlanta *Southern Cultivator* 46 (December 1888): 567, 568; Atlanta *Southern Alliance Farmer*, cited in *Atlanta Constitution*, 19 August 1890; *Atlanta Constitution*, 11 August 1891, 17 August 1893.

10. The functional distinction between exchanges and agencies was not absolute. Most of the exchanges acted in part as commission agencies rather than holding large inventories of goods.

11. North Carolina Farmers' State Alliance Minute Book, 14 August 1888, Farmers' Alliance Papers, North Carolina Division of Archives and History, Raleigh; [W. A. Graham], "North Carolina Farmers' State Alliance Business Agency Fund Circular No. 2," p. 7, John R. Osborne Papers, Manuscript Division, Duke University Library, Durham; W. A. Darden to Elias Carr, 17 December 1888; S. B. Alexander to Carr, 18 January 1889, both in Elias Carr Papers, Archives Department, East Carolina University, Greenville, N.C. President Alexander wrote that "two thirds of my correspondence is in regards to complaints" about the agency.

12. W. A. Darden to Elias Carr, 9 December 1888, 21 January 1889; W. A. Graham to Carr, 18 January 1889, all in Carr Papers.

13. North Carolina Farmers' State Alliance, *Proceedings . . . 1889*, p. 19; NCFSA, *Proceedings . . . 1890*, p. 15. Contributions to the fund ultimately totaled around $35,000.

14. NCFSA, *Proceedings . . . 1890*, pp. 13–17; D. H. Rittenhouse to John R. Osborne, 13 September 1889, Osborne Papers.

15. [Graham], *Business Agency Circular*, p. 7; circular from W. H. Worth to Osborne, 22 January 1890, Osborne Papers; NCFSA, *Proceedings . . . 1890*, p. 14.

16. Clinton (N.C.) *Caucasian* 6 February 1890; NCFSA, *Proceedings . . . 1889*, pp. 13–15. Cf., McMath, "Agrarian Protest," pp. 51, 52, for a discussion of Alliance tobacco marketing.

17. Church, "Farmers' Alliance and the Populist Movement in South Carolina," pp. 29–31.

18. William I. Hair, *Bourbonism and Agrarian Protest*, p. 156; Raleigh *Progressive Farmer*, 23 April 1889.

19. Nashville *Weekly Toiler*, 9 January 1889; James A. Sharp, "The Entrance of the Farmers' Alliance into Tennessee Politics," East Tennessee Historical Society's *Publications* 9 (1937): 78n; Roger Louis Hart, "Bourbonism and Populism in Tennessee, 1875–1896" (Ph.D. diss., Princeton University, 1970), pp. 169–72.

20. Nashville *Weekly Toiler*, 6 March, 11 September 1889; Washington *National Economist* 3 (26 April 1890): 94.

21. Lloyd Walter Cory, "The Florida Farmers' Alliance, 1887–1892" (M.S. thesis, Florida State University, 1963), pp. 20, 36–38, 57; Jacksonville *Florida Dispatch*, 21 February, 9 May 1889.

22. Richard M. Humphrey, "The Colored Farmers' National Alliance," in *Farmers' Alliance History and Agricultural Digest*, ed. Nelson A. Dunning, p. 290.

23. Circular to "The Alliance Men in North Carolina and Virginia," ca. 1890, Carr Papers; Raleigh *Progressive Farmer*, 28 October 1890; Richmond *Virginia Sun*, 1 June 1892. Aside from Humphrey's statement I have found references only to the exchanges in Norfolk, Charleston, and Mobile. The small exchange in Mobile served Colored Alliances in Georgia and Florida as well as in Alabama. George B. Tindall, *South Carolina Negroes, 1877–1900*, p. 119; William Warren Rogers, "The Negro Alliance in Alabama," *Journal of Negro History* 45 (January 1960): 41.

24. Dallas *Southern Mercury*, 23 October 1888; Richmond *Exchange Reporter*, 18 August 1891; Hair, *Bourbonism and Agrarian Protest*, p. 196.

25. National Farmers' Alliance and Co-operative Union, *Proceedings . . . 1888*, p. 45; Washington *National Economist* 2 (25 January 1890): 295; Nashville *Weekly Toiler*, 24 October 1888; Rogers, *One-Galloused Rebellion*, pp. 142–44; William F. Holmes, "The Leflore County Massacre and the Demise of the Colored Farmers' Alliance," *Phylon* 34 (September 1973): 267–74. In addition, in 1890 the white association of state business agents admitted Humphrey and J. J. Rogers to membership. National Farmers' Alliance and Industrial Union, *Proceedings . . . 1890*, p. 43.

26. Farmers' State Alliance of Texas, *Proceedings . . . 1888*, p. 28.

27. The Alliance's cooperative efforts did frighten some mercantile leaders. Late in 1889 *Dunn's Weekly Review* reported: "In some Southern States trade is seriously effected for the time by the operation of Farmers' Alliances, which enlist farmers in co-operative trading and absorb money which might otherwise go to settle indebtedness with merchants." Quoted in Raleigh *Progressive Farmer*, 11 February 1890.

28. FSAT, *Proceedings . . . 1888*, pp. 40, 41; Nashville *Weekly Toiler*, 15 August, 5 September 1888; North Carolina Alliance Minute Book, 14, 15 August 1888, Farmers' Alliance Papers; *Memphis Appeal*, 25 August 1888. Thomas E. Watson's claim to have begun the jute bagging fight in Georgia is not supported by evidence. Beginning in mid-September Watson, who was not a member of the Alliance, spoke out strongly on the issue, but by then bagging was already a major issue in several states. C. Vann Woodward, *Tom Watson, Agrarian Rebel*, pp. 140, 141.

29. Nashville *Weekly Toiler*, 29 August, 3 October 1888; Charles W. Macune, "The Farmers' Alliance," 1920, typescript, University of Texas Archives, Austin, pp. 26–28.

30. *Memphis Appeal*, 30 March 1890; Raleigh *Progressive Farmer*, 9 April 1889; Atlanta *Southern Cultivator* 47 (May 1889): 235, 236.

31. Washington *National Economist* 1 (13 April 1889): 62; (27 April 1889): 89; (1 June 1889): 174, 175.

32. Ibid., 1 (8 June 1889): 184, and 2 (23 November 1889): 149.

33. Ferguson, "Agrarianism in Mississippi," pp. 157–61; Jackson *Clarion-Ledger*, cited in *Memphis Appeal*, 11 April 1889; *Memphis Appeal*, 31 August 1889; W. H. Worth to Elias Carr, 28 February 1890, Carr Papers.

34. NFA&CH, *Proceedings . . . 1888*, pp. 30, 31; Washington *National Economist* 1 (30 March 1889): 36; (7 September 1889): 385; R. J. Sledge, "Secret Instructions from the National Cotton Committee," [September 1889], Osborne Papers; *Memphis Appeal*, 3 September 1889.

35. Raleigh *Progressive Farmer*, 10 September 1889. In some areas cotton did reach ports more slowly than usual in 1889. Cf., *Atlanta Journal*, quoted in Raleigh *Progressive Farmer*, 4 February 1890.

36. *Memphis Appeal*, 10 August, 12 September 1889; Clinton *Caucasian*, 11 July 1889; Atlanta *Southern Cultivator* 48 (February 1890):80; Washington *National Economist* 1 (8 June 1889): 184; (6 July 1889): 245, and 2 (26 October 1889): 88.

37. Range, *Century of Georgia Agriculture*, p. 140. An Alliance leader who attended a regional conference on bagging early in 1890 reported that little cotton bagging had been used in the Gulf states the previous year. S. B. Alexander to Elias Carr, 24 March 1890, Carr Papers.

38. Range, *Century of Georgia Agriculture*, pp. 140, 141; Dallas *Southern Mercury*, 23 May 1889; Raleigh *Progressive Farmer*, 1 September 1891. One reason that the Alliance leaders sought to continue the war on jute in 1890 was that several state exchanges had large inventories of cotton bagging. Nevertheless, by harvest time state exchanges were again handling jute. A. C. Rozin to Elias Carr, 2 August 1890; Albany (Ga.) *News and Advertiser*, quoted in Thomasville (Ga.) *Times-Enterprise*, 5 July 1890.

39. Woodward, *Tom Watson*, p. 141.

40. Clipping from *Atlanta Journal*, William Jonathan Northen Scrapbook, vol. 1, William Jonathan Northen Papers, Georgia State Department of Archives and History, Atlanta; Lewis Nicholas Wynne, "The Alliance Legislature of 1890" (M.A. thesis, University of Georgia, 1970), p. 34; *Atlanta Constitution*, 3 April 1889. The southern press was generally sympathetic to the antijute campaign, although in Alabama and Texas the most influential papers opposed it.

41. Iredell Jones to L. L. Polk, 6 June 1889, Leonidas LaFayette Polk Papers, Southern Historical Collection, University of North Carolina, Chapel Hill.

42. Rogers, *One-Gallused Rebellion*, p. 261; Atlanta *Southern Alliance Farmer*, cited in Valdosta (Ga.) *Times* (weekly), 1 February 1890. Relations between the Alliance and townsmen were not always cordial. In Dothan, Alabama, ill will between the Alliance and city officials, followed by a dispute over a tax and drayage license assessed on the Alliance warehouse, led to the fatal shooting of the warehouse manager and the town marshal. After the acquittal of the manager's alleged killer, a townsman, Alliance members threatened to burn the town to the ground. *Atlanta Constitution*, 15 and 16 October 1889.

43. On Wilson and the national Union Company, see inf., chap. 8. *New York Times*, 3 and 7 December 1890; S. B. Alexander to Elias Carr, 12 March 1891, Carr Papers.

44. A cogent statement on commercialization of agriculture in the plains states which also seems applicable to the South is found in Anne Mayhew, "A Reappraisal of the Causes of Farm Protest in the United States, 1870–1900," *Journal of Economic History* 32 (June 1972): 464–75. Mayhew argues that agrarian protest after 1870 "was a reaction to new, technologically superior inputs which replaced traditional inputs and which could be acquired *only* with money, and a reaction to the need for cash to buy consumer goods which could not be supplied on-the-farm in the Plains area" (p. 469).

45. Iredell Jones to L. L. Polk, 6 June 1889, Polk Papers; W. Scott Morgan, *History of the Wheel and Alliance, and the Impending Revolution*, p. 125.

46. Dunning, ed., *Farmers' Alliance History*, p. 64; NFA&CU, *Proceedings . . . 1887*, pp. 6, 7; Nashville *Weekly Toiler*, 10 October 1888. McCracken, a machinist by trade, had gained the presidency of the Wheel when the Brothers of Freedom, which he had helped to establish, merged with the Wheel in 1886. He may well have feared a personal loss of power, but he was also more closely identified with union labor and with political insurgency than any officer of the national Alliance at the time of the merger.

47. Winn (Ky.) *Labor Journal*, quoted in Nashville *Weekly Toiler*, 21 November 1888; Nashville *Weekly Toiler*, 18, 25 July 1888. In Tennessee the Wheel and Alliance were jointly operating a cooperative exchange located in Memphis.

48. NFA&CU, *Proceedings . . . 1888*, pp. 4, 16–19.

49. Atlanta *Southern Cultivator* 47 (September 1889): 472, 473; Washington *National Economist* 1 (10 August 1889): 327. An accompanying increase in dues to the national organization caused some opposition to the merger.

50. Dallas *Southern Mercury*, 13 June 1889, 20 March, 15 May 1890; [Fred G. Blood, ed.], *Hand Book and History of the National Farmers' Alliance and Industrial Union*, p. 45; Washington *National Economist* 4 (12 February 1891): 364.

51. Washington *National Economist* 2 (28 September 1889): 24, 25.

52. Raleigh *Progressive Farmer*, 23 February 1888; Nashville *Weekly Toiler*, 19 September 1888; Six Mile (Ala.) *Bibb Blade*, 15 March 1888.

53. Ferguson, "Agrarianism in Mississippi," p. 431; *Memphis Appeal*, 11 July 1889; Raleigh *Progressive Farmer*, 27 November 1888; Paul B. Means to Matt Ransom, 28 December 1888, Matt Whitaker Ransom Papers, Southern Historical Collection, University of North Carolina, Chapel Hill.

54. Ferguson, "Agrarianism in Mississippi," p. 435; Atlanta *Southern Cultivator* 47 (August 1889): 408; Hart, "Bourbonism and Populism in Tennessee," p. 211; Nashville *Weekly Toiler*, 10 October 1888.

55. NCFSA, *Proceedings . . . 1889*, pp. 6, 24; Raleigh *Progressive Farmer*, 9 July 1889; Washington *National Economist* 1 (17 August 1889): 344.

56. Rogers, *One-Gallused Rebellion*, p. 166; Nashville *Weekly Toiler*, 4 July 1888; Raleigh *Progressive Farmer*, 30 July 1889. In Arkansas leaders of the Wheel dominated the state's Union Labor party, which waged strong gubernatorial and congressional campaigns. Clifton Paisley, "The Political Wheelers and the Arkansas Election of 1888," *Arkansas Historical Quarterly* 25 (Spring 1966), 3–21.

57. Lawrence C. Goodwyn, "The Origin and Development of American Populism" (Ph.D. diss., University of Texas, Austin, 1971), pp. 178–94. For the role of Texas Alliance leaders in the formation of the national Union Labor party see ibid., pp. 179–80.

58. Dallas *Southern Mercury*, 13 November, 30 October 1888.

59. Murray Edelman, *The Symbolic Uses of Politics*, pp. 4, 51. For the seminal statements on the agrarian movement as reactionary and radical see Richard Hofstadter, *The Age of Reform from Bryan to F.D.R.* (New York: Alfred A. Knopf, 1955), and Norman Pollack, *The Populist Response to Industrial America*. According to Hofstadter, agrarian rhetoric functioned to assuage the status anxiety of rural Americans. But in Pollack's view it became a weapon to unify the working classes for radical political action. To be sure, both views can be supported by selective analysis of Alliance speeches, but the eclectic nature of Alliance rhetoric, coupled with the preponderance of referential symbols, suggests that, as C. Vann Woodward has contended, Alliance rhetoric functioned to support the efforts of a rather specific interest group. Woodward, *Origins of the New South, 1877–1913*, vol. 9 of *A History of the South*, ed. by Wendell Holmes Stephenson and E. Merton Coulter, chap. 7.

60. Following Richard Hofstadter's dichotomy, Alliance spokesmen seemed to be more concerned about conspiracies *in* history than with "saying that history *is*, in effect, a conspiracy." In some instances they acted with good reason. There *was* a jute bagging trust, and there *were* concerted efforts to blunt the political force of the movement. Hofstadter, *Age of Reform*, p. 71.

61. L. L. Polk, manuscript of Ocala presidential address, 2 December 1890, Polk Papers; Raleigh *Progressive Farmer*, 26 June 1888.

62. Leonidas LaFayette Polk, *Agricultural Depression, Its Causes—the Remedy*, p. 26. Cf., Robert C. McMath, Jr., "The Godly Populists: Protestantism in the Farmers' Alliance and People's Party of Texas" (M.A. thesis, North Texas State University, 1968).

63. Ozark (Ala.) *Banner*, 21 September 1893; *Dallas News*, 22 July 1892.

64. Washington *National Economist* 8 (23 July 1892): 295.

65. For an extended treatment of agrarian rhetoric of in the South see Bruce Edward Palmer, "The Rhetoric of Southern Populists: Metaphor and Imagery in the Language of Reform" (Ph.D. diss., Yale University, 1972).

66. Cf., Clifford Geertz, "Ideology as a Cultural System," in *Ideology and Discontent*, ed. David E. Apter, pp. 47–76. Sheldon Hackney has suggested one explanation for the contradiction between the increasingly radical rhetoric of the agrarian movement and its less than revolutionary tactics. Applying the schema of "norm-oriented" and "value-oriented" movements elaborated in Neil Smelser's *Theory of Collective Behavior*, Hackney suggests that as the Alliance's various tactical efforts to alter normative patterns failed the movement attempted to counteract the resulting disillusionment among its members by escalating its rhetoric to the level of demanding fundamental changes in the American value system. Sheldon Hackney, ed., *Populism*, p. xx.

CHAPTER 5

1. Dallas *Southern Mercury*, 20 December 1888; Raleigh *Progressive Farmer*, 31 July 1888.

2. National Farmers' Alliance and Co-operative Union, *Proceedings . . . 1888*, pp. 51, 52; *Dallas Mercury*, 30 July 1886; Charles W. Macune, "The Purposes of the Farmers' Alliance," in *Farmers' Alliance History and Agricultural Digest*, ed. Nelson A. Dunning, pp. 260, 261.

3. Cf., Joyce Oramel Hertzler, *American Social Institutions: A Sociological Analysis*, p. 84.

4. *Constitution of the Farmers' State Alliance of North Carolina* (Raleigh: Edwards and Broughton, 1889), p. 12; J. J. Silvey to L. L. Polk, 19 December 1889, Leonidas LaFayette Polk Papers, Southern Historical Collection, University of North Carolina, Chapel Hill; Raleigh *Progressive Farmer*, 12 January 1888.

5. *Atlanta Constitution*, 7 March 1891.

6. NFA&CU, *Proceedings . . . 1888*, p. 54; Noel P. Gist, *Secret Societies*, pp. 131, 132; Roger Louis Hart, "Bourbonism and Populism in Tennessee, 1875–1896" (Ph.D. diss., Princeton University, 1970), p. 173; Raleigh *Progressive Farmer*, 6 March, 25 September 1888.

7. Pleasant Garden Alliance Minutebook, William D. Hardin Papers, Manuscript Division, Duke University Library, Durham; Atlanta *Southern Cultivator* 47 (March 1889): 142; James S. Ferguson, "Agrarianism in Mississippi, 1871–1900: A Study in Nonconformity" (Ph.D. diss., University of North Carolina, 1952), p. 237.

8. Two disclaimers are in order at this point. First, to say that the Alliance appealed to a

"middle range" of rural people is not to suggest that its membership was predominately "middle class" or economically secure but merely that both upper and lower extremes of the socioeconomic scale were underrepresented in the Alliance. Secondly, in almost no states have county-level Alliance membership records survived, which, if extant, would make possible at least crude ecological correlations with demographic and economic variables.

9. Hart, "Bourbonism and Populism in Tennessee," pp. 164–66; NFA&CU, *Proceedings . . . 1888*, p. 40; Clarence N. Ousley, "A Lesson in Cooperation," *Popular Science Monthly* 36 (April 1890): 822. Cf., Atlanta *Southern Cultivator* 45 (October 1887): 475; Six Mile (Ala.) *Bibb Blade*, 27 June 1889.

10. Raleigh *Progressive Farmer*, 28 August 1888.

11. These conclusions are based on general observation of the Alliance movement in the South.

12. Ferguson, "Agrarianism in Mississippi," pp. 90–97; William Warren Rogers, *The One-Gallused Rebellion*, pp. 132–36; Albert B. Moore, *History of Alabama and Her People*, 1:759; Willard Range, *A Century of Georgia Agriculture, 1850–1950*, pp. 159, 160; Leon Parker Ogilvie, "Populism and Socialism in the Southeast Missouri Lowlands," *Missouri Historical Review* 65 (January 1971), 160, 161. On the "frontier" origins of southern agrarianism, cf., Sheldon Hackney, ed., *Populism*, p. xvii, and Hackney, *Populism to Progressivism in Alabama*, pp. 25–27.

13. For a recent discussion of the frontier character of western Populism see Michael Paul Rogin, *The Intellectuals and McCarthy*, pp. 111–15.

14. According to Alliance statistics, in July 1888, about 12 percent of the members were women, but records of local and county Alliances in Virginia, North Carolina, Georgia, and Texas suggest that the percentage of women increased in later years. Dallas *Southern Mercury*, 12 July 1888; Washington *National Economist* 5 (25 July 1891): 300.

15. Washington *National Economist* 1 (29 June 1889): 235; Bettie Gay, "The Influence of Women in the Alliance," in *Farmers' Alliance History*, ed. Dunning p. 309.

16. Winona (Miss.) *Times*, 18 March 1892, quoted in Ferguson, "Agrarianism in Mississippi," p. 232; Nashville *Weekly Toiler*, 30 April 1890; Bethany Alliance Minute Book, John R. Osborne Papers, Mrary, Durham.

17. Anne F. Scott, "Women, Religion, and Social Change in the South, 1830–1930," in *Religion and the Solid South*, by Samuel S. Hill, Jr., and others, pp. 102–10; Solon J. Buck, *The Granger Movement*, p. 281; Leonard P. Fox, "Origins and Early Development of Populism in Colorado" (Ph.D. diss., University of Pennsylvania, 1916), p. 4; Dallas *Southern Mercury*, 17 September 1891; Raleigh *Progressive Farmer*, 24 September 1889; Nashville *Weekly Toiler*, 26 September 1888; Raleigh *Progressive Farmer*, 12 February 1895; Washington *National Economist* 7 (27 August 1892): 326; Fannie Leak to secretary of Gillespie County, Texas, Alliance, 4 August 1895, inserted in Gillespie Alliance Minute Book, University of Texas Archives, Austin. In 1890 Mrs. Clardy served on the platform committee of the state Prohibition party. Ernest William Winkler, ed., *Platforms of Political Parties in Texas*, p. 285. Two Texas Alliancewomen, Elizabeth A. Dwyer and Dr. Ellen Lawson Dabbs of Fort Worth, spent time as staff writers for the *National Economist*.

18. Washington *National Economist* 3 (12 July 1890): 272, 273; Dallas *Southern Mercury*, 7 June 1888.

19. Dallas *Southern Mercury*, 28 January 1892.

20. Annie L. Diggs, "The Women in the Alliance Movement," *Arena* 6 (June 1892): 170; Ralph Smith, " 'Macuneism,' or the Farmers of Texas in Business," *Journal of Southern History* 13 (May 1947): 241n; Baptist General Convention of Texas, *Proceedings . . . 1886*, p. 14.

21. Gay, "Influence of Women," in *Farmers' Alliance History*, ed. Dunning, pp. 308, 309.

22. There were some exceptions, of course. The Alliance brought into positions of leadership some nonelite members of its rank and file. That was particularly true of rural teachers and lay preachers who had been on the fringes of local elites before achieving prominence in the Alliance. Many of those teachers and preachers were in the vanguard of political insurgency.

23. For biographical data on ninety-five state and national Alliance leaders from the South, see inf., app. A.

24. These two categories of Alliance leadership correspond roughly to Suzanne Keller's distinction between ruling classes and strategic elites, with the former representing a large

group, the membership of which is determined by birth and wealth, which exercises broad authority, and the latter representing a small, concentrated group whose power is limited to specific areas of expertise. However, the distinction between ruling class and strategic elite in the rural South of the late nineteenth century was at best ill-defined. Suzanne Keller, *Beyond the Ruling Class*, pp. 58, 59.

25. Jack P. Maddex, *The Virginia Conservatives, 1867–1879*, chap. 17; William J. Cooper, *The Conservatiove Regime*, pp. 211–15; Alwyn Barr, *Reconstruction to Reform*, pp. 3, 4.

26. Robert C. McMath, Jr., "Mobilizing Agrarian Discontent: The Rise of the Farmers' Alliance in Georgia," presented at convention of the Southern Historical Association, 8 November 1972.

27. Harrison Sterling Price Ashby Biographical Folder, University of Texas Archives, Austin; *Dallas News*, 16 September 1894.

28. North Texas Conference of the Methodist Episcopal Church, South, *Minutes . . . 1887*, p. 13; North Texas Conference of the Methodist Episcopal Church, South, *Minutes . . . 1888*, p. 13.

29. *Dallas News*, 21 August 1891.

30. Ashby Biographical Folder.

31. *National Cyclopedia of American Biography* (New York: James T. White Company, 1893), 4:430; Allen Johnson, ed., *Dictionary of American Biography* (New York: Charles Scribners' Sons, 1929), 3:516; *The National Economist Almanac, 1890*, p. 74.

32. Record Book (unpaginated), August 1886, Elias Carr Papers, Archives Department, East Carolina University, Greenville, N.C.

33. North Carolina Farmers' State Alliance, *Proceedings . . . 1889*, p. 14; NCFSA, *Proceedings . . . 1890*, p. 29.

34. Elias Carr to R. J. Roberson, 29 September 1890, copy in Carr Papers.

35. Elias Carr to L. L. Polk, 28 May 1892, quoted in Stuart Noblin, *Leonidas LaFayette Polk, Agrarian Crusader*, p 280. A week earlier Carr had written to a local Alliance leader: "I am unalterably opposed to this third party movement, yet if it should be formed and their platform coincides more nearly with those of the Alliance demands than either of the present parties then it becomes our duty, and it should be our pleasure to support it." Carr to E. J. Brooks, 22 May 1892, copy in Carr Papers.

36. Noblin, *Leonidas LaFayette Polk*, p. 294.

37. Washington *National Economist* 1 (20 April 1889): 76.

38. Raleigh *Progressive Farmer*, 28 May 1889; Old Hickory Alliance Minute Book, 8 October 1890, Charles Herbert Pierson Papers, University of Virginia, Charlottesville; Bethany Alliance Minute Book, 12 April 1890, Osborne Papers.

39. William L. Garvin, *History of the Grand State Farmers' Alliance of Texas*, p. 42; Jacksboro (Tex.) *Rural Citizen*, 14 January 1886. In its Parker County phase the Texas Alliance used a ceremonial regalia consisting of a white scarf worn around the neck, but the practice had apparently died out before the order expanded beyond Texas.

40. *Ritual of the Farmers' Alliance* (Dallas: Mercury Job Office, n.d.), in Osborne Papers.

41. Dallas *Southern Mercury*, 20 June 1889; Robert Lee Hunt, *A History of Farmer Movements in the Southwest, 1873–1925*, p. 56. When Senator John B. Gordon joined an Alliance near his home in DeKalb County, Georgia, the Athens *Banner* published a vivid, but fictional, description of his initiation, in which the senator was made to change into farmers' clothing to remove the taint of politics and was then whacked with a "subtreasury plank" by the "supreme spanker." Undated clipping from Athens (Ga.) *Banner*, Thomas Edward Watson Papers, vol. 21, Southern Historical Collection, University of North Carolina, Chapel Hill.

42. Robert C. McMath, Jr., "Agrarian Protest at the Forks of the Creek: Three Subordinate Farmers' Alliances in North Carolina," *North Carolina Historical Review* 51 (Winter 1974): 59–63.

43. For a contrary view see Rogers, *One-Gallused Rebellion*, p. 140; and Ferguson, "Agrarianism in Mississippi," p. 242.

44. Washington *National Economist* 6 (26 December 1891): 225, 229, and (16 January 1892): 276.

45. Raleigh *Progressive Farmer*, 6 December 1892.

46. Washington *National Economist* 8 (14 January 1893): 2 and (21 January 1893): 2.

47. Troy (Ala.) *Jeffersonian*, 21 January 1894; Dallas *Southern Mercury*, 26 April 1894.

48. Raleigh *Progressive Farmer*, 21 October 1890. The quarterly business meetings of the county Alliances typically included basket dinners and might be accompanied by dancing and games, as well as political speechmaking. Palo Pinto (Tex.) *Palo Pino County Star*, 21 June 1890; Montgomery *Alliance Herald*, 14 May 1891.

49. A few Alliance encampments were also held in Georgia, North Carolina, and Mississippi. In 1890 Henry C. Demming, Pennsylvania Alliance organizer and former master of the state Grange, organized a massive farmers' encampment at Mount Gretna, Pennsylvania, in which the Alliance played a major role. Atlanta *People's Party Paper*, 25 November 1892; Raleigh *Progressive Farmer*, 1 August 1893; Ferguson, "Agrarianism in Mississippi," p. 236; Washington *National Economist* 3 (2 August 1890): 315.

50. Charles Albert Johnson, *The Frontier Camp Meeting*, pp. 25, 242; Water N. Vernon, *Methodism Moves across North Texas*, pp. 116, 117; *Dallas News*, 22, 23 July 1892; Dallas *Southern Mercury*, 12 September 1889.

51. Dallas *Southern Mercury*, 10 August 1889. After the birth of the People's party, debates between Populists and Democrats often enlivened the speechmaking.

52. *Dallas News*, 31 July 1891.

53. Ibid., 25 July 1892.

CHAPTER 6

1. See sup., chap. 3.

2. Chicago *Western Rural and American Stockman* 22 (26 July 1884): 472; Roy V. Scott, "Milton George and the Farmers' Alliance Movement," *Mississippi Valley Historical Review* 45 (June 1958): 96.

3. Lee Benson, *Merchants, Farmers, and Railroads*, pp. 110, 111, 277, 278.

4. John D. Hicks, *The Populist Revolt*, p. 100.

5. Scott, "Milton George," p. 100; N. B. Ashby, *The Riddle of the Sphinx*, p. 408.

6. Herman C. Nixon, "The Populist Movement in Iowa," *Iowa Journal of History and Politics* 21 (January 1926): 19, 20; J. M. Thompson, "The Farmers' Alliance in Nebraska: Something of Its Origin, Growth and Influence," *Proceedings and Collections of the Nebraska State Historical Society*, 2d ser., 5 (1902): 199; Junction City (Kans.) *Union*, 9 September 1882, Farmers' Alliance Clipping File, p. 84, Kansas State Historical Society Library, Topeka; Minute Book of Haven Farmers' Alliance, Kansas State Historical Society Archives; Scott, "Milton George," p. 101; Chicago *Western Rural and American Stockman*, pass.

7. Chicago *Western Rural and American Stockman* 24 (20 March 1886): 131; Hicks, *Populist Revolt*, p. 134; Glenn Lowell Brudvig, "The Farmers' Alliance and Populist Movement in North Dakota (1884–1896)" (M.A. thesis, University of North Dakota, 1956), pp. 77–80.

8. Scott, "Milton George," p. 104.

9. Chicago *Western Rural and American Stockman* 24 (20 November 1886): 766.

10. Ibid., 25 (10 September 1887): 591; Ashby, *Riddle of the Sphinx*, pp. 410–14; Scott, "Milton George," p. 108.

11. Chicago *Western Rural and American Stockman* 21 (29 September 1883); 329; Theodore Saloutos, *Farmer Movements in the South, 1865–1933*, pp. 69, 70; Scott, "Milton George," p. 108.

12. Chicago *Western Rural and American Stockman* 23 (25 April 1885): 261; 24 (20 November 1886): 766; 24 (11 December 1886): 811.

13. Herman C. Nixon, "The Cleavage within the Farmers' Alliance Movement," *Mississippi Valley Historical Review* 15 (June 1928): 22–27.

14. Raymond C. Miller, "The Populist Party in Kansas" (Ph.D. diss., University of Chicago, 1928), pp. 170–72, 296; Topeka *Weekly Capital*. 20 January 1881 [mislabelled 1880], Farmers' Alliance Clipping File, p. 1; Junction City *Union*, 9 September 1882, Farmers' Alliance Clipping File, p. 84; Topeka *Kansas Farmer*, 30 May, 9 August 1888; 14 February, 27 June 1889.

15. Raymond C. Miller, "The Economic Background of Populism in Kansas," *Mississippi Valley Historical Review* 11 (March 1925): 410–78.

16. National Farmers' Alliance and Co-operative Union, *Proceedings . . . 1888*, p. 35; Dexter (Kans.) *Post*, 23 June 1888; Topeka *Kansas Farmer*, 28 June, 5 July 1888; Peter H. Argersinger,

Populism and Politics, pp. 12, 22, 23. Several historians of Kansas Populism have, with misgivings or even skepticism, cited the account of William Franklin Rightmire, a Populist leader who claimed to have helped establish the southern Alliance in Kansas as a means of promoting political insurgency. Rightmire's claims are demonstrably in error. See Robert C. McMath, Jr., "Preface to Populism: The Origin and Economic Development of the 'Southern' Farmers' Alliance in Kansas," forthcoming in *Kansas Historical Quarterly*.

17. Topeka *Kansas Farmer*, 11 April, 21 August 1889; 2 April 1890; Newton *Kansas Commoner*, 31 May 1889; *Appleton's Annual Cyclopaedia and Register of Important Events of the Year 1890* (New York: Appleton and Company, 1891), p. 301.

18. Topeka *Kansas Farmer*, 30 May, 9 August 1888; 14 February, 27 June 1889; 1 January 1890.

19. Quoted in Peter H. Argersinger, "Pentecostal Politics in Kansas: Religion, the Farmers' Alliance, and the Gospel of Populism," *Kansas Quarterly* 1 (Fall 1969): 27, 28. Professor Argersinger's excellent article was the principal source of information contained in this paragraph. For a more extended but less analytical discussion of the same theme see Leland Levi Lengel, "The Righteous Cause: Some Religious Aspects of Kansas Populism" (Ph.D. diss., University of Oregon 1968).

20. James C. Malin, *A Concern about Humanity*, pp. 55–64.

21. On the Alliance's shift toward political independency, see inf., chap. 7.

22. One of the multitude of short-lived groups which sprang up was the Farmers' and Laborers' Co-operative Union of America, established in 1886 at Mound Valley by one G. Cambell. The group advocated the enactment of such standard antimonopoly and soft money measures as government control of railroads, limitation of land ownership to actual settlers, and a land-loan system similar to that proposed subsequently by William Peffer. Cambell claimed to have helped form a Kansas Alliance in 1872 which later spread to Texas and New York. His unverifiable story appears to be the basis for subsequent claims that Kansas was the birthplace of both the northern and southern Alliances. [G. Cambell], *Manual of the Open Conference of the Farmers' and Laborers' Co-operative Union of America*, in Kansas State Historical Society Library; Topeka *Advocate*, 25 February, 4, 11, 25 March 1891; [Fred G. Blood, ed.], *Hand Book and History of the National Farmers' Alliance and Industrial Union*, p. 35.

23. Among those who wrote in this vein were T. M. Smith, vice-president of the Texas State Alliance, and Andrew J. Carothers, a white Allianceman from Giddings, Texas, who was then organizing one of several Colored Farmers' Alliances. Topeka *Kansas Farmer*, 19, 26 July, 29 August 1888.

24. Dexter (Kans.) *Free Press*, 30 November, 7 December 1888; 15 February, 1, 24 March, 7 June 1889; Cambridge (Kans.) *News*, 22 March 1889. The Grange and local farm groups had established cooperatives before the coming of the Alliance, generally with little success. Malin, *Concern about Humanity*, p. 218.

25. Minute Book of Lone Tree Alliance, 19 June 1890, Kansas State Historical Society Archives; NFA&CU, *Proceedings . . . 1888*, p. 35.

26. W. W. Graves, *History of Neosha County*, pp. 581, 582; Topeka *Kansas Farmer*, 29 January 1890; *Annual Statement of the Farmers' Alliance Insurance Company* [McPherson, Kans.], 1891, filed in Minute Book of Lone Tree Alliance; *Rules of the Barton County Alliance Exchange Company*, in People's party pamphlets, Kansas State Historical Society Library; Newton *Kansas Commoner*, 5 April 1889.

27. Cambridge *News*, 12 April 1889; Meriden (Kans.) *Advocate*, 17 August 1889. The plan of operation which the Kansas Alliance ultimately adopted closely resembled that of the Dakota Farmers' Alliance Company, which opened in January, 1888. Brudvig, "The Farmers' Alliance and Populist Movement in North Dakota," pp. 78–84.

28. Meriden *Advocate*, 31 August 1889; Topeka *Kansas Farmer*, 10 July 1889.

29. Meriden *Advocate*, 17 August 1889, 2 April 1890; Topeka *Kansas Farmer*, 9 October 1889.

30. Meriden *Advocate*, 24 August, 9 October 1889; Topeka *Advocate*, 2 April 1890.

31. Topeka *Advocate*, 6, 20, March, 1 April 1890.

32. Topeka *Kansas Farmer*, 22 October 1890.

33. Topeka *Daily Capital*, 15 October 1890, in Farmers' Alliance Clipping File, pp. 120, 121; Topeka *Advocate*, 18 November 1891; Topeka *Kansas Farmer*, 22 October 1890.

34. Herbert S. Schell, *History of South Dakota*, p 224; Brudvig, "Farmers' Alliance and Populist Movement in North Dakota," p. 40. Brudvig's thesis provides the most complete account of the Alliance in Dakota Territory and subsequently of the movement in North Dakota.

35. Schell, *South Dakota*, p. 224; Brudvig, "Farmers' Alliance and Populist Movement in North Dakota," p. 52.

36. Brudvig, "Farmers' Alliance and Populist Movement in North Dakota," pp. 47, 55–60. Both Muir and Loucks were immigrants, the former a native of Scotland and the latter of Canada.

37. Huron *Dakota Ruralist*, 26 January, 15 June 1889; Brudvig, "Farmers' Alliance and Populist Movement in North Dakota," pp. 79–84. The Dakota Alliance tried, without success, to establish its own twine manufacturing plant. Like southern forays into the manufacturing of cotton bagging, this venture siphoned off capital that was badly needed by the cooperatives.

38. Huron *Dakota Ruralist*, 26 January 1889; Brudvig, "Farmers' Alliance and Populist Movement in North Dakota," p. 84.

39. Huron *Dakota Ruralist*, 26 January 1889; Brudvig, "Farmers' Alliance and Populist Movement in North Dakota," pp. 86–91.

40. Brudvig, "Farmers' Alliance and Populist Movement in North Dakota," pp. 92–100; Elwyn B. Robinson, *History of North Dakota*, pp. 205, 206.

41. Brudvig, "Farmers' Alliance and Populist Movement in North Dakota," pp. 101–19; Schell, *South Dakota*, pp. 225–27; Robinson, *North Dakota*, pp. 206–8. Alliancemen won key leadership positions in both the 1887 and 1889 terms of the legislature. In 1887 George Crose, editor of the state Alliance paper, was elected speaker of the lower house, and in 1889 Smith Stimmel, president of the Cass County Alliance, became president of the upper house.

42. Huron *Dakota Ruralist*, 22 June, 14 September 1889; Brudvig, "Farmers' Alliance and Populist Movement in North Dakota," p. 63.

43. Organizers of the southern Alliance actually began work in New Mexico and Colorado in 1888. Robert W. Larson, *New Mexico Populism*, chaps. 2 and 3; Leonard P. Fox "Origins and Early Development of Populism in Colorado" (Ph.D. diss., Univeristy of Pennsylvania, 1916), pp. 12–33; Gordon B. Ridgeway, "Populism in Washington," *Pacific Northwest Quarterly* 39 (October 1948): 293–96; Roy V. Scott, *The Agrarian Movement in Illinois, 1880–1896*, pp. 127, 128. Beginning in mid-1889 the files of the Washington *National Economist* contain reports on the western organizing campaign.

44. Chicago *Western Rural and American Stockman* 26 (22 December 1888): 813; Huron *Daily Huronite*, 20 June 1889.

45. Hicks, *Populist Revolt*, pp. 113, 114.

46. Details of the abortive merger are given in ibid., pp. 113–27.

47. Ibid., page 119, 120; Lawrence C. Goodwyn, "The Origin and Development of American Populism" (Ph.D. diss., Univeristy of Texas, Austin, 1971), pp. 248–55.

48. Nixon, "Cleavages within the Farmers' Alliance," pp. 22–27.

49. Washington *National Economist* 2 (19 October 1889): 72, 73; (21 December 1889): 210–15; St. Louis *Post-Dispatch*, 4, 5 December 1889; Ashby, *Riddle of the Sphinx*, 415, 416; Ralph Beaumont to Terence V. Powderly, 19 December 1889, Terence Vincent Powderly Papers, Department of Archives and Manuscripts, Catholic University of America, Washington, D.C.

50. Washington *National Economist* 2 (21 December 1889): 217, 218.

51. See Hicks, *Populist Revolt*, pp. 427, 428, for complete list of demands. Washington *National Economist* 2 (14 December 1889): 193.

52. R. F. Gray to Terence Powderly, 10 June 1889; Isaac McCracken to Powderly, 24 June 1889; Powderly to H. L. Loucks, 7 May 1889; all in Powderly Papers; Knights of Labor of America, *Proceedings . . . 1889*, pp. 91–96; Knights of Labor of America, *Proceedings . . . 1888*, p. 1792. Alliance approval of the Knights of Labor was less than unanimous. Cf., Saloutos, *Farmer Movements in the South*, p. 105.

53. See inf., chap. 7.

54. Goodwyn, "American Populism," p. 255.

55. L. L. Polk to Elias Carr, 27 August 1889, Elias Carr Papers, Archives Department, East Carolina University, Greenville, N.C.

56. Raleigh *Progressive Farmer*, 8 September 1887.

CHAPTER 7

1. Washington *National Economist* 2 (28 December 1889): 225.

2. Ibid., 2 (21 December 1889): 216, 217. The commodities eligible for storage were wheat, corn, oats, barley, rye, rice, tobacco, cotton, wool, and sugar. Subtreasuries would be located in counties that produced $500,000 worth of these commodities annually. Cf., John D. Hicks, *The Populist Revolt*, chap. 7, for details of the plan.

3. Midwesterners, even Alliance leaders, were for the most part cool to the idea, except as a political device. As they pointed out, it would not alleviate their long-term credit problems. Nevertheless, plains-states Alliances endorsed it in a show of unity with their southern compatriots.

4. Harry Skinner, "The Hope of the South," *Frank Leslie's Illustrated Newspaper* 69 (30 November 1889): 290; James C. Malin, "The Farmers' Alliance Subtreasury Plan and European Precedents," *Mississippi Valley Historical Review* 31 (September 1944): 255, 256.

5. Malin, "Subtreasury Plan," pp. 256–61.

6. Charles W. Macune, "The Farmers' Alliance," 1920, typescript, University of Texas Archives, Austin, pp. 47–53.

7. The other members of the executive committee were Alonzo Wardall of South Dakota and J. F. Tillman of Tennessee. Macune and Wardall comprised the legislative committee.

8. When the Alliance and the Agricultural Wheel formally merged earlier in 1889, Evan Jones of Texas became president of the new Farmers' and Laborers' Union. Jones, who was not a forceful or effective administrator, was little more than a caretaker in office prior to the formation of the NFA&IU. Macune remained in fact the movement's leader.

9. Washington *National Economist* 5 (15 August 1891): 348, 349.

10. Ibid., 6 (29 September 1891): 40.

11. Ibid., 5 (15 August 1891): 349.

12. W. A. Graham to Elias Carr, 22 January 1890, Elias Carr Papers, Archives Department, East Carolina University, Greenville, N.C.

13. Stuart Noblin, *Leonidas LaFayette Polk, Agrarian Crusader*, pp. 219, 220.

14. Raleigh *Progressive Farmer*, 6 May, 22 July 1890; Macune, "Farmers' Alliance," p. 50; L. L. Polk to Elias Carr, 30 March 1890, Carr Papers.

15. Washington *National Economist* 3 (3 May 1890): 97–103, and (24 May 1890): 145, 152; Leonidas LaFayette Polk, *Agricultural Depression, Its Causes—the Remedy*.

16. L. L. Polk to Elias Carr, 10 March 1890, Carr Papers.

17. Ralph Beaumont to Terence V. Powderly, 19 December 1889, Powderly to Beaumont, 26 December 1889, both in Terence Vincent Powderly Papers, Department of Archives and Manuscripts, Catholic University of America, Washington, D.C.

18. Ralph Beaumont to Terence V. Powderly, 23 December 1889, in Powderly Papers; Gerald N. Grob, *Workers and Utopia*, p. 85.

19. Terence V. Powderly to John H. Hayes, 20 April 1890, John H. Hayes Papers, Department of Archives and Manuscripts, Catholic University of America, Washington, D.C.

20. L. L. Polk to Zebulon B. Vance, 10 April 1890, and notation of reply on reverse, Zebulon Baird Vance Papers, Southern Historical Collection, University of North Carolina, Chapel Hill. Vance courteously declined, telling Polk that such a meeting of Congress was without precedent.

21. L. L. Polk to Elias Carr, 7 June 1890, Carr Papers.

22. Ralph Beaumont to Terence V. Powderly, 4 June 1890; Powderly to Beaumont, 3 June 1890, both in Powderly Papers.

23. James S. Ferguson, "Agrarianism in Mississippi, 1871–1900: A Study in Nonconformity" (Ph.D. diss., University of North Carolina, 1952), pp. 505–9; Farmers' State Alliance of Texas, *Proceedings . . . 1890*, pp. 22–24; Richmond *Southern Planter* 51 (November 1890): 530, 531; Homer Clevenger, "The Farmers' Alliance in Missouri," *Missouri Historical Review* 39

(October 1944): 36–39; North Carolina Farmers' State Alliance, *Proceedings . . . 1890*, p. 28; Farmers' State Alliance of Georgia, *Proceedings . . . 1890*, pp. 26, 27; Lloyd Walter Cory, "The Florida Farmers' Alliance, 1887–1892" (M.S. thesis, Florida State University, 1963), pp. 95, 96.

24. *Atlanta Constitution*, 2 April 1890; M. V. B. Ake to W. H. Felton, 23 August 1890, Rebecca Latimer Felton Papers, Manuscript Division, University of Georgia, Athens.

25. Lewis Nicholas Wynne, "The Alliance Legislature of 1890" (M.A. thesis, University of Georgia, 1970), p. 63; Valdosta (Ga.) *Times*, 12, 19 July 1890; Macon (Ga.) *Weekly Telegraph*, 9 July 1890. On the 1890 legislative elections in Georgia see inf., chap. 8.

26. "The Farmers' Alliance in the Southeast," *Harper's Weekly* 34 (13 December 1890): 970, 971. A summary of Alliance political activities in the southern states during 1890 is found in Theodore Saloutos, *Farmer Movements in the South, 1865–1933*, pp. 106–17. For detailed accounts see appropriate state studies.

27. John H. Reagan to James S. Hogg, 16 November 1890, quoted in Lawrence C. Goodwyn, "The Origin and Development of American Populism" (Ph.D. diss., University of Texas, Austin, 1971), p. 306; John William DuBose to Robert McKee, 13 November 1890, Robert McKee Papers, Alabama State Department of Archives and History, Montgomery.

28. Petition of Mountain Cove Alliance to Henry St. George Tucker, undated; Charles Macune to Tucker, 17, 24 September 1890; John L. Sneed to Tucker, 27 September 1890; Tucker to Sneed, 29 September 1890; all in Tucker Papers, Southern Historical Collection, University of North Carolina, Chapel Hill. After considerable debate the Virginia state Alliance had voted in August not to endorse the subtreasury.

29. Cf., Resolutions of Cumberland County (N.C.) Alliance to Vance, 4 April 1890. Among those expressing their thanks was Alliance patriarch S. O. Daws of Texas. Daws to Vance, ca. April, 1890, both in Vance Papers. A detailed account of Vance's reelection campaign is found in Noblin, *Leonidas LaFayette Polk*, pp. 240–51.

30. J. M. Mewboorne to Elias Carr, 5 August 1890, Carr Papers; J. S. Bell to Zebulon B. Vance, 8 August 1890, Vance Papers.

31. Josephus Daniels to Zebulon B. Vance, 19 July 1890; W. T. Caho to Vance, 14 July 1890; both in Vance Papers.

32. Ed. Chambers Smith to Zebulon B. Vance, 2 September 1890; Charles B. Aycock to Vance, 6 September 1890; Robert Winston to Vance, 17 September 1890; all in Vance Papers.

33. Elias Carr to Zebulon B. Vance, 20 November 1890; copy of Vance to Carr, 6 December 1890; both in Vance Papers.

34. Henry C. Dethloff, "The Alliance and the Lottery: Farmers Try for the Sweepstakes," *Louisiana History* 6 (Spring 1965): 145–55; William I. Hair, *Bourbonism and Agrarian Protest*, pp. 201–3.

35. Dallas *Southern Mercury*, 8 May, 7 August 1890; Goodwyn, "American Populism," pp. 296–99.

36. Daniel Merritt Robison, *Bob Taylor and the Agrarian Revolt in Tennessee*, pp. 147, 148; Roger Louis Hart, "Bourbonism and Populism in Tennessee, 1875–1896" (Ph.D. diss., Princeton University, 1970), p. 239.

37. Joseph Church, "The Farmers' Alliance and the Populist Movement in South Carolina (1887–1896)" (M.A. thesis, University of South Carolina, 1953), pp. 41–47.

38. Ferguson, "Agrarianism in Mississippi," chap. 15.

39. Ibid.; Albert D. Kirwan, *Revolt of the Rednecks*, chap. 7; J. Morgan Kousser, "The Shaping of Southern Politics: Suffrage Restriction and the Establishment of the One-Party South, 1880–1910" (Ph.D. diss., Yale Univeristy, 1971), pp. 218–25.

40. Homer Clevenger, "Agrarian Politics in Missouri, 1880–1896" (Ph.D. diss., University of Missouri, 1940), pp. 100–101, 196–98; Clevenger, "Farmers' Alliance in Missouri," pp. 36–40.

41. Goodwyn, "American Populism," pp. 334, 335. Except in Missouri the antisubtreasury movement did little more than provide grist for the mills of anti-Alliance newspapers.

42. Saloutos, *Farmer Movements in the South*, p. 110.

43. Alex M. Arnett, *The Populist Movement in Georgia*, pp. 102–20; clippings from *Atlanta Constitution*, 9 June 1890, Northen Scrapbook, vol. 1, Northen Papers; Maury Klein, *The Great Richmond Terminal*, pp. 33, 219, 243. Calhoun was a grandson of John C. Calhoun. In additon to

his corporate law practice he had large land holdings in Georgia, South Carolina, and Texas and had interests in oil, railroads, and manufacturing.

44. Noblin, *Leonidas LaFayette Polk*, pp. 256–58; John B. Gordon to W. J. Northen, 25 September 1890, Northen Papers.

45. Washington *National Economist* 1 (6 July 1889): 248; Kenneth E. Hendrickson, "Some Political Aspects of the Populist Movement in South Dakota," *North Dakota History* 34 (Winter 1967): 77–80; Howard Roberts Lamar, *Dakota Territory, 1861–1889*, pp. 267, 268.

46. Late in 1889 Wardall had been soundly defeated in a bid for one of the state's first senate seats. Herbert S. Schell, *History of South Dakota*, p. 227.

47. Hendrickson, "Populist Movement in South Dakota," p. 84; Schell, *History of South Dakota*, pp. 227–29.

48. Glenn Lowell Brudvig, "The Farmers' Alliance and Populist Movement in North Dakota (1884–1896)" (M.A. thesis, University of North Dakota, 1956), pp. 101–43; Elwyn B. Robinson, *History of North Dakota*, p. 221.

49. Peter H. Argersinger, *Populism and Politics*, pp. 9, 12; Meriden (Kans.) *Advocate*, 9 November 1889.

50. W. F. Rightmire, "The Alliance Movement in Kansas—Origin of the People's Party," *Transactions of the Kansas State Historical Society, 1905–1906*, 9, 1–8.

51. Cf., sup., chap. 6; and Robert C. McMath, Jr., "Preface to Populism: The Origin and Economic Development of the 'Southern' Farmers' Alliance in Kansas," forthcoming in *Kansas Historical Quarterly*.

52. Minute Book of Lone Tree Alliance, No. 2005, 4 September 1890, and pass., Kansas State Historical Society Archives, Topeka; Minute Book of the Gove County Farmers' Alliance, No. 2628, 12 July, 23 August 1890. For further evidence of this dual appeal see S. M. Scott, *The Champion Organizer of the Northwest*.

53. Dexter (Kans.) *Free Press*, 18 October 1889; Winfield (Kans.) *Courier*, cited in Elizabeth N. Barr, "The Populist Revolt," in *History of Kansas: State and People*, comp. by William E. Connelley, 2:1143; Meriden *Advocate*, 12 October, 19 November 1889.

54. Topeka *Kansas Farmer*, 30 October 1889; Meriden *Advocate*, 12 October 1889.

55. O. Gene Clanton, *Kansas Populism*, p. 54.

56. Topeka *Kansas Farmer*, 8 January 1890, and pass.; Topeka *Advocate*, 6 March 1890.

57. Topeka *Kansas Farmer*, 2 April 1890; Clanton, *Kansas Populism*, p. 56. Stephen McLallin later claimed that leaders of the state Alliance called the 25 March meeting to ramrod the formation of a new party. Topeka *Advocate*, 22 August 1894. Be that as it may, advocates of insurgency could have made no headway had not a ground swell of third-party sentiment already emerged at the grass roots.

58. Peter H. Argersinger, "Road to a Republican Waterloo: The Farmers' Alliance and the Election of 1890 in Kansas," *Kansas Historical Quarterly* 33 (Winter 1967): 454, 455; Clanton, *Kansas Populism*, p. 58; Scott, *Champion Organizer*.

59. Argersinger, "Republican Waterloo," p. 460; Clanton, *Kansas Populism*, pp. 58–60. There were, of course, non-Alliance and nonrural participants in the new party from the beginning, but initially they were in a distinct minority. For evidence of a similar pattern in Nebraska, the one state in which the "northern" Alliance gave rise to a successful third party, see Stanley B. Parsons, *The Populist Context*, pp. 83–90.

60. Kansas City (Mo.) *Star*, 5 November 1890, quoted in Argersinger, "Republican Waterloo," p. 443.

61. Minute Book of the Lone Tree Alliance, 5 May 1892.

62. Topeka *Kansas Farmer*, 26 November 1890.

63. *Eleventh Census, Report of Statistics of Churches*, 9:159. The comparison is based on estimates of congregations affiliated with the Southern Baptist Convention.

64. *Appleton's Annual Cyclopaedia and Register of Important Events of the Year 1890* (New York: D. Appleton and Company, 1891), p. 301; Gordon B. Ridgeway, "Populism in Washington," *Pacific Northwest Quarterly* 39 (October 1948): 284–311.

65. National Farmers' Alliance and Industrial Union, *Proceedings . . . 1890*, pp. 32, 33.

66. Samuel Proctor, "The National Farmers' Alliance Convention of 1890 and Its 'Ocala' Demands," *Florida Historical Quarterly* 27 (January 1950): 161–67.

67. The council did listen to speeches by "fraternal delegates" of the Colored Farmers' Alliance and Citizens' Alliance, both of which were supporting a third party, but no votes were taken on Alliance participation in a new party.

68. *New York Times*, 5 December 1890.

69. The council adopted the subtreasury plank by a vote of seventy-nine to ten, with delegates from Mississippi, Illinois, Missouri, and Tennessee voting against it. Ibid., pp. 32–34.

70. NFA&IU, *Proceedings . . . 1890*, p. 25.

71. Ibid., pp. 5, 7, 16, 29.

72. Ibid., pp. 17, 27; Clanton, *Kansas Populism*, p. 96.

73. NFA&IU, *Proceedings . . . 1890*, pp. 17, 27; *New York Times*, 3, 7 December 1890. The Associated Press accounts that appeared in the *Times* were written by William S. McAllister of Mississippi, another foe of Macune and the subtreasury.

74. Topeka *Kansas Farmer*, 26 November 1890.

75. NFA&IU, *Proceedings . . . 1890*, pp. 16, 37.

CHAPTER 8

1. Washington *National Economist* 4 (21 January 1891): 310. The Citizens' Alliance, composed of town and city dwellers, had been established in Kansas in 1890 to augment the rural base of the third party.

2. Ibid.; Raleigh *Progressive Farmer*, 31 March 1891.

3. Washington *National Economist* 5 (30 May 1891): 61.

4. Charles Macune to Terence V. Powderly, 27 January 1891, Terence Vincent Powderly Papers, Department of Archives and Manuscripts, Catholic University of America, Washington, D.C.

5. Charles Macune to Terence V. Powderly, 11 August 1891; Powderly to Macune (telegram), 18 August 1891; both in Powderly Papers.

6. Washington *National Economist* 3 (23 August 1890): 367; 4 (24 January 1891): 305; 6 (26 September 1891): 24. Local Alliance papers sometimes found that the ready-print or boiler plate that they bought from national companies such as A. N. Kellogg of Chicago contained articles or editorials critical of the order.

7. Ibid., 4 (24 January 1891): 305; Clinton (N.C.) *Caucasian*, 10 September 1891; Dallas *Southern Mercury*, 30 January 1896; Atlanta *People's Party Paper*, 1 November 1895; Lawrence C. Goodwyn, "The Origin and Development of American Populism" (Ph.D. diss., University of Texas, Austin, 1971), p. 368.

8. S. B. Alexander to Elias Carr, 20 June 1890; L. L. Polk to Carr, 10, 24 March 1891, all in Elias Carr Papers, Archives Department, East Carolina University, Greenville, N.C.; Stuart Noblin, *Leonidas LaFayette Polk, Agrarian Crusader*, p. 256.

9. S. B. Alexander to Elias Carr, 12 March 1891; L. L. Polk to Carr, 3 January 1891; both in Carr Papers.

10. Washington *National Economist* 4 (14 February 1891): 345–47; Raleigh *Progressive Farmer*, 3 March 1891.

11. Raleigh *Progressive Farmer*, 21 April 1891; Tarboro (N.C.) *Farmers' Advocate*, 20 May 1891; Dallas *Southern Mercury*, 25 June 1891. At its Indianapolis meeting in December 1891, the Supreme Council disbanded the Alliance Press Bureau.

12. Washington *National Economist* 4 (14 February 1891): 346, 347; Richard H. Barton, "The Agrarian Revolt in Michigan, 1865–1900" (Ph.D. diss., Michigan State University, 1958), p. 155.

13. St. Louis *Republic*, 6 February 1891, cited in Washington *National Economist* 4 (28 February 1891): 380.

14. C. W. Macune to S. B. Alexander, 9 February 1891, in Carr Papers.

15. Indianapolis *American Nonconformist*, 8 October 1891; Huron *Dakota Ruralist*, 4 July 1891.

16. Herman C. Nixon, "The Populist Movement in Iowa," *Iowa Journal of History and Politics* 21 (January 1926): 48–49.

17. Donald E. Walters, "The Period of the Populist Party," in *The Rumble of California Politics, 1848–1970*, ed. Royce D. Delmatier, et al., pp. 102–4; Michael Paul Rogin and John L. Shover, *Political Change in California*, pp. 15, 16; Washington *National Economist* 4 (11 October 1890): 65; Winfield (Kans.) *American Nonconformist*, 16 April 1891.

18. Washington *National Economist* 5 (18 July 1891): 273; 5 (28 April 1891): 89; 6 (28 November 1891): 164; Huron *Dakota Ruralist*, 15 August 1891; New York *Herald*, quoted in Dallas *Southern Mercury*, 2 July 1891. The *Herald* put the total membership at around 1,270,000.

19. Indianapolis *American Nonconformist*, 5 November 1891; Peter H. Argersinger, "Populism and Politics: William A. Peffer and the People's Party" (Ph.D. diss., University of Wisconsin, 1970), pp. 191–99; William I. Hair, *Bourbonism and Agrarian Protest*, pp. 204, 205.

20. James S. Ferguson, "Agrarianism in Mississippi, 1871–1900: A Study in Nonconformity" (Ph.D. diss., University of North Carolina, 1952), pp. 492–95.

21. Ibid., pp. 499–518; Washington *National Economist* 5 (11 April 1891): 52. The new constitution's voting requirements did not go into effect until 1892, but informal disfranchisement was already taking its toll.

22. Ferguson, "Agrarianism in Mississippi, "pp. 505–10, 520–23.

23. Katheryn T. Abbey, "Florida Versus the Principles of Populism, 1896–1911," *Journal of Southern History* 4 (November 1938): 463; Ferguson, "Agrarianism in Mississippi," pp. 499–523; Noblin, *Leonidas LaFayette Polk*, pp. 250–51.

24. Lewis Nicholas Wynne, "The Alliance Legislature of 1890" (M.A. thesis, University of Georgia, 1970), pp. 98–100; Abbey, "Florida Versus the Principles of Populism," pp. 464–67; Roger Louis Hart, "Bourbonism and Populism in Tennessee, 1875–1896" (Ph.D. diss., Princeton University, 1970). p. 254.

25. Hart, "Bourbonism and Populism in Tennessee," p. 254; Wynne, "Alliance Legislature," pp. 113–19. Wynne concludes that "the Alliance movement was a 'false' agrarian crusade, particularly in Georgia." His evidence supports such a conclusion about those men who were elected to the Georgia legislature with Alliance support in 1890 but not about the movement as a whole.

26. *Atlanta Constitution*, 7 October 1890.

27. Ibid., 2 March 1890, 19 July 1891; Ellaville (Ga.) *Schley County News*, 31 July 1890; Thomasville (Ga.) *Times-Enterprise*, 16 August 1890.

28. Robert C. McMath, Jr., "Mobilizing Agrarian Discontent: The Rise of the Farmers' Alliance in Georgia," presented at convention of the Southern Historical Association, 8 November 1972.

29. Thomas M. Owen, *History of Alabama and Dictionary of Alabama Biography*, 4:1431; Robert Barnwell Rhett, Jr., to Joseph Wheeler, 10 May 1891, Joseph Wheeler Papers, Alabama State Department of Archives and History, Montgomery.

30. John B. Clark, *Populism in Alabama*, p. 119; clipping from *Atlanta Constitution*, 7 March 1891, in William Jonathan Northen Scrapbook, vol. I, William Jonathan Northen Papers, Georgia State Department of Archives and History, Atlanta.

31. Dallas *Southern Mercury*, 3 December 1891; Charles W. Macune, "The Farmers' Alliance," 1920, typescript, University of Texas Archives, Austin, p. 40; Hart, "Bourbonism and Populism in Tennessee," pp. 287, 288; Ferguson, "Agrarianism in Mississippi," p. 513.

32. Fayetteville (Tenn.) *Sun*, 16 September 1891, quoted in Hart, "Bourbonism and Populism in Tennessee," p. 275; Calvin S. Brice to Matt Ransom, 1 July 1891, in Matt Whitaker Ransom Papers, Southern Historical Collection, University of North Carolina, Chapel Hill. A national association of Democratic clubs was formed in 1891 to counteract a similar grassroots effort on the part of Republicans. In the South the Democratic clubs were used to neutralize third-party organizations.

33. Robert McKee to Henry Clay Tomkins, 5 July 1891, copy in Robert McKee Papers, Alabama State Department of Archives and History.

34. Raleigh *Progressive Farmer*, 10 March 1891.

35. Kurt R. Anschel, et al., eds., *Agricultural Cooperatives and Markets in Developing Countries*.

36. F. A. Ingram to Elias Carr, 7 March 1890, Carr Papers.

37. Dallas *Southern Mercury*, 30 July 1891; Clinton (N.C.) *Caucasian*, 21 January 1892; Raleigh *Progressive Farmer*, 29 November 1892.

38. Clipping from *Atlanta Journal*, ca. September 1891, Thomas Edward Watson Papers, Southern Historical Collection, University of North Carolina, Chapel Hill; unidentified clipping, ca. 15 August 1891, Northen Scrapbook, vol. I, Northen Papers; Robert C. McMath, Jr., "Preface to Populism: The Origin and Economic Development of the 'Southern' Farmers' Alliance in Kansas," forthcoming in *Kansas Historical Quarterly*; Glenn Lowell Brudvig, "The Farmers' Alliance and Populist Movement in North Dakota (1884–1896)" (M.A. thesis, University of North Dakota, 1956).

39. State Farmers' Alliance of Virginia, *Proceedings . . . 1890*, pp. 14, 15, 25; Allen W. Moger, *Virginia*, p. 93; A. R. Venable to Charles Herbert Pierson, 22 November 1890, Charles Herbert Pierson Papers, University of Virginia, Charlottesville; SFAV, *Proceedings . . . 1891*, p. 10.

40. J. N. C. Beverley to C. H. Pierson, 4 November 1890, Pierson Papers; Richmond *Exchange Reporter*, 11 July, 12 December 1891. Stock in the exchanges was to be held in the name of suballiances.

41. F. Guy to C. H. Pierson, 8 June 1891, Pierson Papers. Not all Virginia cooperatives followed the Rochdale plan. In the southside county of Pittsylvania the Central Alliance Trade Union conducted an extensive business in groceries and supplies on credit in 1891 and 1892. The store had adequate capital but collapsed after sixteen months of operation, partially because it had overextended credit. Ledger Book, Pittsylvania Central Alliance Trade Union Records, University of Virginia, Charlottesville.

42. Macune, "Farmers' Alliance," p. 33; Lloyd Walter Cory, "The Florida Farmers' Alliance, 1887–1892" (M.S. thesis, Florida State University, 1963), p. 38; Dallas *Southern Mercury*, 15 May 1890; receipt for seed, 28 April 1891, John R. Osborne Papers, Manuscript Division, Duke University Library, Durham; Oswald Wilson to C. H. Pierson, 15 November 1890, Pierson Papers.

43. St. Louis *National Reformer*, 1 April 1892; Dallas *Southern Mercury*, 28 May 1891; Washington *National Economist* 6 (20 February 1892): 354.

44. *New York Times*, 10 November 1891; Washington *National Economist* 6 (20 February 1892): 354; H. H. Balch to W. H. Worth, 7 May 1891; Oswald Wilson to Worth, 18 April 1891; copies of both in Carr Papers. Attached to the copy of Balch's letter is a blank contract that is to be made between Wilson and operators of local stores.

45. Brudvig, "Farmers' Alliance and Populist Movement in North Dakota," p. 85; Topeka *Advocate*, 11 March, 26 August 1891; North Carolina Farmers' State Alliance, *Proceedings . . . 1891*, p. 38; Roy V. Scott, *The Agrarian Movement in Illinois, 1880–1896*, p. 77; clippings from *Macon Telegraph*, 11 July 1891, and *Atlanta Constitution*, 19 August 1891, both in Northen Scrapbook, vol. I; SFAV, *Proceedings . . . 1891*, p. 10.

46. Dallas *Southern Mercury*, 19 March 1891; Richmond *Virginia Sun*, 27 February 1892; S. B. Alexander to Elias Carr, 4 February 1891, Carr Papers.

47. *Memphis Appeal-Avalanche*, 23 November 1892; *Atlanta Constitution*, 19 November 1891; Topeka *Advocate*, 30 December 1891, 16 November 1892.

48. Homer Clevenger, "The Farmers' Alliance in Missouri," *Missouri Historical Review* 39 (October 1944): 42–44; Hart, "Bourbonism and Populism in Tennessee," pp. 241, 242; Joseph Church, "The Farmers' Alliance and Populist Movement in South Carolina (1887–1896)" (M.A. thesis, University of South Carolina, 1953), p. 51; SFAV, *Proceedings . . . 1891*, p. 11; quarterly reports from district lecturers (N.C.), 31 December 1891, Marion Butler Papers, Southern Historical Collection, University of North Carolina, Chapel Hill; *Atlanta Constitution*, 18 August 1892. Alliance spokesmen publicly denied any such decline and claimed the order was still growing, but evidence to the contrary is conclusive.

49. J. Morgan Kousser, *The Shaping of Southern Politics*, chaps. 3–5.

50. Farmers' State Alliance of Texas, *Proceedings . . . 1888*, p. 99; Raleigh *Progressive Farmer*, 5 November 1889.

51. Raleigh *Progressive Farmer*, 25 February 1890; William Warren Rogers, *The One-Gallused Rebellion*, pp. 176, 177. District lecturers were first appointed in North Carolina in 1889. Cf., Atlanta *Southern Cultivator* 48 (July 1890): 321, for similar developments in Georgia.

52. FSAT, *Proceedings . . . 1888*, p. 99; FSAT, *Proceedings . . . 1890*, pp. 29, 30.
53. Dallas *Southern Mercury*, 13 November, 4 December 1890; Washington *National Economist* 4 (6 December 1890): 188.
54. NCFSA, *Proceedings . . . 1890*, pp. 24, 25. For their services as district lecturers the North Carolinians received three dollars per day from the state Alliance. For information on Massey see Robert C. McMath, Jr., 'Agrarian Protest at the Forks of the Creek: Three Subordinate Farmers' Alliances in North Carolina," *North Carolina Historical Review* 51 (Winter 1974): 44, 45.
55. Dallas *Southern Mercury*, 4 June 1891; Washington *National Economist* 5 (6 June 1891): 187; Raleigh *Progressive Farmer*, 10 March 1891.
56. *Memphis Appeal–Avalanche*, 22 January 1892; Raleigh *Progressive Farmer*, 28 April 1891. In Georgia, where Alliancemen seemed ripe for political insurgency, the radicalizing influence of the district lecture system was weakened by the state executive committee, dominated by Lon Livingston. The committee appointed the district lecturers and instructed them to confine their efforts to "exemplification of the secret work, [and] explanation of the Ocala and State Alliance platforms and policies, including the insurance feature of the State Alliance." Atlanta *Southern Cultivator* 49 (February 1891): 97.
57. J. J. Silvey to C. H. Pierson, 10 June 1891, Pierson Papers. The political meaning of "education" in the Alliance, as opposed to the advancement of scientific farming advocated by the Grange is discussed in Roy V. Scott, *The Reluctant Farmer*, pp. 42–44.
58. Dallas *Southern Mercury*, 14 May 1891. In a similar appeal J. H. Turner of Georgia, secretary-treasurer of the national Alliance, called in 1891 for the admission of blacks to Democratic primaries. J. H. Turner, "The Race Problem," in *Farmers' Alliance History and Agricultural Digest*, ed. Nelson A. Dunning, pp. 275, 276.
59. W. A. Patillo to Elias Carr, 30 April, 2 May, 9 June 1891, all in Carr Papers.
60. W. A. Patillo to Elias Carr, 23 February, 30 April 1891, both in Carr Papers.
61. J. J. Rogers to Elias Carr, 30 April 1891, Carr Papers. Italics in original.
62. J. J. Rogers to Elias Carr, 17 May 1891, Carr Papers; Raleigh *Progressive Farmer*, 11 August 1891.
63. *Atlanta Constitution*, 24 July 1891.
64. William F. Holmes, "The Arkansas Cotton Pickers' Strike of 1891 and the Demise of the Colored Farmers' Alliance," *Arkansas Historical Quarterly* 32 (Summer 1973): 107–19.
65. Melton A. McLaurin, "The Knights of Labor in North Carolina Politics," *North Carolina Historical Review* 49 (July 1972): 308; Charles Crowe, "Tom Watson, Populists, and Blacks Reconsidered," *Journal of Negro History* 60 (April 1970): 109; Hair, *Bourbonism and Agrarian Protest*, p. 196; Hart, "Bourbonism and Populism," pp. 198–210. The role of Alliancemen in the constitutional disfranchisement of Mississippi blacks in 1890 is disputed. Ferguson, "Agrarianism in Mississippi," pp. 464, 465; Kirwan, *Revolt of the Rednecks*, pp. 63, 64.
66. J. B. Raynor to C. W. Macune, 12 November 1891, Powderly Papers. Macune passed Raynor's suggestion on to Powderly without comment.
67. Raleigh *Progressive Farmer*, 11 August 1891; Washington *National Economist* 6 (19 September 1891): 8; L. L. Polk to James W. Denmark, 21 August 1891, Leonidas LaFayette Polk Papers, Southern Historical Collection, University of North Carolina, Chapel Hill.
68. Washington *National Economist* 5 (8 August 1891): 328; clipping from Atlanta *Southern Alliance Farmer*, 10 February 1891, Northen Scrapbook, vol. I, Northen Papers.
69. C. Vann Woodward, *Origins of the New South, 1877–1913*, p. 244.
70. Dallas *Southern Mercury*, 30 April 1891; Lawrence C. Goodwyn, "The Origin and Development of American Populism" (Ph.D. diss., University of Texas, Austin, 1971), pp. 309–12; Huron *Dakota Ruralist*, 2 May 1891.
71. Washington *National Economist* 5 (9 May 1891): 133, 134. Cf., Goodwyn, "American Populism," pp. 309–25, for an extended discussion of the Waco meeting.
72. Goodwyn, "American Populism," pp. 354–57.
73. John D. Hicks, *The Populist Revolt*, pp. 211–14; Goodwyn, "American Populism," pp. 327–31.
74. Washington *National Economist* 4 (21 February 1891): 357; Raleigh *Progressive Farmer*, 19 May 1891.

75. Hair, *Bourbonism and Agrarian Protest*, p. 212; Union Springs (Ala.) *Herald*, 27 May 1891.

76. Dallas *Southern Mercury*, 4 June 1891; Washington *National Economist* 5 (30 May 1891): 161; Raleigh *Progressive Farmer*, 26 May, 2 June 1891.

77. Washington *National Economist* 6 (21 November 1891): 145; (28 November 1891): 168; (5 December 1891): 183; Indianapolis *American Nonconformist*, 19 November 1891. This last request was not met. When Congress convened in December all of the southern "Alliance" congressmen except Thomas E. Watson entered the Democratic caucus and helped elect conservative George F. Crisp of Georgia as speaker.

78. Hicks, *Populist Revolt*, p. 221; Indianapolis *American Nonconformist*, 19 November 1891.

79. Copy of address in Polk Papers. Privately, Polk went on to predict that the Democrats would nominate Grover Cleveland for president and the Republicans would nominate Benjamin Harrison. L. L. Polk to Elias Carr, 24 November 1891, Carr Papers.

80. L. L. Polk to Elias Carr, 24 November 1891, Carr Papers.

81. Robert Schilling to Terence Powderly, 3 September 1891, Powderly Papers; *Memphis Appeal-Avalanche*, 28 February 1892.

82. St. Louis *Post-Dispatch*, 23 February 1892; Alex M. Arnett, *The Populist Movement in Georgia*, pp. 131, 132; L. L. Polk to James W. Denmark, 8, 12 February 1892, both in Polk Papers.

83. Thomas Gilruth to Powderly, 11 January 1892; H. E. Taubeneck to Robert Schilling, 8 December 1891; both in Powderly Papers; St. Louis *Post-Dispatch*, 23, 24 February 1892; *Memphis Appeal-Avalanche*, 22 February 1892. The credentials committee announced that its deliberations had been delayed by the flood of would-be delegates from minor organizations. In fact, the struggle between supporters and opponents of the People's party, centering on contested seats of southern Alliancemen, was probably the basic cause of the delay.

84. Washington *National Economist* 6 (27 February 1892): 380; (5 March 1892): 394–96. For details of the meeting see Hicks, *Populist Revolt*, pp. 223–29.

85. Washington *National Economist* 6 (5 March 1892): 397; St. Louis *Post-Dispatch*, 25 February 1892.

CHAPTER 9

1. Clinton (N.C.) *Caucasian*, 19 March 1892.

2. Atlanta *Southern Alliance Farmer*, cited in Washington *National Economist* 7 (9 April 1892): 58; Tarboro (N.C.) *Farmers' Advocate*, 20 April 1892; Dallas *Southern Mercury*, 10 March 1892.

3. Atlanta *People's Party Paper*, 28 April 1892; Pittsboro (N.C.) *Chatham Record*, 21 April 1892. Cf., Gillespie County (Tex.) Alliance Minutebook, 8 April 1892, University of Texas Archives, Austin.

4. Atlanta *People's Party Paper*, 13 May 1892; H. Larry Ingle, "A Southern Democrat at Large: William Hodge Kitchin and the Populist Party," *North Carolina Historical Review* 45 (April 1968): 186; Union Springs (Ala.) *Herald*, 16 March 1892.

5. Many of the southern Presbyterian, Methodist, and Baptist journals editorialized in this vein. Cf., Harold W. Mann, *Atticus Greene Haygood*.

6. A more detailed discussion of this conflict is found in Robert C. McMath, Jr., "The Farmers' Alliance in the South: The Career of an Agrarian Institution" (Ph.D. diss., Univeristy of North Carolina, 1972), chap. 11. The line of demarcation *was* between town and countryside rather than between the city and rural areas. Cf., Robert R. Dykstra, "Town-Country Conflict: A Hidden Dimension in American Social History," *Agricultural History* 34 (October 1964): 195–204.

7. Raleigh *Christian Advocate*, 11 May 1892. In 1898 during the Democratic campaign to wrest control of the legislature away from fusionists, the same paper endorsed the Democrats in all but name: "The state is in the throes of a political agitation, such as it has not seen since the memorable days of 1878. Once again the color line has been drawn. . . . No one who loves God and his native State can look with indifference on the scene or muzzle his conscience-directed activities." Ibid., 2 November 1898.

8. Washington *National Economist* 5 (25 April 1891): 85; Butler (Ala.) *Choctaw Alliance*, 3 August 1893.

9. Atlanta *Christian Index*, 18 August 1892; Raleigh *Biblical Recorder*, 5 October 1892. For further indications of town-country cleavages among churchmen see Ozark (Ala.) *Banner*, 26 April 1894; Dallas *Southern Mercury*, 25 April 1895.

10. Atlanta *Christian Index*, 1 September 1892; Clinton (N.C.) *Caucasian*, 11, 18 August 1892. Populists also applied pressure against Democratic ministers. Cf., Raleigh *Progressive Farmer*, 2 January 1894.

11. See sup., chap. 5.

12. Broadside quoting St. Louis *Globe Democrat*, 21 November 1890, and Eureka Springs (Ark.) *Star*, 23 November 1890, Marion Butler Papers, Southern Historical Collection, University of North Carolina, Chapel Hill.

13. Ozark *Banner*, 27 July, 31 August, 14 September 1893. Methodist conferences had authority to locate a minister who was "complained of as being so unacceptable, ineffecient, or secular, as to be no longer useful in his work." Located ministers could still preach but could not hold circuit appointments. William P. Harrison, ed., *The Doctrines and Disciplines of the Methodist Episcopal Church, South*, p. 153.

14. Raleigh *Caucasian*, 22 August 1895.

15. Raleigh *News and Observer*, 22 September 1895. The previous year Kilgo had included in his description of a "Christian College" the responsibility to "hush the howl of the mob and send them back to their places of toil by teaching them to do unto others as they would have others do unto them." John Carlisle Kilgo Papers, Manuscript Division, Duke University Library, Durham. For a detailed discussion of Thompson's battle with church leaders see Frederick Augustus Bode, "Religion and Class Hegemony: A Populist Critique in North Carolina," *Journal of Southern History* 38 (August 1971): 417–38.

16. Raleigh *News and Observer*, 22 September 1895.

17. Raleigh *Caucasian*, 19 September 1895.

18. Ibid., 17 October 1895. In 1896 Tuttle invited Thompson, who was moving to Raleigh to assume the office of secretary of state, to join his church. "*With us you'd find a welcome*," wrote Tuttle. "We are decidedly *most* in sympathy with your political views and associations." Tuttle to Thompson, 9 November 1896, Cyrus W. Thompson Papers, Southern Historical Collection, University of North Carolina, Chapel Hill.

19. Henry F. May, *Protestant Churches and Industrial America*, p. 91.

20. When the minor flowering of a southern social gospel came after the turn of the century, its source was not the countryside, home of an indigenous, if short-lived, social Christianity, but the cities. Kenneth K. Bailey, *Southern White Protestantism in the Twentieth Century*, chap. 2; Wayne Flynt, "Dissent in Zion: Alabama Baptists and Social Issues, 1900–1914," *Journal of Southern History* 35 (November 1969): 542.

21. Alex M. Arnett, *The Populist Crusade in Georgia*, p. 152. The ratification drive was less successful in some states, particularly Tennessee and South Carolina, where most leaders of the order still opposed the third party.

22. Theodore Saloutos, *Farmer Movements in the South, 1865–1933*, pp. 124–32; Roger Louis Hart, "Bourbonism and Populism in Tennessee, 1875–1896" (Ph.D. diss., Princeton University, 1970), pp. 285, 286.

23. Washington *National Economist* 5 (9 May 1891): 133, 134; 6 (27 February 1892): 380.

24. James W. Denmark to L. L. Polk, 1 June 1892, Leonidas LaFayette Polk Papers, Southern Historical Collection, University of North Carolina, Chapel Hill; Sydenham B. Alexander to Elias Carr, 6 May 1892, Elias Carr Papers, Archives Department, East Carolina University, Greenville, N.C.

25. Marion Butler to Elias Carr, 7 June 1892, Carr Papers; Phillip R. Muller, "New South Populism: North Carolina" (Ph.D. diss., University of North Carolina, 1971), p. 68; Stuart Noblin, *Leonidas LaFayette Polk, Agrarian Crusader*, pp. 278; L. L. Polk to John D. Thorne, 29 March 1892, Marion Butler Papers, Southern Historical Collection, University of North Carolina, Chapel Hill. Reports from county Alliance secretaries in North Carolina revealed divisions within the order on the St. Louis demands and sharp fighting in the county Democratic

conventions on the issue, resulting in limited support for the demands among delegates to the state Democratic convention. Secretaries' reports, May 1892, Butler Papers.

26. M. L. Wood to Elias Carr, 16 July 1892; W. A. Forney to Elias Carr, 10 June 1892; both in Carr Papers.

27. Clinton (N.C.) *Caucasian*, 26 May 1892; James W. Denmark to O. W. Sutton, 16 September 1892, copy in Leonidas Polk Denmark Papers, North Carolina Division of Archives and History, Raleigh; North Carolina Farmers' State Alliance Treasurer's Book, 31 March 1892, p. 48, Farmers' Alliance Papers, North Carolina State Division of Archives and History.

28. Resolutions from Grimesland Alliance to Pitt County (North Carolina) Alliance, 8, 22 October 1892, John Bryan Grimes Papers, Southern Historical Collection, University of North Carolina, Chapel Hill; Sydenham B. Alexander to Elias Carr, 6 May 1892, Carr Papers.

29. Allen W. Moger, *Virginia*, p. 108; James A. Sharp, "The Farmers' Alliance and the People's Party in Tennessee," East Tennessee Historical Society's *Publications* 10 (1938): 100, 101; Roscoe C. Martin, *The People's Party in Texas*, pp. 146–48; clipping from Rome (Ga.) *Tribune*, 1 April 1892; William Jonathan Northen Scrapbook, vol. II, William Jonathan Northen Papers, Georgia State Department of Archives and History, Atlanta.

30. *Montgomery Advertiser*, 4, 5 May 1892; Raleigh *Progressive Farmer*, 10 May 1892.

31. Noblin, *Leonidas LaFayette Polk*, p. 291. On several occasions during his tenure as president of the Alliance, Polk had been physically incapacitated, although news of his illnesses was not made public. There is some indication that he suffered from mental depression as well. During one of Polk's illnesses Syd Alexander wrote that "his mental troubles are as great as [his] physical [ailments]." S. B. Alexander to Elias Carr, 1, 7 February 1890; J. J. Dunn to Carr, 4 October 1890, both in Carr Papers.

32. Noblin, *Leonidas LaFayette Polk*, pp. 223–28; Huron *Dakota Ruralist*, 7 January, 2 June 1892; Terence V. Powderly to Thomas E. Watson, 27 May 1892, Terence Vincent Powderly Papers, Department of Archives and Manuscripts, Catholic University of America, Washington, D.C.

33. At Omaha on 4 July the People's party ratified the St. Louis demands and nominated Weaver for president and James Gaven Field of Virginia over Ben Terrell for vice-president. John D. Hicks, *The Populist Revolt*, pp. 235, 236.

34. Edmund R. Cocke to Henry St. George Tucker, 12 July 1892, Tucker Papers, Southern Historical Collection, University of North Carolina, Chapel Hill.

35. Clinton *Caucasian*, 30 June, 14 July, 11 August 1892; Jackson (Miss.) *Daily State Ledger*, 25 July 1892, quoted in James S. Ferguson, "Agrarianism in Mississippi, 1871–1900: A Study in Nonconformity" (Ph.D. diss., University of North Carolina, 1952), p. 541.

36. Washington *National Economist* 7 (28 May 1892): 162; (2 July 1892): 241, 242; (10 September 1892): 404; 8 (8 October 1892): 3.

37. Farmers' State Alliance of Texas, *Proceedings . . . 1892*, p. 10; North Carolina Farmers' State Alliance, *Proceedings . . . 1892*, p. 25; Atlanta *People's Party Paper*, 26 August 1892; *Montgomery Advertiser*, 13 August 1892; William I. Hair, *Bourbonism and Agrarian Protest*, pp. 230, 231; Joseph Church, "The Farmers' Alliance and the Populist Movement in South Carolina (1887–1896)" (M.A. thesis, University of South Carolina, 1953), p. 57.

38. Cf., Ingle, "A Southern Democrat at Large," pp. 178–94.

39. The name "mid-roader" was applied to Populists who eschewed any contact with either Republicans or Democrats but "stuck to the middle of the road."

40. William Warren Rogers, *The One-Gallused Rebellion*, p. 221; C. Vann Woodward, *Tom Watson, Agrarian Rebel*, p. 237; Lloyd Walter Cory, "The Florida Farmers' Alliance, 1887–1892" (M.S. thesis, Florida State University, 1963), pp. 130–32.

41. Arthur M. Schlesinger, Jr., ed., *History of American Presidential Elections, 1789–1968*, 3:1784; J. Morgan Kousser, *The Shaping of Southern Politics*, p. 43.

42. Kousser, *Shaping of Southern Politics*, p. 41.

43. This point is developed further in Lawrence C. Goodwyn, "The Origin and Development of American Populism" (Ph.D. diss., Univeristy of Texas, Austin, 1971), pp. 349–52.

44. Schlesinger, ed., *American Presidential Elections*, 3:1784. Potential Alliance voting strength was computed by subtracting women and young men under the age of twenty-one

(about 25 percent) from the total Alliance membership in 1890. The Populist total, of course, included a handful of urban votes and an indeterminable number of non-Alliance rural votes.

45. For an account of the order's demise which gives more weight to the third-party issue, see Saloutos, *Farmer Movements in the South*, p. 135.

46. Washington *National Economist* 8 (5 November 1892): 4.

47. Ozark *Banner*, 9 March 1893; circular from J. F. Tillman, 29 October 1892, Butler Papers.

48. Washington *National Economist* 8 (18 February 1893): 3.

49. Robert D. Marcus, *Grand Old Party*, p. 181; Hair, *Bourbonism and Agrarian Protest*, pp. 229–33.

50. Gerald N. Grob, *Workers and Utopia*, p. 96; Vincent Joseph Falzone, "Terence V. Powderly: Mayor and Labor Leader, 1849–1893" (Ph.D. diss., Univeristy of Maryland, 1970), p. 317; Terence V. Powderly to Matthew S. Quay, 15 April 1892; Powderly to F. R. Agnew, 11 March 1892; Powderly to Thomas E. Watson, 27 May 1892; all in Powderly Papers.

51. References in Powderly's correspondence suggesting such an arrangement are elliptical but substantial. Cf., E. M. Halford to Powderly, 13 March 1892; Powderly to Benjamin Harrison, 29 March 1892; Powderly to James B. Weaver, 14 September 1892; John E. Williamson to Powderly, 21 September 1892; Powderly to Thomas W. Gilruth, 30 September 1892; all in Powderly Papers.

52. Willard Range, *A Century of Georgia Agriculture, 1850–1950*, p. 141; Moger, *Virginia*, p. 110. Between April and June the receipts of the North Carolina Alliance for dues dropped by about one-third. NCFSA, *Proceedings . . . 1892*, p. 9.

53. Huron *Dakota Ruralist*, 29 June 1893; Topeka *Advocate*, 16 November 1892.

54. Huron *Dakota Ruralist*, 27 October 1892; Indianapolis *American Nonconformist*, October–December 1892, pass.

55. Huron *Dakota Ruralist*, 24 November 1892; Washington *National Economist* 7 (26 November 1892): 3; Dallas *Southern Mercury*, 1 December 1892; National Farmers' Alliance and Industrial Union, *Proceedings . . . 1892*, p. 19. Loucks's inflammatory address was not printed in the official minutes of the meeting.

56. Butler (Ala.) *Choctaw Alliance*, 4 January 1893; Goldsboro (N.C.) *Caucasian*, 1 December 1892; Dallas *Southern Mercury*, 4 May 1893. Macune did in fact remain a member of the order but held no offices after November, 1892.

57. NFA&IU, *Proceedings . . . 1892*, p. 22; Washington *National Economist* 8 (18 February 1893): 1, 2; Ozark *Banner*, 9 March, 25 May 1893; Atlanta *People's Party Paper*, 23 June, 7 July 1893; Huron *Dakota Ruralist*, 29 June 1893.

58. Washington *National Economist* 8 (18 February 1893): 2, and (4 March 1893): 4, 5; Ozark *Banner*, 9 March 1893. The file of the *National Economist* available for this study ends with the issue of 11 March 1893, but references in other reform papers indicate that it survived at least until June.

59. Theodore Saloutos, "Charles W. Macune: Large-Scale Cooperative Advocate," in *Great American Cooperators*, by Joseph Grant Knapp and associates, p. 12.

60. Atlanta *People's Party Paper*, 6 January 1893; Richmond *Virginia Sun*, 17 May 1893.

61. H. H. Boyce to L. L. Polk, 8 April 1892, Polk Papers; Ferguson, "Agrarianism in Mississippi," p. 449n; Old Hickory Alliance Minutebook, 25 February 1893, Charles Herbert Pierson Papers, University of Virginia, Charlottesville.

62. NFA&IU, *Proceedings . . . 1892*, p. 24; Washington *National Economist* 8 (10 December 1892): 3; Raleigh *Progressive Farmer*, 18 April 1893.

63. Washington *National Economist* 7 (26 March 1892): 24, 25; Richmond *Virginia Sun*, 26 October 1892; Huron *Dakota Ruralist*, 2 March 1893; Raleigh *Progressive Farmer*, 14 March, 10 October 1893; Dallas *Southern Mercury*, 14 September 1893.

64. Record Book of the Alliance Gin, Buda, Texas, 1890–1910, photostatic copy, University of Texas Archives, Austin; Butler *Choctaw Alliance*, 22 November 1893; Raleigh *Progressive Farmer*, 5 September 1893; Woodward, *Tom Watson*, pp. 224, 225; Old Hickory Alliance Minute Book, 28 January 1893, Pierson Papers. Some of the cooperatives continued to operate after the collapse of the order. For example, the Alliance Mill of Denton, Texas, became the Morrison

Milling Company and is still operating. An Alliance insurance company in McPherson, Kansas, survived into the twentieth century and in 1937 had over 65,000 policy holders. "More Business, More Space," *Progress in Kansas* 3 (September 1937): 23.

65. Huron *Dakota Ruralist*, 7 December 1893; Buford (Ga.) *Alliance Plowboy*, 11 September 1895; Raleigh *Progressive Farmer*, 4 July, 14 September 1893; NCFSA, *Proceedings . . . 1894*, pp. 17, 18.

66. NCFSA, *Proceedings . . . 1895*, pp. 11–13, 25, 26; Adolph Jenkins Honeycutt, "The Farmers' Alliance in North Carolina" (M.S. thesis, North Carolina State College of Agriculture and Engineering, 1926), p. 26; John Graham to Cyrus Thompson, 14 December 1896, Thompson Papers.

67. Ozark *Banner*, 18 May 1893; Dallas *Southern Mercury*, 15 February 1894; Raleigh *Progressive Farmer*, 12 February 1895.

68. Dallas *Southern Mercury*, 23 April 1896, 25 February 1897. None of the reform papers examined mentioned a national Alliance meeting in 1898. In its issue of 15 February 1898 the *Progressive Farmer* ceased listing the officers of the national Alliance on its masthead.

69. Nelson A. Dunning to Marion Butler, 20 September 1895, Butler Papers.

70. Ottowa (Kans.) *Journal and Triumph*, 17 May 1894, Farmers' Alliance Clipping File, Kansas State Historical Society Library, Topeka; Rogers, *One-Gallused Rebellion*, pp. 318, 319; Atlanta *People's Party Paper*, 10 July 1896; Hair, *Bourbonism and Agrarian Protest*, pp. 254, 255; Church, "Farmers' Alliance and the Populist Movement in South Carolina," pp. 69, 70.

71. Dallas *Southern Mercury*, 20 August, 10 September 1896; 6 May 1897; Lampasas (Tex.) *People's Journal*, 7 October 1892.

72. Robert L. Hunt, *A History of Farmer Movements in the Southwest, 1873–1925*, pp. 46–52; Dallas *Southern Mercury*, 2 January 1902. In 1905 Andrew J. Carothers, who in 1886 organized one branch of the Colored Farmers' Alliance, announced the formation of a National Colored Farmers' Union, with himself as general superintendent. Dallas *Southern Mercury United with Farmers' Union Password*, 17 August 1905.

73. Adolphus Philoneous Hungate Memoir-Notebook, sec. 11, pp. 1–3, in possession of James P. Cole, Austin, Texas; Harrison Sterling Price Ashby Biographical Folder, University of Texas Archives, Austin; Dallas *Southern Mercury United with Farmers' Union Password*, 4 May, 15 June 1905. Recent studies of Oklahoma radicalism have not dealt with the effect of the Texas immigration. Cf., Garin Burbank, "Agrarian Radicals and Their Opponents: Political Conflict in Southern Oklahoma, 1910–1924," *Journal of American History* 58 (June 1971): 5–23.

74. NCFSA, *Proceedings . . . 1922–1941* (Raleigh).

75. Carl Cleveland Taylor, *The Farmers' Movement, 1620–1920*, p. 325.

76. Ibid., p. 326.

CHAPTER 10

1. Alex M. Arnett, *The Populist Movement in Georgia*, p. 76.

2. Joseph Grant Knapp, *The Rise of American Cooperative Enterprise, 1620–1920*, p. 67. Knapp, a pioneer agricultural economist, suggests that the Alliance's cooperative ventures "greatly influenced the character of subsequent cooperative thinking." Alliance cooperatives in the southern and plains states bore a striking resemblence to present day cooperatives in developing nations. Kurt R. Anschel, et al., eds., *Agricultural Cooperatives and Markets in Developing Countries*; J. C. Abbot, "The Development of Marketing Institutions," and John M. Brewster, "Traditional Social Structures as Barriers to Social Change," both in *Agricultural Development and Economic Growth*, ed. Herman M. Southworth and Bruce F. Johnston, pp. 364–98, 66–98.

3. For a differing view of this point see Lawrence C. Goodwyn, "The Origin and Development of American Populism" (Ph.D. diss. University of Texas, Austin, 1971).

4. Cf., Robert C. McMath, Jr., "Agrarian Protest at the Forks of the Creek: Three Subordinate Farmers' Alliances in North Carolina," *North Carolina Historical Review* 51 (Winter 1974): 41–63.

5. Robert D. Marcus, *Grand Old Party*, p. viii; R. Hal Williams, " 'Dry Bones and Dead Language': The Democratic Party," in *The Gilded Age*, ed. H. Wayne Morgan, p. 130.

6. Alliancemen's suspicion of the overproduction theory is shared by at least one economic historian, who argues that a shifting of southern agriculture away from cotton would not have improved economic conditions. Stephen DeCanio, "Cotton 'Overproduction' in Late Nineteenth-Century Southern Agriculture," *Journal of Economic History* 33 (September 1973): 608–33. "By rejecting the panacea of diversification," DeCanio suggests, "southern farmers implicitly displayed a solid grasp of the realities of their regional economy" (p. 633).

7. The agrarians' "monetarist" explanation of deflation is not without its modern supporters. Cf., Theodore Saloutos, "The Professors and the Populists," *Agricultural History* 40 (October 1966): 251.

8. This suggestion was first made by southern Democratic leaders and their Republican counterparts in the Midwest, who did not want the Alliance "going into politics." The argument has found its way into several accounts of the agrarian movement. It is reflected in Richard Hofstadter's distinction between the "hard side" and "soft side" of Populism. Cf., Theodore Saloutos, *Farmer Movements in the South, 1865–1933*, chap. 8, especially p. 135; Hugh Talmage Lefler and Albert Ray Newsome, *North Carolina: The History of a Southern State*, p. 547.

9. Richard Hofstadter, *The Age of Reform from Bryan to F.D.R.*; Norman Pollack, *The Populist Response to Industrial America*; Bruce Edward Palmer, "The Rhetoric of Southern Populists: Metaphor and Imagery in the Language of Reform" (Ph.D. diss., Yale University, 1972). One major exception to this trend is Goodwyn, "American Populism."

10. I have been influenced on this point by Donald G. Mathews, "The Second Great Awakening as an Organizing Process, 1780–1830," *American Quarterly* 21 (Spring 1969): 23–43; and T. Scott Miyakawa, *Protestants and Pioneers*. It seems to me that the Alliance was involved in the search for order in ways that Robert Wiebe did not fully appreciate. Cf., Robert H. Wiebe, *The Search for Order, 1877–1920*, pp. 71–74.

11. Sheldon Hackney, ed., *Populism*, pp. xvii–xix. Neil Smelser's model is set forth in his *Theory of Collective Behavior*.

12. Sociologists disagree about the usefulness of structural-functionalism. Cf., Anthony D. Smith, *The Concept of Social Change*. For criticism of the structuralist model as applied to Populism, cf., Walter T. K. Nugent, *The Tolerant Populists*, pp. 31, 32; and Michael Paul Rogin, *The Intellectuals and McCarthy*, pp. 26–32.

13. Smelser, *Theory of Collective Behavior*, pp. 8, 9, chap. 9.

14. Pollack, *Populist Response*, p. 11.

15. Mancur Olson, Jr., *The Logic of Collective Action*. Olson is an economist, but his model has application to social and political studies as well as economic ones.

16. Ibid., p. 2. Italics in original.

17. Ibid., chap. 6. Olson excepts corporate lobbyists from this pattern, suggesting that, since the number of powerful companies in any given industry is usually small, they can in fact operate rationally as an interest group. Olson's theory does not readily accommodate "citizens' " lobbies or the expression of authentic altruism.

Bibliography

I. PRIMARY SOURCES

A. MANUSCRIPTS

Athens, Ga. Manuscript Division, University of Georgia. Rebecca Latimer Felton Papers.

Atlanta, Ga. Georgia State Department of Archives and History. Crawfordville Alliance Minute Book.

Atlanta, Ga. Georgia State Department of Archives and History. William Jonathan Northen Collection.

Austin, Tex. In possession of James P. Cole. Adolphus Philoneous Hungate Memoir-Notebook.

Austin, Tex. University of Texas Archives. Harrison Sterling Price Ashby Biographical Folder.

Austin, Tex. University of Texas Archives. Record Book of the Buda, Texas, Alliance Gin, photostatic copy.

Austin, Tex. University of Texas Archives. Centennial Farmers' Alliance Minute Book.

Austin, Tex. University of Texas Archives. Gillespie County (Tex.) Farmers' Alliance Minute Book.

Austin, Tex. University of Texas Archives. Charles W. Macune, "The Farmers' Alliance," 1920, typescript.

Austin, Tex. University of Texas Archives. Patrons of Husbandry Records (Texas).

Austin, Tex. University of Texas Archives. Archibald Johnson Rose Papers.

Chapel Hill, N.C. Southern Historical Collection, University of North Carolina. Marion Butler Papers.

Chapel Hill, N.C. Southern Historical Collection, University of North Carolina. John Bryan Grimes Papers.

Chapel Hill, N.C. Southern Historical Collection, University of North Carolina. Leonidas LaFayette Polk Papers.

Chapel Hill, N.C. Southern Historical Collection, University of North Carolina. Matt Whitaker Ransom Papers.

Chapel Hill, N.C. Southern Historical Collection, University of North Carolina. Cyrus W. Thompson Papers.

Chapel Hill, N.C. Southern Historical Collection, University of North Carolina. Tucker Family Papers.

Chapel Hill, N.C. Southern Historical Collection, University of North Carolina. Zebulon Baird Vance Papers.

Charlottesville, Va. Alderman Library, University of Virginia. Charles Herbert Pierson Papers.

Charlottesville, Va. Alderman Library, University of Virginia. Pittsylvania Central Alliance Trade Union Records.

Durham, N.C. Manuscript Division, Duke University Library. William D. Hardin Papers.

Durham, N.C. Manuscript Division, Duke University Library. Jamestown Alliance Minute Book.

Durham, N.C. Manuscript Division, Duke University Library. John Carlisle Kilgo Papers.

Durham, N.C. Manuscript Division, Duke University Library. John R. Osborne Papers.

Greenville, N.C. Archives Department, East Carolina University. Elias Carr Papers.

Montgomery, Ala. Alabama State Department of Archives and History. Robert McKee Papers.

Montgomery, Ala. Alabama State Department of Archives and History. Joseph Wheeler Papers.

Raleigh, N.C. North Carolina Division of Archives and History. Leonidas Polk Denmark Collection.

Raleigh, N.C. North Carolina Division of Archives and History. Farmers' Alliance Papers (N.C.).

Raleigh, N.C. North Carolina Division of Archives and History. Clarence Hamilton Poe Papers.

Topeka, Kans. Kansas State Historical Society Archives. Minute Book of the Gove County (Kans.) Farmers' Alliance, No. 2628.

Topeka, Kans. Kansas State Historical Society Archives. Minute Book of Hoven Farmers' Alliance, No. 132.

Topeka, Kans. Kansas State Historical Society Archives. Minute Book of the Lone Tree Alliance, No. 2005.

Topeka, Kans. Kansas State Historical Society Library. Farmers' Alliance Clipping File (Kans.).

Topeka, Kans. Kansas State Historical Society Library. People's Party Pamphlets.

Tuscaloosa, Ala. Alabama University Library. Oliver Day Street Collection.

Washington, D.C. Department of Archives and Manuscripts, Catholic University of America. John W. Hayes Papers.

Washington, D.C. Department of Archives and Manuscripts, Catholic University of America. Terence Vincent Powderly Papers.

B. GOVERNMENT DOCUMENTS

Graham, Hugh Davis, and Gurr, Ted Roberts, eds. *Violence in America: Historical and Comparative Perspectives, A Report to the National Commission on the Causes and Prevention of Violence.* 2 vols. Washington: Government Printing Office, 1969.

United States Census Office. *Tenth Census of the United States, 1880.* MSS Agricultural Schedules. Jack, Lampasas, Parker, and Wise Counties, Texas. Microfilm copy at University of North Carolina Library, Chapel Hill.

———. *Tenth Census of the United States, 1880.* MSS Population Schedules. Jack, Lampasas, Parker, and Wise Counties, Texas. Microfilm copy at University of North Carolina Library, Chapel Hill.

———. *Eleventh Census of the United States, Report on Population of the United States.* Washington: Government Printing Office, 1897.

————. *Eleventh Census of the United States, Report on Statistics of Churches*. Washington: Government Printing Office, 1897.
United States Congress. House. *Biographical Directory of the American Congress, 1774–1927*. House Document 783, 69th Congress, 2d Session, 1928.

C. PUBLISHED MINUTES AND PROCEEDINGS

Baptist General Convention of Texas. *Proceedings*. Dallas, 1886–92.
Farmers' State Alliance of Georgia. *Proceedings*. Atlanta, 1890.
Farmers' State Alliance of Texas. *Proceedings*. Dallas, 1888, 1891, 1892.
Inter-State Farmers' Association. *Proceedings*. Atlanta, 1887–89.
Knights of Labor of America. *Proceedings*. Philadelphia, 1886–90.
National Farmers' Alliance and Co-operative Union. *Proceedings*. Dallas, 1887, 1888.
National Farmers' Alliance and Industrial Union. *Proceedings*. Washington, 1890, 1892.
North Carolina Farmers' State Alliance. *Proceedings*. Raleigh, 1889–1941.
North Texas Conference of the Methodist Episcopal Church, South, *Proceedings*. Dallas, 1886–94.
State Farmers' Alliance of Virginia. *Proceedings*. Petersburg, 1890, 1891.

D. INTERVIEWS AND LETTERS TO THE AUTHOR

Cotten, Fred R. Weatherford, Texas. Interview, 2 August 1971.
Hall, Rev. Leon. Durham, North Carolina. Interview, 1 July 1971.
Horner, William E., Sr. Sanford, North Carolina. Interview, 30 June 1971.
————. Letters to author, 4 July 1971, 6 August 1971.
Lipscomb, Mrs Mary. Durham County, North Carolina. Interview, 22 September 1971.
Massey, Charles Knox. Chapel Hill, North Carolina. Interview, 1 July 1971.

E. NEWSPAPERS AND PERIODICALS

Aberdeen, Huron (S.D.) *Dakota Ruralist*. 1888–94.
Atlanta *Christian Index*. 1888–92.
Atlanta Constitution, 1887–96.
Atlanta *Georgia Alliance Quarterly*. 1890.
Atlanta *People's Party Paper*. 1892–96.
Atlanta *Southern Cultivator*. 1887–96.
Athens (Ga.) *Weekly Banner*. 1888–92.
Austin *Firm Foundations*. 1887–96.
Buford (Ga.) *Alliance Plowboy*. 1895.
Butler (Ala.) *Choctaw Alliance*. 1893, 1894, 1896.
Butler (Ala.) *Choctaw Herald*. 1888, 1889.
Cambridge (Kans.) *News*. 1888, 1889.
Carrollton (Ga.) *Carroll Free Press*. 1887–92.
Chicago *Western Rural*. 1881–1891. (Becomes Chicago *Western Rural and American Stockman*, 1883.)
Clarksville, (Tex.) *Standard*. 1886–88.
Clinton, Goldsboro, Raleigh *Caucasian*. 1887–98.
Comanche (Tex.) *Pioneer Exponent*. 1888, 1889, 1896.
Comanche (Tex.) *Town and Country*. 1886.
Dallas Herald. 1882.

Dallas News. 1886–96.

Dallas *Southern Mercury.* 1884–1907. (Begins as *Dallas Mercury,* 1884. Becomes *Southern Mercury* in 1887. Becomes *Southern Mercury United With Farmers' Union Password* in 1905.)

Dallas *Texas Advance.* 1893, 1894.

Dallas *Texas Baptist and Herald.* 1887–96.

Dallas *Texas Christian Advocate.* 1887–92.

Decatur (Tex.) *Wise County Messenger.* 1880–90. (Begins as Paradise *Messenger,* 1880. Becomes Alvord *Messenger,* 1883. Becomes *Wise County Messenger,* 1885.)

Dexter (Kans.) *Free Press.* 1888, 1889.

Dexter (Kans.) *Post.* 1888.

Durham Recorder. 1889–91.

Ellaville (Ga.) *Schley County News.* 1889–93.

Fort Worth *Daily Democrat-Advance.* 1881, 1882. (Begins as *Daily Democrat,* 1881.)

Galveston *Daily News.* 1886–96.

Greensboro *North Carolina Christian Advocate.* 1889–96.

Huron (S.D.) *Daily Huronite.* 1889–90.

Indianapolis *American Nonconformist.* 1891, 1892.

Jacksboro (Tex.) *Rural Citizen.* 1880–86.

Lampasas (Tex.) *Dispatch.* 1877, 1878.

Lampasas (Tex.) *People's Journal.* 1892, 1893.

Macon *Weekly Telegraph.* 1883–93.

Memphis Appeal. 1888–92. (Becomes *Memphis Appeal-Avalanche,* 1890.)

Meriden, Topeka *Advocate.* 1889–94.

Mocksville (N.C.) *Davie Times.* 1888–92.

Montgomery Advertiser. 1887–95.

Montgomery *Alabama Baptist.* 1887.

Montgomery *Alliance Herald.* 1891–94.

Moulton (Ala.) *Advertiser.* 1887–89.

Nashville *Weekly Toiler.* 1888–90.

New York Times. 1891–93.

Newton (Kans.) *Kansas Commoner.* 1888–90.

Ozark (Ala.) *Banner.* 1892–95.

Palo Pinto, Strawn (Tex.) *Palo Pinto County Star.* 1885–87, 1889, 1890, 1894.

Pittsboro (N.C.) *Chatham Record.* 1887–92.

Raleigh *Biblical Recorder.* 1888–93.

Raleigh *Christian Advocate.* 1888–94.

Richmond *Exchange Reporter.* 1891, 1892.

Richmond *Southern Planter.* 1883–93.

Richmond *Virginia Sun.* 1892, 1893.

St. Louis *National Reformer.* 1892.

St. Louis *Post-Dispatch.* 1889–92.

Salem (N.C.) *People's Press.* 1888–92.

Sandersville (Ga.) *Middle Georgia Progress.* 1888–92.

Six Mile, Centreville (Ala.) *Bibb Blade.* 1888–90.

Tarboro (N.C.) *Farmers' Advocate.* 1881, 1892.

Thomasville (Ga.) *Times* (weekly.) 1887–92. (Becomes Thomasville *Times-Enterprise,* 1889.)

Topeka *Kansas Farmer.* 1888–92.

Troy (Ala.) *Jeffersonian.* 1893, 1894.

Union Springs (Ala.) *Herald*. 1888, 1891, 1892.
Valdosta (Ga.) *Times* (weekly). 1887–91.
Waco (Tex.) *Daily Examiner*. 1887.
Washington *National Economist*. 1889–93.
Weatherford (Tex.) *Times*. 1883, 1886.
Winfield (Kans.) *American Nonconformist and Kansas Industrial Liberator*. 1886–91.
Winston, Raleigh *Progressive Farmer*. 1886–99.

F. PAMPHLETS

[Cambell, G.]*Manual of the Open Conference of the Farmers' and Laborers' Cooperative Union of America*. Wichita, Kans.: Beacon Steam Job Print, 1886.
Constitution of the Farmers' State Alliance of North Carolina. Raleigh: Edwards and Broughton, 1889.
Constitution of the Farmers' State Alliance of Texas, 1887. Dallas: Southern Mercury Print., n.d.
Farmers' Alliance Co-operative Manufacturing Company, Iron Gate, Virginia. [Prospectus.] New Market, Va.: Henkel and Company, 1890.
Polk, Leonidas LaFayette. *Agricultural Depression, Its Causes—The Remedy; Speech . . . Before the Senate Committee on Agriculture and Forestry*. . . . Raleigh: Edwards and Broughton, 1890.
Rules of the Barton County Alliance Exchange Company. Great Bend, Kans.: Beacon Job Print, 1890.

G. ARTICLES

Diggs, Annie L. "The Women in the Alliance Movement." *Arena* 6 (June 1892): 161–79.
"The Farmers' Alliance in the Southeast." *Harper's Weekly* 34 (13 December 1890): 970–71.
Ousley, Clarence N. "A Lesson in Cooperation." *Popular Science Monthly* 36 (April 1890): 821–28.
Skinner, Harry. "The Hope of the South." *Frank Leslie's Illustrated Newspaper* 69 (30 November 1889): 290.
Snyder, Edwin. "The Farmers' Alliance." *Proceedings of the Nineteenth Annual Meeting of the Kansas State Board of Agriculture . . . 8–11 January 1890*. Topeka: Kansas Publishing House, 1890.

H. GENERAL WORKS, COMPILATIONS, SURVEYS

American Newspaper Annual. Philadelphia: N. W. Ayer and Son, 1887.
Appleton's Annual Cyclopedia and Register of Important Events of the Year 1890. N.s., vol. 15. New York: D. Appleton and Company, 1891.
Aptheker, Herbert, ed. *A Documentary History of the Negro People of the United States*. New York: The Citadel Press, 1951.
Ashby, N. B. *The Riddle of the Sphinx*. Des Moines, Iowa: Industrial Publishing Company, 1890.
[Blood, Fred G., ed.] *Hand Book and History of the National Farmers' Alliance and Industrial Union*. Washington: n.p., 1893.
Branson's North Carolina Business Directory. Vol. 7. Raleigh: Levi Branson, 1890.
Bryan, J. E. *The Farmers' Alliance: Its Origin, Progress and Purposes*. Fayetteville, Ark.: n.p., 1891.

Connor, Robert Diggs Wimberly, ed. *A Manual of North Carolina*. Raleigh: E.M. Uzzle and Company, 1913.

Dunning, Nelson A., ed. *Farmers' Alliance History and Agricultural Digest*. Washington: Alliance Publishing Company, 1891.

Garvin, William L. *History of the Grand State Farmers' Alliance of Texas*. Jacksboro, Tex.: J. N. Rogers and Company, 1885.

———, and Daws, S. O. *History of the National Farmers' Alliance and Co-operative Union of America*. Jacksboro, Tex.: J. N. Rogers and Company, 1887.

Harrison, William P., ed. *The Doctrines and Disciplines of the Methodist Episcopal Church, South*. Nashville: Publishing House of the Methodist Episcopal Church, South, 1890.

Morgan, W. Scott. *History of the Wheel and Alliance, and the Impending Revolution*. Hardy, Ark.: Published by the author, 1889.

The National Economist Almanac, 1890: National Farmers' Alliance and Industrial Union Hand-Book. Washington: National Economist Printing Company, 1890.

Nugent, Catherine, ed. *Life Work of Thomas L. Nugent*. Stephenville, Tex.: Published by the author, 1896.

Thomas, E. B. *A Complete Directory of the Legislature of the State of Georgia for 1890–'91*. Atlanta: C. P. Byrd, 1890.

Winkler, Ernest William, ed. *Platforms of Political Parties in Texas*. Austin: University of Texas Press, 1916.

I. MEMOIRS AND AUTOBIOGRAPHIES

Barry, James Buckner. *A Texas Ranger and Frontiersman: The Days of Buck Barry in Texas, 1845–1906*. Dallas: The Southwest Press, 1932.

Huckabay, Ida Lasater. *Ninety-Four Years in Jack County*. Jacksboro, Tex.: Published by the author, 1949.

Poe, Clarence Hamilton. *My First Eighty Years*. Chapel Hill: University of North Carolina Press, 1963.

Robertson, Ben. *Red Hills and Cotton: An Upcountry Memory*. New York: Alfred A. Knopf, 1942.

Scott, S. M. *The Champion Organizer of the Northwest: Or My First Sixty Days Work as an Organizer*. McPherson, Kans.: n.p., 1890.

II. SECONDARY SOURCES

A. PERIODICAL ARTICLES

Abbey, Katheryn T. "Florida Versus the Principles of Populism, 1896–1911." *Journal of Southern History* 4 (November 1938): 462–75.

Abramowitz, Jack. "The Negro in the Populist Movement." *Journal of Negro History* 38 (July 1953): 257–89.

Allport, Gordon W. "The Functional Autonomy of Motives." *American Journal of Psychology* 50 (1937): 141–56.

Argersinger, Peter H. "Pentecostal Politics in Kansas: Religion, the Farmers' Alliance, and the Gospel of Populism." *Kansas Quarterly* 1 (Fall 1969): 24–35.

———. "Road to a Republican Waterloo: The Farmers' Alliance and the Election of 1890 in Kansas." *Kansas Historical Quarterly* 33 (Winter 1967): 443–69.

Barr, Chester Alwyn. "Ben Terrell: Agrarian Spokesman." *West Texas Historical Association Yearbook* 45(1969): 58–71.

Bode, Frederick Augustus. "Religion and Class Hegemony: A Populist Critique in North Carolina." *Journal of Southern History* 38 (August 1971): 417–38.

Burbank, Garin. "Agrarian Radicals and Their Opponents: Political Conflict in Southern Oklahoma, 1910–1924." *Journal of American History* 58 (June 1971): 5–23.

Clark, Thomas D. "The Furnishing and Supply System in Southern Agriculture since 1865." *Journal of Southern History* 12 (February 1946): 24–44.

Clevenger, Homer. "The Farmers' Alliance in Missouri." *Missouri Historical Review* 39 (October 1944): 24–44.

———. "The Teaching Techniques of the Farmers' Alliance: An Experiment in Adult Education." *Journal of Southern History* 11 (November 1945): 505–18.

Crowe, Charles. "Tom Watson, Populists, and Blacks Reconsidered." *Journal of Negro History* 60 (April 1970): 99–116.

DeCanio, Stephen. "Cotton 'Overproduction' in Late Nineteenth-Century Southern Agriculture." *Journal of Economic History* 33 (September 1973): 608–33.

Dethloff, Henry C. "The Alliance and the Lottery: Farmers Try for the Sweepstakes." *Louisiana History* 6 (Spring 1965): 141–59.

Dykstra, Robert R. "Town-Country Conflict: A Hidden Dimension in American Social History." *Agricultural History* 34 (October 1964): 195–204.

Elkins, F. Clark. "The Agricultural Wheel: County Politics and Consolidation, 1884–1885." *Arkansas Historical Quarterly* 29 (Summer 1970): 152–75.

Ellis, Louis Tuffly. "The Revolutionization of the Texas Cotton Trade, 1865–1885." *Southwestern Historical Quarterly* 73 (April 1970): 478–508.

Farmer, Margaret Pace. "Furnishing Merchants and Sharecroppers in Pike County, Alabama." *Alabama Review* 23 (April 1970): 143–51.

Flynt, Wayne. "Dissent in Zion: Alabama Baptists and Social Issues, 1900–1914." *Journal of Southern History* 35 (November 1969): 523–42.

Goodwyn, Lawrence Corbett. "Populist Dreams and Negro Rights: East Texas as a Case Study." *American Historical Review* 76 (December 1971): 1435–56.

Hendrickson, Kenneth E. "Some Political Aspects of the Populist Movement in South Dakota." *North Dakota History* 34 (Winter 1967): 77–92.

Hicks, John D. "The Origin and Early History of the Farmers' Alliance in Minnesota." *Mississippi Valley Historical Review* 9 (December 1922): 203–26.

Holmes, William F. "The Arkansas Cotton Pickers' Strike of 1891 and the Demise of the Colored Farmers' Alliance." *Arkansas Historical Quarterly* 32 (Summer 1973): 107–19.

———. "The Leflore County Massacre and the Demise of the Colored Farmers' Alliance." *Phylon* 34 (September 1973): 267–74.

Ingle, H. Larry. "A Southern Democrat at Large: William Hodge Kitchin and the Populist Party." *North Carolina Historical Review* 45 (April 1968): 178–94.

Laird, William E., and Rinehart, James R. "Deflation, Agriculture, and Southern Development." *Agricultural History* 42 (April 1968): 115–24.

Lightfoot, Billy Bob. "From Frontier to Farmland: Highlights of the History of Comanche County," West Texas Historical Association *Year Book* 32 (1956): 30–43.

———. "The Human Party: Populism in Comanche County, 1886." West Texas Historical Association *Year Book* 31 (1955): 28–40.

McLaughlin, William G. "Pietism and the American Character." *American Quarterly* 17 (Summer 1965): 163–86.

McLaurin, Melton A. "The Knights of Labor in North Carolina Politics." *North Carolina Historical Review* 49 (July 1972): 298–315.

McMath, Robert C., Jr. "Agrarian Protest at the Forks of the Creek: Three Subordi-

nate Farmers' Alliances in North Carolina." *North Carolina Historical Review*
    51 (Winter 1974): 41–63.

———. "Preface to Populism: The Origin and Economic Development of the 'South-
    ern' Farmers' Alliance in Kansas." Forthcoming in *Kansas Historical Quarterly*.

———. "Southern White Farmers and the Organization of Black Farm Workers: A
    North Carolina Document." Forthcoming in *Labor History*.

Malin, James C. "The Farmers' Alliance Subtreasury Plan and European Prece-
    dents." *Mississippi Valley Historical Review* 31 (September 1944): 255–60.

Mathews, Donald G. "The Second Great Awakening as an Organizing Process,
    1780–1830." *American Quarterly* 21 (Spring 1969): 23–43.

Mayhew, Anne. "A Reappraisal of the Causes of Farm Protest in the United States,
    1870–1900." *Journal of Economic History* 32 (June 1972): 464–75.

Meyers, Frederic. "The Knights of Labor in the South." *Southern Economic Journal* 6
    (April 1940): 470–87.

Miller, Floyd J. "Black Protest and White Leadership: A Note on the Colored
    Farmers' Alliance." *Phylon* 33 (June 1972): 169–74.

Miller, Raymond C. "The Economic Background of Populism in Kansas." *Mis-
    sissippi Valley Historical Review* 11 (March 1925): 469–89.

"More Business, More Space." *Progress in Kansas* 3 (September 1937): 23.

Nixon, Herman C. "The Cleavages within the Farmers' Alliance Movement."
    Mississippi Valley Historical Review 15 (June 1928): 22–23.

———. "The Populist Movement in Iowa." *Iowa Journal of History and Politics* 21
    (January 1926): 3–107.

Ogilvie, Leon Parker. "Populism and Socialism in the Southeastern Missouri Low-
    lands." *Missouri Historical Review* 65 (January 1971): 159–83.

Paisley, Clifton. "The Political Wheelers and the Arkansas Election of 1888" *Arkansas
    Historical Quarterly* 25 (Spring 1966): 3–21.

Proctor, Samuel. "The National Farmers' Alliance Convention of 1890 and Its 'Ocala'
    Demands." *Florida Historical Quarterly* 27 (January 1950): 161–81.

Ransom, Roger L., and Sutch, Richard. "Debt Peonage in the Cotton South after the
    Civil War." *Journal of Economic History* 32 (September 1972): 641–69.

Ridgeway, Gordon B. "Populism in Washington." *Pacific Northwest Quarterly* 39
    (October 1948): 284–311.

Rightmire, W. F. "The Alliance Movement in Kansas—Origin of the People's Party."
    Transactions of the Kansas State Historical Society, 1905–1906, 9: 1–8.

Rogers, William Warren. "The Negro Alliance in Alabama." *Journal of Negro History*
    45 (January 1960): 38–44.

Saloutos, Theodore. "The Agricultural Wheel in Arkansas." *Arkansas Historical Quar-
    terly* 2 (June 1943): 127–40.

———. "The Professors and the Populists." *Agricultural History* 40 (October 1966):
    235–54.

Saunders, Robert M. "Progressive Historians and the Late Nineteenth-Century
    Agrarian Revolt: Virginia as a Historical Test Case." *Virginia Magazine of His-
    tory and Biography* 79 (October 1971): 484–92.

———. "Southern Populists and the Negro, 1893–1895." *Journal of Negro History*
    54 (July 1969): 240–61.

Schlesinger, Arthur Meier. "Biography of a Nation of Joiners." *American Historical
    Review* 50 (October 1944): 1–25.

Scott, Roy V. "Milton George and the Farmers' Alliance Movement." *Mississippi Valley Historical Review* 45 (June 1958): 90–109.

Shannon, Fred Albert. "C. W. Macune and the Farmers' Alliance." *Current History* 33 (June 1955): 330–35.

Sharp, James A. "The Entrance of the Farmers' Alliance into Tennessee Politics." East Tennessee Historical Society's *Publications* 9 (1937): 77–92.

———. "The Farmers' Alliance and the People's Party in Tennessee." East Tennessee Historical Society's *Publications* 10 (1938): 91–113.

Smith, Ralph. "The Farmers' Alliance in Texas, 1875–1900: A Revolt against Bourbon and Bourgeois Democracy." *Southwestern Historical Quarterly* 48 (January 1954): 346–69.

———. " 'Macuneism,' or the Farmers of Texas in Business." *Journal of Southern History* 13 (May 1947): 220–44.

Stewart, Ernest D. "The Populist Party in Indiana." *Indiana Magazine of History* 14 (1918): 332–67.

Thompson, J. M. "The Farmers' Alliance in Nebraska: Something of Its Origin, Growth, and Influence." *Proceedings and Collections of the Nebraska State Historical Society*, 2d ser., 5 (1902): 199–206.

Warner, Donald F. "Prelude to Populism." *Minnesota History* 32 (September 1951): 129–54.

B. GENERAL WORKS

Allen, Ruth A. *The Great Southwest Strike.* University of Texas Publication No. 4214. Austin: University of Texas Press, 1942.

Anschel, Kurt R., et al., eds. *Agricultural Cooperatives and Markets in Developing Countries.* New York: Frederick A. Praeger, 1969.

Apter, David E., ed. *Ideology and Discontent.* New York: Free Press of Glencoe, 1964.

Argersinger, Peter H. *Populism and Politics: William Alfred Peffer and the People's Party.* Lexington: University Press of Kentucky, 1974.

Arnett, Alex M. *The Populist Movement in Georgia: A View of the "Agrarian Crusade" in the Light of Solid-South Politics.* Columbia University Studies in History, Economics, and Public Law, vol. 104. New York: Columbia University Press, 1922.

Bailey, Kenneth K. *Southern White Protestantism in the Twentieth Century.* New York: Harper and Row, 1964.

Barr, Alwyn. *Reconstruction to Reform: Texas Politics, 1876–1906.* Austin: University of Texas Press, 1971.

Bell, Daniel, ed. *The New American Right.* New York: Criterion Books, 1955.

Benson, Lee. *Merchants, Farmers, and Railroads: Railroad Regulation and New York Politics, 1850–1887.* Cambridge: Harvard University Press, 1955.

Bonner, James C., and Roberts, Lucien E., eds. *Studies in Georgia History and Government.* Athens: University of Georgia Press, 1940.

Buck, Solon J. *The Granger Movement: A Study of Agricultural Organization and Its Political, Economic, and Social Manifestations, 1870–1880.* Cambridge: Harvard University Press, 1913.

Clanton, O. Gene. *Kansas Populism: Ideas and Men.* Lawrence: University of Kansas Press, 1969.

Clark, John B. *Populism in Alabama*. Auburn, Alabama: Auburn Printing Company, 1927.

Clark, Thomas Dionysius. *The Southern Country Editor*. Indianapolis: Bobbs-Merrill Company, 1948.

Connelley, William E., comp. *History of Kansas, State and People*. 2 vols. 3rd ed. Chicago: The American Historical Society, 1928.

Cooper, William J. *The Conservative Regime: South Carolina, 1877–1890*. Baltimore: The Johns Hopkins University Press, 1968.

Delmatier, Royce D., et al., eds. *The Rumble of California Politics, 1848–1970*. New York: John Wiley and Sons, 1970.

De Santis, Vincent P. *Republicans Face the Southern Question: The New Departure Years, 1877–1897*. Baltimore: Johns Hopkins University Press, 1959.

Edelman, Murray. *The Symbolic Uses of Politics*. Urbana: University of Illinois Press, 1964.

Farish, Hunter Dickinson. *The Circuit Rider Dismounts: A Social History of Southern Methodism, 1865–1900*. Richmond: The Deitz Press, 1938.

Gaustad, Edwin Scott. *Historical Atlas of Religion in America*. New York: Harper and Row, 1962.

Gist, Noel P. *Secret Societies: A Cultural Study of Fraternalism in the United States*. University of Missouri Studies, vol. 15. Columbia: University of Missouri Press, 1940.

Gould, Lewis L. *Progressives and Prohibitionists: Texas Democrats in the Wilson Era*. Austin: University of Texas Press, 1973.

Graves, W. W. *History of Neosha County*. 2 vols. St. Paul, Kansas: Journal Press, 1951.

Gray, Lewis C. *History of Agriculture in the Southern United States to 1860*. 2 vols. Washington: Carnegie Institute of Washington, 1933.

Grob, Gerald N. *Workers and Utopia: A Study of Ideological Conflict in the American Labor Movement, 1865–1900*. Evanston, Ill.: Northwestern University Press, 1961.

Gusfield, Joseph R. *Symbolic Crusade: Status Politics and the American Temperance Movement*. Urbana: University of Illinois Press, 1963.

Hackney, Sheldon, ed. *Populism: The Critical Issues*. Boston: Little, Brown and Company, 1971.

———. *Populism to Progressivism in Alabama*. Princeton: Princeton University Press, 1969.

Hair, William I. *Bourbonism and Agrarian Protest: Louisiana Politics, 1877–1900*. Baton Rouge: Louisiana State University Press, 1969.

Hertzler, Joyce Oramel. *American Social Institutions: A Sociological Analysis*. Boston: Allyn and Bacon, 1961.

Hicks, John D. *The Populist Revolt: A History of the Farmers' Alliance and the People's Party*. Minneapolis: University of Minnesota Press, 1931.

Hill, Samuel S., Jr. *Southern Churches in Crisis*. New York: Holt, Rinehart and Winston, 1966.

———, and others. *Religion and the Solid South*. Nashville: Abingdon Press, 1972.

Hofstadter, Richard. *The Age of Reform from Bryan to F.D.R.* New York: Alfred A. Knopf, 1955.

Holland, G. A. *History of Parker County and the Double Log Cabin*. Weatherford, Tex.: The Herald Publishing Company, 1937.

Horton, Thomas F. *History of Jack County*. Jacksboro, Tex.: Gazette Printing Company, 1954.

Hunt, Robert Lee. *A History of Farmer Movements in the Southwest, 1873–1925*. College Station, Tex.: n.p., 1935.

Jensen, Richard J. *The Winning of the Midwest: Social and Political Conflict, 1888–1896*. Chicago: University of Chicago Press, 1971.

Johnson, Allen, ed. *Dictionary of American Biography*. New York: Charles Scribner's Sons, 1929.

Johnson, Charles Albert. *The Frontier Camp Meeting: Religion's Harvest Time*. Dallas: Southern Methodist University Press, 1955.

Keller, Suzanne. *Beyond the Ruling Class: Strategic Elites in Modern Society*. New York: Random House, 1963.

Kirwan, Albert D. *Revolt of the Rednecks: Mississippi Politics, 1876–1925*. Lexington: University of Kentucky Press, 1951.

Klein, Maury. *The Great Richmond Terminal: A Study in Businessmen and Business Strategy*. Charlottesville: University of Virginia Press, 1970.

Kleppner, Paul. *The Cross of Culture: A Social Analysis of Midwestern Politics, 1850–1900*. 2d ed. New York: Free Press, 1970.

Knapp, Joseph Grant. *The Rise of American Cooperative Enterprise, 1620–1920*. Danville, Ill.: The Interstate Printers and Publishers, 1969.

———. and associates. *Great American Cooperators: Biographical Sketches of 101 Major Pioneers in Cooperative Development*. Washington: American Institute of Cooperation, 1967.

Kousser, J. Morgan. *The Shaping of Southern Politics: Suffrage Restriction and the Establishment of the One-Party South, 1880–1910*. Yale Historical Publications, Miscellany, 102. New Haven: Yale University Press, 1974.

Lamar, Howard Roberts. *Dakota Territory, 1861–1889: A Study of Frontier Politics*. New Haven: Yale University Press, 1956.

Larson, Robert W. *New Mexico Populism: A Study of Radical Protest in a Western Territory*. Foreword by Howard R. Lamar. Boulder: Colorado Associated University Press, 1974.

Lefler, Hugh Talmage, and Newsome, Albert Ray. *North Carolina: The History of a Southern State*. 3rd ed. Chapel Hill: University of North Carolina Press, 1973.

McLaurin, Melton Alonzo. *Paternalism and Protest: Southern Cotton Mill Workers and Organized Labor, 1875–1905*. Contributions in Economics and Economic History, No. 3. Westport, Conn.: Greenwood Publishing Corporation, 1971.

McSeveney, Samuel T. *The Politics of Depression: Political Behavior in the Northeast, 1893–1896*. New York: Oxford University Press, 1972.

Maddex, Jack. *The Virginia Conservatives, 1867–1879*. Chapel Hill: University of North Carolina Press, 1970.

Malin, James C. *A Concern about Humanity: Notes on Reform, 1872–1912, at the National and Kansas Levels of Thought*. Lawrence, Kansas: Published by the author, 1964.

Mann, Harold W. *Atticus Green Haygood: Methodist Bishop, Editor, and Educator*. Athens: University of Georgia Press, 1966.

Marcus, Robert D. *Grand Old Party: Political Structure in the Gilded Age, 1880–1896*. New York: Oxford University Press, 1971.

Martin, Roscoe C. *The People's Party in Texas: A Study in Third Party Politics*. Austin: University of Texas Press, 1933.

May, Henry F. *Protestant Churches and Industrial America*. New York: Harper and Brothers, 1949.

Meier, August, and Rudwick, Elliott. *From Plantation to Ghetto*. Rev. Ed. New York: Hill and Wang, 1970.

Miyakawa, T. Scott. *Protestants and Pioneers: Individualism and Conformity on the American Frontier*. Chicago: University of Chicago Press, 1964.

Moger, Allen W. *Virginia: Bourbonism to Byrd, 1870–1925*. Charlottesville: University of Virginia Press, 1968.

Moore, Albert B. *History of Alabama and Her People*. 3 vols. Chicago: American Historical Society, 1927.

Morgan, H. Wayne, ed. *The Gilded Age*. Rev. ed. Syracuse: Syracuse University Press, 1970.

————. *From Hayes to McKinley: National Party Politics, 1877–1896*. Syracuse: Syracuse University Press, 1969.

Mott, Frank Luther. *American Journalism, A History: 1690–1960*. 3rd ed. New York: Macmillan Company, 1962.

National Cyclopedia of American Biography. New York: James T. White Company, 1893.

Noblin, Stuart. *Leonidas LaFayette Polk, Agrarian Crusader*. Chapel Hill: University of North Carolina Press, 1949.

Nordin, D. Sven. *Rich Harvest: A History of the Grange, 1867–1900*. Jackson: University Press of Mississippi, 1974.

Northen, William Jonathan, ed. *Men of Mark in Georgia*. 6 vols. Atlanta: A. B. Caldwell, 1912.

Nugent, Walter T. K. *The Tolerant Populists: Kansas Populism and Nativism*. Chicago: University of Chicago Press, 1963.

Olson, Mancur, Jr. *The Logic of Collective Action: Public Goods and the Theory of Groups*. Cambridge: Harvard University Press, 1965.

Owen, Thomas M. *History of Alabama and Dictionary of Alabama Biography*. 4 vols. Chicago: S. J. Clarke Publishing Company, 1921.

Parsons, Stanley B. *The Populist Context: Rural Versus Urban Power on a Great Plains Frontier*. Westport, Conn.: Greenwood Press, 1973.

Phelan, Macum. *A History of the Expansion of Methodism in Texas, 1867–1902*. Dallas: Mathis, Van Nort and Company, 1937.

Pollack, Norman. *The Populist Response to Industrial America*. Cambridge: Harvard University Press, 1962.

Pope, Liston. *Millhands and Preachers: A Study of Gastonia*. New Haven: Yale University Press, 1942.

Pressley, Thomas J., and Scofield, William H., eds. *Farm Real Estate Values in the United States by Counties, 1850–1959*. Seattle: University of Washington Press, 1965.

Range, Willard. *A Century of Georgia Agriculture, 1850–1950*. Athens: University of Georgia Press, 1954.

Rice, Lawrence D. *The Negro in Texas, 1874–1900*. Baton Rouge: Louisiana State University Press, 1971.

Richardson, Rupert N. *The Frontier of Northwest Texas, 1846 to 1876: Advance and Defense by the Pioneer Settlers of the Cross Timbers and Prairies*. Vol. 5 of Frontier Military Series. Glendale, Calif.: The Arthur H. Clark Company, 1963.

————. *Texas, the Lone Star State*. 2d ed. Englewood Cliffs, N.J.: Prentice-Hall, 1958.

Robinson, Elwyn B. *History of North Dakota*. Lincoln: University of Nebraska Press, 1966.

Robison, Daniel Merritt. *Bob Taylor and the Agrarian Revolt in Tennessee*. Chapel Hill: University of North Carolina Press, 1935.

Rogers, William Warren. *The One-Gallused Rebellion: Agrarianism in Alabama, 1865–1896*. Baton Rouge: Louisiana State University Press, 1970.

Rogin, Michael Paul. *The Intellectuals and McCarthy: The Radical Specter*. Cambridge: Massachusetts Institute of Technology Press, 1967.

————, and Shover, John L. *Political Change in California: Critical Elections and Social Movements, 1890–1966*. Westport, Conn.: Greenwood Publishing Company, 1970.

Rothman, David J. *Politics and Power: The United States Senate, 1896–1901*. Cambridge: Harvard University Press, 1966.

Saloutos, Theodore. *Farmer Movements in the South, 1865–1933*. Berkeley: University of California Press, 1960.

Schell, Herbert S. *History of South Dakota*. Lincoln: University of Nebraska Press, 1961.

Schlesinger, Arthur M., Jr., ed. *History of American Presidential Elections, 1789–1968*. 4 vols. New York: Chelsea House Publishers and McGraw-Hill Book Company, 1971.

Scott, Roy V. *The Agrarian Movement in Illinois, 1880–1896*. Urbana: University of Illinois Press, 1962.

————. *The Reluctant Farmer: The Rise of Agricultural Extension to 1914*. Urbana: University of Illinois Press, 1970.

Shannon, Fred Albert. *The Farmers' Last Frontier: Agriculture, 1860–1897*. Vol. 5 of *The Economic History of the United States*. New York: Holt, Rinehart and Winston, 1945.

Sheldon, William DuBose. *Populism in the Old Dominion: Virginia Farm Politics, 1885–1900*. Princeton: Princeton University Press, 1935.

Smelser, Neil. *Theory of Collective Behavior*. New York: The Free Press, 1963.

Smith, Anthony D. *The Concept of Social Change: A Critique of the Functionalist Theory of Social Change*. London: Routledge and Kegan Paul, 1973.

Sonnichsen, Charles L. *Ten Texas Feuds*. Albuquerque: University of New Mexico Press, 1957.

Southworth, Herman M., and Johnston, Bruce F., eds. *Agricultural Development and Economic Growth*. Ithaca, New York: Cornell University Press, 1967.

Spain, Rufus Buin. *At Ease in Zion: A Social History of Southern Baptists, 1865–1900*. Nashville: Vanderbilt University Press, 1966.

Spratt, John S. *The Road to Spindletop: Economic Change in Texas, 1875–1901*. Dallas: Southern Methodist University Press, 1955.

Taylor, Carl Cleveland. *The Farmers' Movement, 1620–1920*. New York: American Book Company, 1953.

Tilley, Nannie May. *The Bright Tobacco Industry, 1860–1929*. Chapel Hill: University of North Carolina Press, 1948.

Tindall, George B. *South Carolina Negroes, 1877–1900*. Columbia: University of South Carolina Press, 1952.

Vernon, Walter N. *Methodism Moves across North Texas*. Dallas: The Historical Society, North Texas Conference, The Methodist Church, 1967.

Weinstein, Allan. *Prelude to Populism: Origins of the Silver Issue, 1867–1878*. Yale Historical Publications. Miscellany, 90. New Haven: Yale University Press, 1970.

Wiebe, Robert H. *The Search for Order, 1877–1920*. New York: Hill and Wang, 1967.

Williams, Moses W., and Watkins, George W. *Who's Who Among North Carolina Negro Baptist Organizations*. n.p.: Published by the authors, 1940.

Woodman, Harold D. *King Cotton and His Retainers: Financing and Marketing the Cotton Crop of the South, 1800–1925.* Lexington: University of Kentucky Press, 1968.

Woodward, C. Vann. *Origins of the New South, 1877–1913.* Vol. 9 of *A History of the South,* ed. by Wendell Holmes Stephenson and E. Merton Coulter. 10 vols. Baton Rouge: Louisiana State University Press and the Littlefield Fund for Southern History of the University of Texas, 1951.

————. *Tom Watson, Agrarian Rebel.* New York: Macmillan Company, 1938.

C. UNPUBLISHED MONOGRAPHS AND SPECIAL STUDIES

Bacote, Clarence A. "The Negro in Georgia Politics, 1880–1908." Ph.D. dissertation, University of Chicago, 1955.

Barton, Richard H. "The Agrarian Revolt in Michigan, 1865–1900." Ph.D. dissertation, Michigan State University, 1958.

Bayliss, Garland Erastus. "Public Affairs in Arkansas, 1874–1896." Ph.D. dissertation, University of Texas, Austin, 1972.

Brudvig, Glenn Lowell. "The Farmers' Alliance and Populist Movement in North Dakota (1884–1896)." M.A. thesis, University of North Dakota, 1956.

Calvert, Robert A. "The Southern Grange: The Farmers' Search for Identity in the Gilded Age." Ph.D. dissertation, University of Texas, Austin, 1968.

Church, Joseph. "The Farmers' Alliance and the Populist Movement in South Carolina (1887–1896)." M.A. thesis, University of South Carolina, 1953.

Clevenger, Homer. "Agrarian Politics in Missouri, 1880–1896." Ph.D. dissertation, University of Missouri, 1940.

[Cole, James P.] "The Lampasas Farmers' Alliance." MS in Lampasas County File, Texas State Historical Commission, Austin.

Cory, Lloyd Walter. "The Florida Farmers' Alliance, 1887–1892." M.S. thesis, Florida State University, 1963.

Evans, Samuel Lee. "Texas Agriculture, 1880–1930." Ph.D. dissertation, University of Texas, Austin, 1960.

Falzone, Vincent Joseph. "Terence V. Powderly: Mayor and Labor Leader, 1849–1893." Ph.D. dissertation, University of Maryland, 1970.

Ferguson, James S. "Agrarianism in Mississippi, 1871–1900: A Study in Nonconformity." Ph.D. dissertation, University of North Carolina, Chapel Hill, 1952.

Fine, Bernice R. "Agrarian Reform and the Negro Farmer in Texas, 1886–1896." M.A. thesis, North Texas State University, 1971.

Fox, Leonard P. "Origins and Early Development of Populism in Colorado." Ph.D. dissertation, University of Pennsylvania, 1916.

Gaither, Gerald Henderson. "Blacks and the Populist Revolt: Ballots and Bigotry in the New South." Ph.D. dissertation, University of Tennessee, 1972.

Goodwyn, Lawrence C. "The Origin and Development of American Populism." Ph.D. dissertation, University of Texas, Austin, 1971.

Hart, Roger Louis. "Bourbonism and Populism in Tennessee, 1875–1896." Ph.D. dissertation, Princeton University, 1970.

Honeycutt, Adolph Jenkins. "The Farmers' Alliance in North Carolina." M.S. thesis, North Carolina State College of Agriculture and Engineering, 1925.

Lengel, Leland Levi. "The Righteous Cause: Some Religious Aspects of Kansas Populism." Ph.D. dissertation, University of Oregon, 1968.

Lever, Webbie Jackson. "The Agrarian Movement in Noxumbee County." M.S. thesis, Mississippi State College, 1952.

McMath, Robert C., Jr. "The Farmers' Alliance in the South: The Career of an Agrarian Institution." Ph.D. dissertation, University of North Carolina, Chapel Hill, 1972.

——. "The Godly Populists: Protestantism in the Farmers' Alliance and the People's Party of Texas." M.A. thesis, North Texas State University, 1968.

Miller, Raymond C. "The Populist Party in Kansas." Ph.D. dissertation, University of Chicago, 1928.

Muller, Phillip R. "New South Populism: North Carolina." Ph.D. dissertation, University of North Carolina, Chapel Hill, 1971.

Nolan, Patrick Bates. "Vigilantes on the Middle Border: A Study of Self-Appointed Law Enforcement in the States of the Upper Mississippi from 1840 to 1880." Ph.D. dissertation, University of Minnesota, 1971.

Palmer, Bruce Edward. "The Rhetoric of Southern Populists: Metaphor and Imagery in the Language of Reform." Ph.D. dissertation, Yale University, 1972.

Saunders, Robert Miller. "The Ideology of Southern Populists. 1892–1895." Ph.D. dissertation, University of Virginia, 1967.

Wynne, Lewis Nicholas. "The Alliance Legislature of 1890." M.A. thesis, University of Georgia, 1970.

Index

NINETEENTH AND TWENTIETH CENTURY
AMERICAN HISTORY IN THE NORTON LIBRARY